THE CLASSIC SH

The Classic Short Story, 1870-1925:

Theory of a Genre

Florence Goyet

OpenBook Publishers

smaller ↑

Digital material and resources associated with this volume are available on our website at:

http://www.openbookpublishers.com/isbn/9781909254756

ISBN Paperback: 978-1-909254-75-6
ISBN Hardback: 978-1-909254-76-3
ISBN Digital (PDF): 978-1-909254-77-0
ISBN Digital ebook (epub): 978-1-909254-78-7
ISBN Digital ebook (mobi): 978-1-909254-79-4
DOI: 10.11647/OBP.0039

Cover portraits (left to right): Henry James, Flickr Commons (http://tiny.cc/76rg7w), Guy de Maupassant, Wikimedia (http://tiny.cc/2bsg7w), Giovanni Verga, Wikimedia (http://tiny.cc/eesg7w), Anton Chekhov, Wikimedia (http://tiny.cc/1fsg7w) and Akutagawa Ryūnosuke, Wikimedia (http://tiny.cc/ohsg7w).

All paper used by Open Book Publishers is SFI (Sustainable Forestry Initiative), and PEFC (Programme for the Endorsement of Forest Certification Schemes) Certified.

Printed in the United Kingdom and United States by Lightning Source for Open Book Publishers

To my parents, Janine and Roger Bressand-Saureil.

Table of Contents

Acknowledgements

This book is a fully revised and updated translation, by Yvonne Freccero and Florence Goyet, of *La Nouvelle, 1870-1925: description d'un genre à son apogée* (Paris: Presses Universitaires de France, 1993), which sold out in 2012.

For their encouragement and advice over the years, I am very grateful to Pierre Brunel, Lionel Gossman, Vladimir Kataev, Guido Baldi, Michel Cadot, Peter Por, Béatrice Didier, Thierry Maré, Simone Bonnassieux, Odile Dussud, Kato Masako and Gregory McNamee, as well as the late Elisabeth Shaw, Jean-Jacques Origas and Kato Shuichi. I am indebted to the University of Grenoble-Alpes, the Centre National de la Recherche Scientifique (CNRS), and the Fondation Thiers for giving me the research time to write this book, and to Princeton University and the University of Wisconsin at Madison for their Visiting Fellowships. I thank my research team, Rhétorique de l'Antiquité à la Révolution (RARE), for the grant they gave me. I would also like to thank the librarians at the Institut d'études slaves and Bibliothèque nationale de France (especially M. Jean Watelet) for their assistance in finding materials. For their help with the translation, my sincerest thanks go to my translator Yvonne Freccero, my editor Corin Throsby and Open Book Publishers.

Introduction

This book aims to characterise what I consider to be the "classic" short story, which was written throughout the world by both major and minor short story writers in the period covering roughly 1870-1925. Although the short story has tended to be characterised as offering psychological complexity and nuanced characters, the classic short stories operated under extremely strict conventions. Despite the fact that this form of the short story was practiced so widely, its importance to the genre has yet to be sufficiently acknowledged in the extensive literature on the topic.

In the Anglophone world, two major works gave birth and shape to a revival of short story criticism in the late 1960s and 1970s.[1] Mary Rohrberger's book on Nathaniel Hawthorne defined the short story as an epiphany, revealing to the reader that "there is more to the world than which can be discovered through the senses".[2] Ten years later, Charles

---

1   On the history of short story criticism, see Susan Lohafer, "Introduction to Part I", in *Short Story Theory at a Crossroads*, ed. by Susan Lohafer and Jo Ellyn Clarey (Baton Rouge, LA: Louisiana State University Press, 1990), pp. 3-12. See also Lohafer's (very brief, but particularly clear) outline in her introduction to *The Tales We Tell: Perspectives on the Short Story*, ed. by Rick Feddersen, Susan Lohafer, Barbara Lounsberry and Mary Rohrberger (Westport, CN: Greenwood Press, Praeger, 1998), pp. ix-xii. See also Erik van Achter, "Revising Theory: Poe's Legacy in Short Story Criticism", in *Short Story Theories: A Twenty-First-Century Perspective*, ed. by Viorica Patea (Amsterdam: Rodopi, 2012), pp. 75-88.

2   Mary Rohrberger, *Hawthorne and the Modern Short Story: A Study in Genre* (The Hague: Mouton, 1966), p. 11.

DOI: 10.11647/OBP.0039.14

E. May put together a collection of essays that made him a powerful advocate of a genre that he described as "mythic and spiritual [...] intuitive and lyrical".[3] In these works, critics of the contemporary story found a description of what they saw and appreciated in late twentieth century stories. The scholars had what seemed to be a complete view of the form: stretching back from Frederick Barthelme and Alice Munro to Virginia Woolf, James Joyce, Sherwood Anderson and Anton Chekhov, and rooted in Hawthorne's "invention" of the genre at the beginning of the nineteenth century.

This apparently comprehensive view of the genre, however, left a crucial missing link: critics tend to ignore the end of nineteenth century, despite the fact that this period has a strong claim as a major stage — if not *the* major stage — of the form. There is of course nothing ground-breaking in such an assertion: it is well documented that the short story was enormously popular at this time, and that innumerable periodicals were publishing countless stories.[4] It was also the time when more masters of the form were active than perhaps at any other time: Chekhov, Guy de Maupassant, Luigi Pirandello, Henry James, Mori Ōgai and Akutagawa Ryūnosuke, to name just a few.[5] The particular form of the genre has also been recognised. In 1985, Clare Hanson reminded us with force that not only was the short story of that time important, but also that it had initiated a whole tradition in itself: the "short story", as opposed to "short fiction".[6]

Yet compared to the wealth and importance of these stories in their time, critical appraisals of this form have been very few.[7] The classic short

3   Charles E. May (ed.), *Short Story Theories* (Athens, OH: Ohio University Press, 1976). The quote is from Charles E. May, "The Nature of Knowledge in Short Fiction", in *The New Short Story Theories*, ed. by Charles E. May (Athens, OH: Ohio University Press, 1994), pp. 131-43 (p. 133).

4   Between 1885 and 1901 the publication numbers for cheap magazines in the United States went from 3,600 to 7,500. See Andrew Levy, *The Culture and Commerce of the American Short Story* (Cambridge: Cambridge University Press, 1993). In Europe, the figures are maybe even more impressive: in Italy alone, about 1,800 periodicals were published in 1891; in France, several papers had a circulation of nearly one million by 1900. On all this, and on the consequences for the form itself, see Part II.

5   Throughout the book, Japanese names will be given following the academic habit of using the surname first followed by the given name.

6   "Throughout this period [1880-1980], despite the development of Symbolist and Modernist short story forms, the 'traditional' tale continued to appear. Indeed, the major point which I wish to make about this period is that it is possible to distinguish in it two quite separate lines of development in the short story". Clare Hanson, *Short Stories and Short Fictions, 1880-1980* (New York: St. Martin's Press, 1985), p. 5.

7   The form widely studied is that which is, to use May's words, "essential and seldom

story tradition is often dismissed, in one word, as pertaining only to the "naturalistic" story — or as being, in Rohrberger's words, only "simple narrative".[8] Only a few writers have had their stories studied in any detail, while the short stories of Naturalists like Émile Zola, Gerhart Hauptmann and Giovanni Verga — so influential across Europe — have been largely ignored, as have Leonid Andreyev, Nikolai Leskov and Mikhail Saltykov-Shchedrin. Even Pirandello and Maupassant's short stories have been paid only cursory glances. And even for the authors that are the focus of short story studies, only a handful of their stories are analysed. To take Chekhov as an example, only a few of his stories, especially from the later period of his career, from *Dama s sobachkoi* (*Lady with Lapdog*, 1899) to *Nevest* (*Bethrothed*, 1903, his last story), are widely cited, even though he wrote a hundred or so stories in his "major" period alone — these "epiphanic" stories have become the focus of analysis rather than his "classic" stories.[9]

As a global study of the classic form was still missing, I undertook to concentrate on the short story at this time of its greatest efflorescence, across a number of different countries and languages, working with a corpus of more than a thousand stories. This research led me to see that this "classic" short story, albeit with infinitely various surface features, was built on a constant structure, had a characteristic relationship with its readers, and a generic outlook on its subject. This was nearly universal. It

---

read". Charles E. May, "Why Short Stories Are Essential and Why They Are Seldom Read", in *The Art of Brevity: Excursions in Short Fiction Theory and Analysis*, ed. by Per Winther, Jakob Lothe and Hans H. Skei (Columbia, SC: University of South Carolina Press, 2004), pp. 14-25. The "classic" short story, written by artists that have been extraordinarily influential in their time, and which was universally read, is scarcely studied. Hanson's work is a brilliant exception, but she writes on English writers alone, and soon proceeds to the description of "short fiction" rather than the classic short story. My research concurs with many of her results: from the characters "tend[ing] to be viewed externally", to the subject tending to be "the strange [...] in human personality", to the "narrative symmetry", and the importance of plot in these classic stories, and to the fact that the stories depend "on a fundamental agreement between reader and writer". See Hanson (1985), p. 6.

8   May argues that "The narrative and description in the first two thirds of the story [James Joyce's *The Dead*] suggests that the story will end naturalistically with the end of the party. However [...]". Charles E. May, "The Secret Life in the Modern Short Story", in *Contemporary Debates on the Short Story*, ed. by José R. Ibáñez, José Francisco Fernández and Carmen M. Bretones (Bern: Lang, 2007), pp. 207-25 (p. 217). Rohrberger draws the distinction between the short story as "epiphany" and the "simple narrative". Mary Rohrberger, "Origins, Development, Substance, and Design of the Short Story: How I Got Hooked on the Short Story and Where It Led Me", in *The Art of Brevity* (2004), pp. 1-13 (p. 5).

9   This is after a very prolific period in the "small press", to which Chekhov contributed under a pseudonym more than five hundred stories and anecdotes.

was not a question of giving a *definition* of the short story: many critics have stressed that this would not be very interesting, even if it were possible. It was a question of describing the tools of brevity in this particular form, and the relationship between the reader, the author, and the spectacle that one puts before the other. This survey showed that Chekhov and James, even in their greatest stories, used the same tools as Maupassant or Verga. Chekhov's *Lady with Lapdog* is making a particularly powerful use of the antithetic structure common to classic short stories; James's *The Figure in the Carpet* is particularly representative of the paroxystic representation of short story characters.[10]

To test my hypothesis, and disengage the in-depth characteristics of this form, the first requirement seemed to me to survey in detail an international selection of the "greatest" short story authors. I chose to look at the entire body of stories of five major authors, one in each of the languages with which I was familiar (French, Russian, Italian, English and Japanese): Maupassant, Chekhov, Verga, James and Akutagawa. Maupassant was an obvious choice as he has largely been figured by critics as the master of the "classic" short story, as well as Chekhov, who is seen to embody "short fiction" (or the "modern" short story as I call it).[11] Verga was also an obvious choice, because he is such a popular author in his home country and because, unlike many classic short story writers, his work has been analysed by great critics from Luigi Russo to Leo Spitzer and the progressive Marxists.[12] James was not only central to the discussion of the form by Anglophone critics, but also made what is maybe the most exquisite use of the form. In Japan, Mori Ōgai was my first choice, since he was one of the greatest authors of the time; but instead I decided to focus on Akutagawa because, like Maupassant and Chekhov, he wrote both "classic" stories and "short fiction".[13]

---

10 Considering that I am treating short stories as works of art in their own right, and that they are often published separately, I have italicised their titles rather than putting them in inverted commas. When I am speaking of a cycle or sequence of short stories, I shall say so.

11 It is difficult in English to find a word to specify this type of short story without entering into the debate on "modernism/postmodernism". What I mean by "modern" is a story that renounces the anecdote, and thus, the "classic" format. I discuss this in detail in the book's epilogue.

12 I also looked at the complete short works of Pirandello, because it was interesting to see that even an author who was central to the renewal of the theatrical form used the most "classic" tools when writing short stories.

13 Akutagawa's career began a little later than the others: his first texts date from 1914.

The second step was to place these great authors in the context of their time: to read Maupassant along with Alphonse Daudet, and James along with Rudyard Kipling. More importantly, I decided to read them in the same place as the audience of the time: in the newspapers and the intellectual journals of the late nineteenth and early twentieth centuries. This was more fruitful than I could have imagined. First, it allowed me to see these stories in the vicinity of the other genres of the newspapers (chronicles, reports, anecdotes, etc), with which they have interesting resemblances and differences. Secondly, it explained what is maybe the essential feature of the "classic" short story: its exoticism. Most of these stories deal with characters that are in some ways removed from the reader (either by place, time, race or class).

"Modern" short stories that follow less generic conventions may very well be more satisfying for twenty-first century readers than the classic form. Throughout this book, I shall not shy away from acknowledging the classic short story's limitations: these stories can be extraordinarily powerful, but the form is also somewhat stifling. However, the very fact that the greatest authors of the time abundantly and continuously produced classic short stories should draw our attention to the possibilities of the form. They did great things with potentially restrictive structural "laws". In doing so, they were part of a democratisation of literature: this was a form that could be read, like the serial, by a large number of readers — but which could also give quick, swift pleasure to readers accustomed to more demanding writing.

The authors that I am focussing on in this book participated in the Naturalist period's criticism of what they perceived to be the backward state of their countries. Verga and Chekhov published throughout their lives in intellectual journals (*tolstye zhurnaly* or "thick journals" as they were called in Russia) where their stories were side-by-side with austere articles about science and statistics, and their possible application to ease the nation's poverty. Maupassant and the French Naturalists, from Paul Alexis to Zola, published in newspapers that sometimes bore the very title of *Le Progrès* (*The Progress*), and the transformation of the nation was paramount in their minds. The short story gave them a powerful tool for denunciation of a state of society they felt was unbearable. Yet paradoxically these stories often played the role of reinforcing the social — and sometimes racial — prejudices of the reader. It was precisely this drawback that led to the form's deconstruction in the twentieth century. The greatness of the authors studied in this book lies in their having become sensible to this stifling effect of the classic form, and having opened new avenues to the genre. Maupassant, for example, experimented with the form in his tales of madness and Chekhov wrote stories based on a dilemma, thus putting into question the very idea of a stable, affirmative self and the superiority of one "voice" over the others. But this should not lead us to forget that this was only one part of their work, and that they also led long and admirable careers as "classic" short story writers.

This book shall approach the classic short story from three different and complementary perspectives: its structure; its site of first publication; and the relationship it creates between author, reader and characters. Part I is dedicated to structure. In Chapter One, we shall see that characterisation in the short story is always paroxystic. There are few narrative elements in the classic short story but every trait is there in its extreme form; even mediocre men are mediocre *par excellence*. Chapter Two will show that the classic short story is based on a fundamental antithesis, which creates a powerful tension. This may be achieved through a narrative reversal, or the contrast between two characters (for example, Jekyll and Hyde) or between two world visions (for example, European and American). This is the essential point from which to understand the "twist-in-the-tail", which will be the focus of Chapter Three. The reason that the ending of the short story is so powerful is because it brings into contact the two poles of the antithesis, the two opposites that should never come into contact. The "surprise" ending simply unleashes the accumulated tension that has been building throughout the story. Chapter Four will analyse the means through which the short story accelerates our entry into the narrative. In order to help the reader immediately understand the scene, these stories often resort to "preconstructed" material, including stereotypes (not necessarily literary types, but understood social types). They are also very focussed, eliminating everything that is not their subject.

The second part of the book will analyse the short story within the framework of the media in which it first appeared: newspapers and intellectual journals. Chapter Six presents a detailed review of the mostly expensive, elegant periodicals that were the primary publishing outlet for the short stories of our corpus. These stories that focus on peasants, poor office workers, prostitutes and provincials were for the most part read by wealthy urbanites. These periodicals also published travelogues — which will be the focus of Chapter Seven — in which a chronicler introduced his readers to a foreign country. Often the writers in our corpus wrote "factual" travelogues at the same time as their fictional stories, creating in both a similar distance between the reader and the exotic characters being depicted.

It is this distance that will be the focus of the final section of the book: Part III looks at the relationship between the reader, the author and the characters of the classic short story. The main feature of the genre is its *monologism* — only the author (or narrator) has a full and autonomous voice, whereas the characters in all their "otherness" are put at a distance. Chapters Eight and Nine will concentrate on rhetorical devices that are used to create distance from the characters — even though many of these devices (such as the use of direct speech and dialect) are often thought of as creating intimacy. Chapter Ten looks at the intermediary role the narrator and/or the "reflector" play in creating the sense of distance between reader and author, as the reader joins with the (reliable) narrator to "look down" upon the other characters in the tale. Chapter Eleven attempts to define the special kind of emotion aroused in the short story. Although the reader may feel sympathy for certain characters, our compassion almost never results from a true understanding; they are never our equals, but are doomed to represent social or psychological types. The conclusion to Part III will show that even the short stories of Dostoevsky — the herald of polyphony — are still monological. Monologism is not a feature of our authors but of the genre itself.

The epilogue to the book will hint at the way in which the short story would transform itself out of its effective but restrictive framework into the twentieth century. The stories I call "modern", as opposed to "classic", renounce most of the traits described in this book. Structure is no longer based on antitheses and paroxysms, and, most importantly, polyphony can re-enter the scene. When the nineteenth-century belief in reason and progress gave way to a fundamental uncertainty about the subject, the short story lost its firm grasp on easily defined characters. Instead of telling neatly manufactured little tales, it preferred to turn to the exploration of uncertain and complex minds.

PART I: STRUCTURE

1. Paroxystic Characterisation

At the end of the nineteenth century, through the influence of Naturalism, literature was striving to become the "science of the human heart", and as a consequence many critics and writers began to condemn rhetoric.[1] In *The Experimental Novel* (1880), using Claude Bernard as a guide, Émile Zola called his fellow writers to become "observers" in the spirit of the physiologist.[2] He urged writers to renounce rhetoric, if not style: "The observer relates purely and simply the phenomena which he has under his eyes... He should be the photographer of phenomena, his observation should be an exact representation of nature".[3] As a consequence, the period's motto was "simplicity". The ancient school of writing began to be identified with rhetorical pomposity,[4] and Zola's call for the aesthetics of "slice of life" Naturalism is well known:

---

1 See, for example, Giovanni Verga, *The She-Wolf and Other Stories*, trans. by Giovanni Cecchetti (Berkeley: University of California Press, 1973), p. 87 (hereafter Cecchetti). For the original Italian, see Giovanni Verga, *Tutte le Novelle*, ed. by Carla Ricciardi, 2 vols (Milan: Mondadori, 1983), I, p. 192 (hereafter Ricciardi). Verga is one of the greatest proponents of this radical Italian Naturalist school of Verism.

2 See Émile Zola, *The Experimental Novel, and Other Essays*, trans. by Belle M. Sherman (New York: Cassell, 1893); and Claude Bernard, *An Introduction to the Study of Experimental Medicine*, trans. by Henry Copley Greene (Birmingham, AL: Classics of Medicine Library, 1980). Zola said, "I only repeat what I have said before, that apart from the matter of form and style, the experimental novelist is only one special kind of savant, who makes use of the tools of all other savants, observation and analysis" (p. 50).

3 Ibid, p. 6.

4 "We are actually rotten with lyricism; we are very much mistaken when we think that the

DOI: 10.11647/OBP.0039.1

words — and Verga insists on this point — it must renounce grandiloquent "effects" in favour of psychological truth.[15]

But this constantly proclaimed simplicity and denial of rhetoric does not withstand a close reading of the short stories written at the end of the nineteenth century. Verga's theory and Chekhov's commentaries, like far too many authors' comments on their texts, are accepted as ready currency, a definitive description of their work. In this chapter we shall see that the classic short story, far from being unadorned, relies heavily on rhetorical techniques and paroxystic effects. The claim of simplicity corresponds to reality as far as themes and scope are concerned; in this regard the short story is truly an "economical" genre and all the commentators rightly stress the small number of characters and events and, during this period, their commonplace character. But these very elements are always characterised in excess, they are what they are *prodigiously* — every state, every quality, every feeling is carried to the ultimate. This is not simply a feature of Italian Verism but rather the standard way of dealing with narrative material in the short story: Henry James and Chekhov will bear witness to this. The following chapters will show why the short story is in need of this aggrandizement of its objects, and how it uses it to achieve brevity. It will remain to be shown, in the conclusion of this section, how the short story makes its reader forget, in the excitement of the narrative, both its extremism and the extremely rhetorical structure in which it is used.

Since Verga's theory is quoted constantly by Italian critics from Luigi Capuana and Luigi Russo on, it is worthwhile testing it by beginning with an examination of the short story *Gramigna's Mistress*, by which Verga illustrates his manifesto.[16] The three characters in the story are Sicilians: two peasants and one brigand. However, they are not merely "ordinary" Sicilians, representatives of the anonymous masses. Peppa is rich and "one of the most beautiful girls of Licodia"; she is supposed to marry the most

---

15 Ibid, pp. 87-88 (pp. 191-92). This idea of truth and spontaneity is still often stressed in the insistence on the short story's filiation with oral story-telling, which is considered the model of the "spontaneous" text. The classic reference is to W. Somerset Maugham, *Points of View* (London: Heinemann, 1938), p. 147. See also Valerie Shaw, *The Short Story: A Critical Introduction* (London: Longman, 1983). In her chapter entitled "Artless Narration", Shaw insists on the absence of rhetoric and the proximity of the audience. See also Eduard Anatol'evich Shubin, *Sovremennyi russkii rasskaz: voprosy poetiki zhanra* (Moscow: Nauka, 1974).

16 Goethe similarly offered his *Novelle* as an example of the genre. See Johann Wolfgang von Goethe, *Great Writings of Goethe*, ed. by Stephen Spender, trans. by Christopher Middleton (New York: New American Library, 1958), pp. 138-60.

desired bachelor in the village, nicknamed "Tallow Candle" because of his wealth.[17] Instead she abruptly decides to partner with Gramigna, a rebel who is terrorising the region. Gramigna is far from simply being someone who robs people and who just happens to marry someone called Peppa, as Verga suggests in his preamble to the story. Throughout the beginning of the story, he is increasingly portrayed as a prodigy: he becomes the *ultimate* rebel, of superhuman proportions. He is a thief, but not content just to live off his pillaging: he terrorises an entire province. Not a single peasant "from one end of the province to the other" dares to harvest his crop for fear of Gramigna's bloody vengeance. Even his name (Italian for "crab grass") places him automatically in opposition to the peasants: "a name as cursed as the grass that bears it".[18]

The story soon gives Gramigna the stature of the paladins of former times: "he was alone, but he was worth ten [...] he alone, Gramigna, was never tired, never slept".[19] He is immediately shown as far superior to those hunting him. But the text does not stop there, it withdraws him from human references; the hero will finally reach the very level of primordial elements:

> He slunk like a wolf down the beds of dry creeks [...] for two hundred miles around ran the legend of his deeds [...] he alone against a thousand, tired, hungry, burning with thirst in the immense burnt plain, under the June sun.[20]

This enlargement characterises all the signifying elements of the described world. The harvests they are protecting from him are exceptional:

> ... the wheat was a joy to look at, if only Gramigna wouldn't set it on fire, and that the wicker [basket] by the bed wouldn't be large enough to hold all the grain of the harvest.[21]

A mass of troops is assembled against him. Faced with the terror he inspires, the Prefect calls up the officers of all the reserves to hunt him:

> *Carabinieri*, soldiers and cavalrymen had been after him for two months [...] patrols and squads were immediately in motion, sentries were placed along every ditch and behind every wall [...] by day, by night, on foot, on horseback, and by telegraph.[22]

---

17 Cechetti, p. 89 (Ricciardi, pp. 193-94).
18 Ibid, p. 88 (p. 192). Verga, in an early version, called his hero "Raja". The change in name makes it more powerful: he is the typical enemy of the peasants.
19 Ibid, pp. 88-89 (p. 193).
20 Ibid, p. 89 (p. 193).
21 Ibid, p. 90 (p. 194).
22 Ibid, p. 88 (p. 193).

The mention of the telegraph contributes to the impression of universality: even the air is involved. The difficulty of the hunt is repeatedly emphasised: "The *carabinieri*'s horses dropped dead tired [...] the patrols slept on their feet".[23]

This represents more or less the entire text of the beginning of the story, with all the notations on Gramigna and his enemies gathered in a single page. So it is not just a question of salient features, scattered throughout a portrait to give it more vigour, but of the very spirit of this "portrait", which is not a representation of a man of the people, nor even the description of a rebel, but the creation of an almost mythic character, beyond any normal bounds: in short, an abstraction. By the end of this page, Gramigna is the Rebel *par excellence*, the personification of the evil hero. The story treats the character "Tallow Candle" in the same way. At first he is characterised as "the best match in the village", but he is soon beyond any comparisons with his peers. He too is associated with superhuman imagery: he is "as big and beautiful as the sun", and his unusual strength enables him to carry "the banner of Saint Margaret without bending his back, as if he were a pillar".[24]

Could this be a series of clichés not to be taken literally? Are they simply the exaggerations of this spicy, popular story that Verga claimed was a peasant tale in which he had changed almost none of the "simple and picturesque" terms?[25] If so, there would be no reason to take these paroxysms at face value. But, in fact, the accumulation of prodigious elements is such as to force us to take each of them at face value. At the end of this portrait of Gramigna, we are led to endow an expression such as "he never slept" with its full meaning, because each element reinforces the other: from the enormity of the troops opposing him, we unconsciously come to the conclusion that Gramigna really is more than a man, and we attribute to him a thirst which equals the immense plain and a wakefulness that surpasses the human condition. On the other hand, given his own heroic stature, both the enemy forces and the wealth of the bridegroom become absolutes: every possible police and army unit; the very richest young people.[26] We are given *only* extremes, and the tissue they finally

---

23 Ibid, p. 89 (p. 193).

24 Ibid, p. 90 (p. 194).

25 Ibid, p. 86 (p. 191).

26 Claude Gandelman describes the phenomenon in Kafka: "In Kafka, the metaphors of current language help to make an unreal 'literary situation' accepted as the most normal thing in the world, since it already exists in the language. [...] Only, in Kafka, these

weave bears the mark of this paroxysm in its entirety. If exaggerations were removed, there would be nothing left.

As a consequence, the narrative itself takes on something of the absolute: it is the manhunt *par excellence* that we are following. In the same way, we glide from the idea that Gramigna is at the centre of all conversations, to the idea that he is the *only* subject: "wherever people met, they spoke only of him, of Gramigna".[27] In the rarefied world of the short story, it is not enough that the important elements occupy the forefront: they establish such a strong presence that they conceal all else, and they obliterate everything that is not a paroxysm like themselves. Like the fairytale, the short story accustoms us to working with unequivocal entities: paragons of virtue or vice.[28]

Even the most subtle authors are no different in their construction of characters in their short stories. In *The Figure in the Carpet*, a story from the height of his maturity as a writer, James is dealing with the subtleties of a "literary" subject matter, not with Sicilian peasants — and yet he nevertheless constructs his narrative on an uninterrupted series of paroxysms.[29] The story's narrator, a young critic early in his career, is told by the writer Hugh Vereker that throughout his work there is a secret thread, like "a complex figure in a Persian carpet", which gives it its value. The narrator does his best to discover the secret but fails, although one of his colleagues, the critic Corvick, manages to solve the mystery.

Even in a short story like this, which at the beginning is relatively subdued, intense instances of hyperbole become "natural", almost inescapable. Vereker is initially presented simply as a good writer, even

---

linguistic metaphors are taken literally and even become men's destiny" (concerning "this vermin Gregor Samsa"). Claude Gandelman, *Les Techniques de la provocation chez quelques romanciers et nouvellistes de l'entre-deux-guerres* (doctoral thesis, Paris III Sorbonne-Nouvelle, 1972), p. 110 (translation ours).

27 Cechetti, p. 89 (Ricciardi, p. 193).

28 As is evident in the above-mentioned *Novelle* by Goethe, which accumulates extremes, and explicitly says them to be so: "A new extraordinary object again merits our attention"; "miraculously"; "no man ever saw a royal tiger laid out to sleep so splendidly as you lie now". Goethe (1958), p. 252. For the inheritance of this idea from ancient genres (exemplum, tale and fable), see Hans-Jörg Neuschafer, *Boccaccio und der Beginn der Novelle: Strukturen der Kurzerzählung auf der Schwelle zwischen Mittelalter und Neuzeit* (Munich: Fink Verlag, 1983); André Sempoux, *La Nouvelle*, in *Typologie des sources du moyen âge occidental*, 9 (Turnhout: Brepols, 2009), ch. 9; and Salvatore Battaglia, "Dall'esempio alla novella" in *Filologia Romanza*, 7 (1960), 45-82; also in *La coscienza letteraria del Medioevo* (Naples: Liguori, 1965), pp. 487-548.

29 Henry James, *The Complete Tales of Henry James*, ed. by Leon Edel, 12 vols (London: Rupert Hart Davis, 1960), IX, pp. 273-315 (hereafter Edel).

though, in general, James usually announces from the outset that his author characters are geniuses.[30] Here he merely says: "He was awfully clever [...] but he wasn't a bit the biggest of the lot".[31] However, the entire beginning of the text proceeds steadily to build Vereker into a genius, and the search for his secret is depicted as a feat of total dedication and self-sacrifice on the part of the narrator and Corvick.

James's plainly prodigious terms are not so different from those in *Gramigna's Mistress*. The narrator, who thinks it's enough to have passed "half the night" in reading Vereker's book before he writes his review, is called to order by the writer whom he meets at a lady's house and told that he "didn't see anything" of the work. This conversation makes it possible gradually to portray the man and his secret, the "figure", as a wonder of merit: "Triumph of patience and ingenuity [...] the finest, fullest intention" of all his works is, in the Master's eyes, "an exquisite scheme".[32] The apparent — and temporary — modesty of Vereker, who in the beginning called his figure "a little trick", is merely a means of establishing a crescendo; from the next page on he gives up this pose.[33] To the narrator who asks him "You mean it's a beauty so rare, so great?", he replies "the loveliest thing in the world";[34] and we know the force of "beauty" and "lovely" in James.

This conversation arouses extraordinary emotion in the young writer, and is a real turning point in the short story: from then on he will reread the entire work, despair, look again, and then give up, but not without reporting the conversation to Corvick, the critic who gave him the review to write in his place. Nevertheless, this conversation "says" nothing about the nature of the secret, nor about the nature or ambition of the work of art. Its effect is to place the man and his work in the light of the absolute, to make Vereker into "the Author" *par excellence*, as Gramigna was "the Rebel".

The rest of the short story takes very seriously indeed the statement of the prodigious value of the figure in the work. After the pure and simple affirmation of that paroxystic value, it is the very structure of the text which will take on the role of making it a marvel. For this, it will use what semioticians have called "narrative saturation": all of the potentialities

---

30 In, for example, *The Death of the Lion* (Edel, IX, pp. 77-118) or *The Lesson of the Master* (Edel, VII, pp. 213-84).

31 Edel, IX, p. 275.

32 Ibid, pp. 281-82.

33 Ibid, p. 282.

34 Ibid, p. 285.

of a situation are exploited in turn, all the terms set by the narration are linked with each other.[35] After the narrator has failed, Corvick passionately takes up the quest to uncover the mystery figure himself. He joins with his fiancée Gwendolen in a search so intense that the narrator's initial efforts look somewhat weak. Not content with rereading the twenty volumes, they read them "page by page, as they would take one of the classics; inhale him in slow draughts and let him sink all the way in".[36] Gwendolen says of Corvick: "he knows every page, as I do, by heart".[37]

As with Verga, this is not some spicy exaggeration with no real significance. The short story takes its emphatic assertions literally and ultimately gives the words their fullest, if extreme, meaning. The proof of this is that Corvick discovers the secret when he is on a journey to India, and has not taken the twenty volumes with him. On solving the mystery, he leaves India immediately, giving up the large fee he had been offered to write an article there. Corvick proclaims that he will share the secret with Gwendolen, but only after he is married to her.[38] He also agrees to tell the narrator, but then only in person. The narrator has to go abroad to attend a sick brother; and by the time he returns, Corvick is dead.

Everything then conspires to prevent the narrator (and reader) from discovering the secret: the widow has been told, but she refuses to speak about it to anyone. When all efforts at persuasion have failed, the narrator even considers marrying her. Faced with Gwendolen's refusal, he thinks of marrying Vereker's widow, whom he has never seen, and about whom he knows nothing. The two women die one after the other, and he turns to the second husband of Corvick's widow. This is the "surprise ending" of the story: the husband learns for the first time of the secret's existence and its extraordinary importance. Both of them are in despair, but the narrator's is tempered by the pleasure of supposing that the second husband is perhaps even more frustrated than he.

---

35 See, for example, Stephen Hutchings, *A Semiotic Analysis of the Short Stories of Leonid Andreev: 1900-1909* (London: Modern Humanities Research Association, 1990).

36 Edel, IX, p. 2.

37 Ibid, p. 297.

38 Vereker had already associated the possibility of discovering the figure with the intensity of Corvick and Gwendolen's love. Convinced that no one, ever, would discover the secret before his death, he does nevertheless consider what he is told about the almost mystic quality of Corvick and his fiancée's search, and says that if they love each other so much that they will marry then it is possible that they may really bring the figure to light.

One characteristic of the classic short story is that the paroxysm permeates the entire narrative, affecting not only the heroes, but also all the elements that play a role in the narration. Here, it affects Corvick's projected study of Vereker, which will be "the greatest literary portrait ever painted" as well as the role of the secret for Corvick's widow (a real "counterpoise to her grief"), or the singularity of Corvick himself: "if Corvick had broken down I should never know; no one would be of any use if *he* wasn't".[39] James goes so far as to defy logic in order to magnify everything, as in his characterisation of the secret once it has been discovered:

> When once it came out it came out, was there with a splendour that made you ashamed; and there hadn't been, save in the bottomless vulgarity of the age, with every one tasteless and tainted, every sense stopped, the smallest reason why it should have been overlooked.[40]

This is tantamount to denying the gigantic task imposed on Corvick and his fiancée, a task that would only shed light for Corvick much later, and never for the young woman.

One comes across this phenomenon so often in the classic short story that it is as if authors could not escape it: banality itself is expressed in the most extreme ways. Chekhov's *Skuchnaya istoriya* (*A Boring Story*), for example, seems almost automatically to assume the marks of paroxysm.[41] The example is particularly remarkable because the subject is truly simple, similar to Chekhov's description of the ideal short story as "how Peter married Mary": it describes the human anguish of a sixty-two-year-old man who knows that he is fatally ill. Chekhov often repeated in his letters that he wished that this anguish were accessible to his reader. Yet, from the very first line, the portrait that the doctor draws of himself bears the stamp of the prodigious:

> There is in Russia an eminent professor [... a] privy counselor, who has been awarded many decorations in his lifetime; indeed, he possesses *so many* Russian and foreign orders that whenever he has to put them all on, the students call him the *iconostasis*. [...] [For at least 25-30 years] there has *not* been a single famous scholar or scientist in Russia with whom he has not been intimately acquainted. [...] He is an honorary Fellow of *all* the Russian

---

39 Edel, IX, p. 295.
40 Ibid, p. 300.
41 Anton Pavlovich Chekhov, *Lady with Lapdog and Other Stories*, trans. by David Magarshack (London: Penguin, 1964), pp. 46-104 (hereafter Magarshack). For the text in its original Russian, see Anton Pavlovich Chekhov, *Polnoe sobranie sochinenii i pisem*, 30 vols (Moscow: Nauka, 1974-1983), VII, pp. 251-310 (hereafter Nauka).

[...] universities. [...] This name of mine is well known [...]. It is among those *few* fortunate names which it is considered bad taste to abuse [...] my name is closely associated with the idea of a man who is famous.[42]

I have emphasised here the most salient words and phrases, those that obviously hinder us from thinking of the hero as "just Peter". This process will underlie the presentation of *all* the textual elements: this again is not a side addition, a pleasant way to highlight a self-portrait; it is a fundamental feature of the narrative fabric. To reflect the commonplace world around us, the author accumulates paroxysms into a compact mass. Each of the text's elements could be mentioned; all of them are used in their extreme form. From the narrator's disgust with himself to the extraordinary memory of the beadle he meets every time he goes to the university, to the portrait of the parasite who wants to marry his daughter (he has neither a job, nor any real family, his *only* quality is complacency) or the extraordinary enthusiasm and pleasure felt by the narrator when he teaches:

> *No* debate, *no* entertainment, *no* game has ever given me so much pleasure as giving a lecture [...] And I can't help thinking that *Hercules*, after the most sensational of his exploits, never had such an *exquisite feeling of lassitude* as I experienced *every time* after a lecture".[43]

The effect of these superlatives is sometimes reinforced by other means — for example, the contrast between the damning portrait of his aging wife, and the evocation of her youthful perfection:

> Bewildered, I ask myself: Is it possible that this very fat, clumsy old woman, whose dull expression is so full of petty cares and anxiety about a crust of bread, whose eyes are blurred with perpetual thoughts of debts and poverty, who can only talk of expenses and only smile when things get cheaper — is it possible that this woman was once that very slim Varya, whom I loved so passionately for her fine, clear intellect, her pure soul, her beauty, and — as Othello loved Desdemona — [her "compassion" for the Science I served]?[44]

As in Verga, the drive for extremes is indicated by superhuman comparisons. The column, the sun, Hercules or Othello play the role of *impossibilia* in ancient lyric poetry: guarantees of the extraordinary, they draw the object away from possible comparisons, and make of it an absolute.

---

42 Magarshack, p. 46 (emphases mine) (Nauka, VII, p. 251).

43 Ibid, pp. 56-57 (emphases mine) (pp. 262-63).

44 Ibid, p. 49 (p. 255).

Extremes in the fantastic short story

The short story format is particularly suited to the fantastic.[45] In the whole course of this book, we shall see that fantastic stories and stories of madness make a peculiar use of the features of the short story, and in many ways deconstruct the very system of the genre. What we have just seen in this chapter is that, in the realist story, every feature is pushed to its extreme to the point where it becomes almost abstract. Characters are *prodigiously* what they are, to the extent that they are bordering on the prodigy. In the fantastic story, the high-intensity descriptions will cross that border. Here, the subject will be not so much the characters in themselves, but rather the sensations and emotions they feel — and make us feel.

Let us take just one quick look at a story to which we will return in Chapter Three, and which gives a good example of this crossing of the border between the abstract and the fantastic: Maupassant's *Sur l'eau* (*On the River*).[46] Maupassant tells the story of a passionate fishermen, for whom the extreme beauty of the river is such that it carries with it a real magic — and the word must be understood in its deeper sense. Every element in the description is made through the paroxystic descriptions we are now used to seeing in the classic short story — either realistic or fantastic. First, Maupassant emphasises the character's deep passion for the river: "his heart was full of an all-absorbing, irresistible, devouring passion — a love for the river". Then, the alluring quality of the river itself: "To him it means mystery, the unknown, a land of mirage and phantasmagoria". Finally, there is the river's danger: "the river is a cemetery without graves".[47] In the same way as the realistic stories accumulate extraordinary references (the sun, Hercules), here Maupassant quotes five lines of Victor Hugo's poem "Oceano Nox", only then to assert that the river is even more threatening than the powerful ocean: "It flows stealthily, without a murmur, and the eternal, gentle motion of the water is more awful to me than the big ocean waves".[48] An unusually acute silence ("the extraordinary stillness that

---

45 Elizabeth Bowen, for example, talks of finding it as easy to introduce the fantastic into a short story as it is difficult to do so in a novel. See her preface to *A Day in the Dark and Other Stories* (London: Cape, 1965), p. 9.

46 Guy de Maupassant, *Complete Short Stories of Guy de Maupassant*, trans. by Artine Artinian (Garden City, NY: Hanover House, 1955), pp. 169-72. The French text can be found in Guy de Maupassant, *Contes et nouvelles*, ed. by Louis Forestier, 2 vols (Paris: Gallimard, collection La Pléiade, 1974), I, pp. 54-59.

47 Ibid, p. 169 (p. 54).

48 Ibid.

enveloped me") is followed by the most "marvelous, stupendous sight that it is possible to imagine. It was a vision of fairyland, one of those phenomena that travelers in distant countries tell us about but that we are unable to believe".[49] Nature is described in its most overwhelming forms: the fog is "formed on each side an unbroken hill, six or seven yards in height, that shone in the moonlight with the dazzling whiteness of snow".[50]

The descriptions of the supernatural beauty of nature are then followed by moments of anguish, and the fisherman is gradually seized by terror. The very stillness is at this moment transformed into a "tempest":

> the slight pitching of the boat disturbed me. I felt as if it were swaying to and fro from one side of the river to the other and that an invisible force or being was drawing it slowly to the bottom and then raising it to let it drop again. I was knocked about as if in a storm.[51]

The fact that we are in the midst of prodigies allows supernatural events to arise: the "matter of fact" explanations that could account for them (the fisherman has been drinking, for example) will not prevent the reader's disquiet.

******

The short story never simply tells how someone named Peter married a woman called Mary. At the end of the nineteenth century the short story author even seems incapable of telling how such-and-such a man of no special qualities is unhappy on the eve of his death. What the short story can tell, to the contrary, and what it repeats from Tolstoy's *Three Deaths: A Tale* and *The Death of Ivan Ilyich* to *A Boring Story* is how such-and-such a man who had every reason to be happy and knew it, is hurled from this Capitol onto the Tarpeian Rock of anguish and disgust.

Paroxystic characterisation is a feature widely recognised in hardboiled "magazine stories",[52] and this might very well be the reason why this technique is frequently *not* discussed in the works of the "great authors"

---

49 Ibid, pp. 170 and 171 (pp. 56 and 58).

50 Ibid, p. 171 (p. 59).

51 Ibid, p. 170 (p. 56)

52 Bill Mullen shows that Chester Himes's revolutionary success at getting published in the big magazines of the 1930s, despite endemic racism, was due to his mastering of the codes of pulp fiction, including the "hardboiled" (paroxystic) style. Bill Mullen, "Marking Race/Marketing Race: African American Short Fiction and the Politics of Genre, 1933-1946" in *Ethnicity and the American Short Story*, ed. by Julie Brown (New York: Garland, 1997), pp. 25-46.

(even though, as we will see in Part II, these authors often published their work in magazines). In magazine stories, critics recognise the extreme treatment of the narrative material; but they tend to feel that for "respectable" authors it is something to be avoided. Even a magazine editor like Rust Hills explained to would-be writers of short stories that they should not resort to types ("an extension or exaggeration of a commonly-held quality or manner or accent"), at least for their main character.[53] We have been trained by two centuries of the western novel to consider that a great work cannot use characters without nuances. But the peculiarity of the short story at the end of nineteenth century is precisely that it *does* use such paired-down characters and extreme narratives — with great success — even under the pen of the greatest authors like James and Chekhov. We will now look at one of these paroxystic techniques in more detail: the oxymoronic structure of the classic short story that, with remarkable economy of means, is able to drive the story's action from a summit to the bottom of a precipice.

---

53 Rust Hills, *Writing in General and the Short Story in Particular* (Boston: Houghton Mifflin, 2000), p. 63. Rust Hills was fiction editor for *Esquire* from the 1950s to the 1990s. See also the "how-to" guides to writing short stories, such as Maren Elwood, *Characters Make Your Story* (Boston: Houghton Mifflin, 1942).

2. Antithetic Structure

By the paroxystic characterisation we have just observed, the classic short story makes its characters into the exemplary representatives of their category: the Rebel and the Rich Young Man; the Great Author and the Devoted Critic. These become almost abstract entities. What is lost in the individualisation of the characters, however, is gained in the efficacy of the plot. The interest shifts from individuals to the development of the story itself, for which such characters are remarkably well adapted. The essential feature of the short story then becomes its structure, which, at the period we are considering in the late nineteenth century, is nearly always based on antithesis.

Of the thousand stories of this period I have reviewed, almost all are organised by antithesis at a deeper level. This structuring antithesis is not a decorative figure of speech, merely there to create a harmonious balance, but a powerful dynamic device. It is a tension as enormous as the paroxysms it builds on, and it can be best described in terms borrowed from physics. It is as if the short story were "charging" its magnetic poles — the narrative elements — through paroxysms. The relationship that is established between the fully charged poles — the magnetic field — is more important than each of the poles themselves. In this way, the narrative structure takes precedence over the characters. Robert Louis Stevenson's *Strange Case of Dr*

DOI: 10.11647/OBP.0039.2

Jekyll and Mr Hyde is emblematic of this deep antithetical tension.[1] In this most famous of short stories, the reader is very aware of the structuring force of the antithesis: what has become proverbial is no single trait of any one of the characters, but the truly radical *opposition* between the two characteristics — angelic and satanic — of the hero. The short story's power comes from placing an oxymoron — the taut coexistence of two opposing forces — on the level of the entire text. Stevenson insists that the doctor is a true benefactor of humanity, as much as he insists that Hyde is a monster, because there can be no oxymoron without tension, or lively antithesis without extremes.

O. Henry's *The Gift of the Magi* provides another example of symmetrical characters.[2] The extremes are embodied in a couple of young people, Della and Jim, so poor that they each possess only one item of value. In order to give the other a worthy gift, each sacrifices this treasure, buying an object that is meant to enhance the luster of the other's prize possession. Della has *only* her hair, which she sells to a merchant in order to buy a chain worthy of Jim's Watch (the capital letter is O. Henry's). Jim *only* possesses a watch, a treasure that he saved through all his misfortunes; he sells it to buy Della combs worthy of her hair. When they meet, they discover their symmetrical sacrifice.

The story's delight comes from the recognition of this symmetry, and O. Henry dwells on it in his conclusion by praising this reciprocal love that sacrifices its only treasure to the other. Note that the moment the symmetry has been declared, the anecdote ends: the effect is achieved, the short story is complete. This structure is necessary and adequate to the text: its seven pages call for no further development. And this is also what makes this text a classic short story. If we had only been given the first part of the text, it would merely have been an account of a "good deed", like many others found in Christmas issues of early twentieth-century magazines. By

---

1   See Irving Saposnik's insistence on the absolute necessity not to separate the two sides of the character: "[the story] has become the victim of its own success, allowing subsequent generations to [...] see Jekyll or Hyde where one should see Jekyll-Hyde". Saposnik goes on to show the elaborate structure of the text. Irving S. Saposnik, *Robert Louis Stevenson* (New York: Twayne, 1974), p. 88.

2   A much-maligned author, O. Henry (William Sydney Porter) is nevertheless regularly rehabilitated by critics. In *Literatura* (1927), Boris Eikhenbaum describes *The Gift of the Magi* as the archetype of all O. Henry's short stories; see Charles E. May, *The New Short Story Theories* (Athens, OH: Ohio University Press, 1994), pp. 81-88. *The Gift of the Magi* can be read via Project Gutenberg: http://www.auburn.edu/~vestmon/Gift_of_the_Magi.html (accessed 22/10/13).

adding the second part, O. Henry creates a dramatic knot: by revealing that Jim has bought combs for the shorn hair, he creates a tension that is enough to leave the impression of completion. Note also that this symmetry dispenses with the need to construct complex characters. Della is described at length at the beginning of the text, but the characterization is no more than the development of a single concept: that of the Young-Girl-Beautiful-and-Beloved. Jim is *never* described. It is enough for him to be symmetrical with Della for us to have a clear picture of him. He is her mirror image, a sort of male Della. We do not need a description, we can create him in our minds on the same lines as her.[3]

The juxtaposition of two antithetic poles avoids the need for psychological justification of the characters' actions. In Giovanni Verga's *Gramigna's Mistress*, which we looked at in the last chapter, we see Peppa suddenly abandoning her rich fiancé, Tallow Candal, to join "the Rebel"). Peppa's "decision" takes up half a line and has no justification or explanation.[4] On the first page we see the full extent of the menace Gramigna wagers over the country. Without the slightest transition, we move on to the portrait of Tallow Candle and his extreme riches, and to the announcement of the marriage. By the end of the same paragraph Peppa announces her refusal of Tallow Candle and her desire for no one else but Gramigna. There is not a single reflection on the part of the characters or of the narrator that explains the necessity or reasons for such a relinquishment.

This rapid transition is somehow not jarring for the reader because the men are presented as two elements of an opposition, each equally prodigious: they are "equivalent". This connection has only to be suggested for it to seem justified and natural, because it is already understood that they are two faces of the same phenomenon. Peppa's sudden change is justified because she has passed from the height of riches to the depths of

---

3   Saposnik (1974) says the same thing about *Dr Jekyll and Mr Hyde*. Struck by the number of interpretations of Hyde's character, he remarks that nevertheless they are all metaphorical: Hyde is "usually described in metaphors because essentially that is what he is: a metaphor of uncontrolled appetites, an amoral abstraction. [...] Purposely left vague, he is best described as Jekyll-deformed, dwarfish, stumping, ape-like — a frightening parody of a man unable to exist on the surface" (p. 101).

4   "[...] it seemed [to Tallow Candle] he couldn't wait to take his bride home on the back of his bay mule. But one fine day Peppa told him: 'Never mind your mule, because I don't want to get married.' Imagine the commotion! The old woman tore her hair, and Tallow Candle remained openmouthed". Giovanni Verga, *The She-Wolf and Other Stories*, trans. by Giovanni Cecchetti (Berkeley: University of California Press, 1973), p. 90. For the original Italian, see Giovanni Verga, *Tutte le Novelle*, ed. by Carla Ricciardi, 2 vols (Milan: Mondadori, 1983), I, pp. 191-99.

when they are in the middle of a tunnel, and the narrator chokes on the soot that pours in. Just as he is about to scold her, she throws some tangerines, which she had hidden in her blouse, to her young brothers who have come to see her off.

This is the *Wendepunkt* of the short story, which brings about the complete reversal: from that moment, the narrator understands the girl's behaviour, and is saddened by her lot. All the symbols scattered through the text are reversed: the "warm sunny color" of the tangerines is contrasted with the gloominess, paroxystically described at the beginning. The end of the story presents the same terms as at the beginning, but inverts the signs: "I was able to forget some of my boredom and my indescribable exhaustion, and also the absurdity, the vulgarity, and the monotony of the human condition".[12] The antithesis here operates on the unfolding of the narrative, in accordance with Tieck's definition.

However, usually antithetic tension is established between textual elements that have nothing to do with the unfolding of the narrative. Neither *Dr Jekyll and Mr Hyde* nor *The Gift of the Magi* offer a narrative reversal. Similarly, in a story like Henry James's *The Beast in the Jungle*, it is the central concept, the "event" which is reversed in the antithesis.[13] *Because* John Marcher, the hero, has spent his whole life waiting for the extraordinary event for which he thinks he was born, *nothing* happens. A woman, May Bartram, spends years beside him as he keeps his eyes riveted on the "beast of destiny" that never appears. All she will have been in her life is the companion of that waiting. After her death, he suddenly realises that the destiny for which he has waited so long may have been to love her; blinded by his expectation of an exceptional happening, he failed where an ordinary man would have succeeded. A statement at the end of the short story is typical of the genre: "[…] he had been the man of this time, *the* man, to whom nothing on earth was to have happened. That was the rare stroke — that was his visitation".[14] Ultimately, Marcher's life had been exceptional in a negative sense. The antithesis is essential but it does not affect the

---

12 Kojima, p. 211 (p. 99).

13 Henry James, *The Complete Tales of Henry James*, ed. by Leon Edel, 12 vols (New York: Rupert Hart Davis, 1960), XI, pp. 351-402 (hereafter Edel). On this story, see also Arthur A. Brown, "Death and the Reader: James's 'The Beast in The Jungle'", in *Postmodern Approaches to the Short Story*, ed. by Farhat Iftekharrudin, Joseph Boyden, Joseph Longo and Mary Rohrberger (Westport, CN: Praeger, 2003), pp. 39-50.

14 Edel, p. 401 (the emphasis is James's).

unfolding of the narrative nor does it play any part in the chain of actions: it simply places two opposite possibilities side by side.

The antithesis can also be the abstract law of a paradigm. A good example of this can be found in another important story of Akutagawa's, *Kareno shō* (*Withered Fields*), which again demonstrates the primacy of the structure over character in the short story.[15] In the story, Bashō — the great seventeenth-century poet — is dying. He is surrounded by his faithful disciples, all of whom are well-known figures in Japan that are considered to be great men in their own right. The narrative is quite simple: Akutagawa evokes the setting and the gloomy day, and then he describes each disciple, one after the other, as he goes to pay his last respects to his dying master. It is a story that most Japanese readers would know well. Akutagawa, however, describes something nobody in the Japanese tradition ever imagined when telling the story before. Traditionally the story was used to illustrate the dedication and love of the disciples for their master. However, in Akutagawa's version, the disciples react completely unexpectedly: negatively, selfishly. Each is discovering himself engrossed in his own preoccupations far from the solemn grief everyone thought he was experiencing.

What is interesting in *Withered Fields* is that it is the type of text that is considered complex. Critics (both Japanese and western) often cite it as bearing the echo of the contradictory sentiments that disturbed Akutagawa about the death of his own master, Natsume Sōseki. The unexpected scene is supposed to be a "revelation" for each of them, and for the readers as well. But close analysis shows things to be quite different, and particularly interesting because the matter is treated in a way that is typical of the classic short story.[16]

---

15 Akutagawa Ryūnosuke, *Exotic Japanese Stories: The Beautiful and the Grotesque*, trans. by Takashi Kojima and John McVittie (Liveright: New York, 1964), pp. 291-303 (hereafter Kojima). The Japanese text can be found in Iwanami, II, pp. 201-11.

16 Edwige de Chavannes-Fujimoto is a good example. Her claim that *Withered Fields* is a profound psychological study does not prevent her from recognising that there is a sort of mechanical law in this text, through which assumed attitudes are automatically transformed into their contrary. She notes that the beginning of the story lacks psychological complexity and that all the descriptive traits (the costume or bearing of the characters) are caricatures, the equivalent of the attributes given to "puppets". As the text unfolds, she argues that Bashō's death reveals each disciple's true depth. According to Chavannes-Fujimoto, the story provides a true study of the human heart, because Akutagawa was "distributing" the different emotions of his heart among the various characters. Edwige de Chavannes-Fujimoto, *Akutagawa Ryūnosuke. L'organisation de la phrase et du récit* (Paris: Inalco, 1979), pp. 145-46.

The essential point is that the various "revelations" which occur to the characters are in fact homologous. Certainly, we see the deep interior reactions of each of them to the death of their venerated master. But these reactions always follow an identical law: in each case they radically contradict what was anticipated. The disciples' mourning of their master's death is proverbial: we expect an account of terrible grief. But each of them acknowledges with surprise its absence. There is certainly "revelation", but this comes in the fact that every detail of their grief is the exact opposite of what they had expected. Kikaku experiences total indifference, augmented by physical disgust for the appearance of the dying man; Kyorai recognises that his constant activity on behalf of his master's well-being has mostly resulted in his own immense self-satisfaction; Shikō is only concerned about the funeral peroration which he must compose, and the material fall-out from his master's death; Inenbo only sees in another's death the respite which he will experience from his own inevitable demise; and finally Jōsō, "that old and faithful Zen devotee" is filled with a profound serenity — the "unlimited sadness and unlimited comfort" of being freed from the chain with which his spirit had been weighed down by Bashō's crushing personality.[17]

By taking their various attitudes to be the manifold reactions of one man (Akutagawa) on the death of his own master, critics have reverted to the idea of diversity, and therefore of a certain psychological richness. But if we forget about the author (and this text in no way claims to be autobiographical) we immediately become aware of the "narrative saturation". Drawn together within the circle of disciples, these unexpected, diverse feelings basically make us feel that we are faced with *all* possible egotistical reactions. What the text provides, then, is not a series of differentiated nuanced portraits but in turn two successive concepts: first, what the critic Edwige de Chavannes-Fujimoto calls the "puppet", in which the initial characterization is a caricature, a symbol of a conventional attitude; then, through the intermediary of a reversal that is identical in each case, the opposite attitude, which is equally a caricature. The text does not follow the meanderings of a soul, but creates two paradigms linked one to the other through antithesis.[18] One cannot transform mechanical

---

17 Kojima, p. 302 (p. 210).
18 Chavannes-Fujimoto (1979), moreover, insists on the importance of the contrasts in this text: she recognises a series of "reversals", and "antitheses", and concludes: "a simple click is enough to make the other face appear" (p. 146).

symmetry into complexity by simply noting — as Akutagawa does when speaking of Kyorai — that "satisfaction and remorse, like the shade and sunlight, bore with them a destiny that had entangled him".[19]

Even Jōsō, who benefits from somewhat special treatment, is nevertheless reduced to a caricature. He is the only disciple whose feelings reveal a certain ambivalence: a sad and voluptuous joy. Pains are taken to characterise him as the "most faithful" of the disciples, excessively devoted. Yet, this embryo of ambiguity cannot hide the tension between devotion and real relief at the death of another, with that "other" being dearest to his heart. What we have is a pure and total reversal of the traditional version of the death of Bashō. The contrast as a quasi-abstract "law" of the text is underlined by the reminder *sub fine* of this traditional version:

> In such a way it happened that Bashō-an Matsuō Tosei, the greatest haiku master, unprecedented in ancient and modern times, enveloped in 'the boundless grief' of followers who mourned his passing, suddenly began his journey towards death.[20]

Akutagawa returns ironically to the vulgate: the "boundless grief" is exactly what has been deconstructed by irony.

Secondary tensions

Antithesis is not a stylistic device but an organising principle in the classic short story. And so it is not surprising to find it at all levels of the text, where it creates microstructures and establishes secondary oppositions that contribute to the coherence and stability of the text as a whole. Anton

19 Kojima, p. 296 (p. 205).
20 Ibid, pp. 302-03 (p. 211). Critics frequently insist on the presence of contrasts in the short story, but never, to my knowledge, see it as a profound part of the structure. In addition to the work of Tieck, the contemporary writer Ōe Kenzaburō argues that the density of writing found in good short stories is the result of tension. However, to his mind, this tension might be found not in the text, but within the author. He gives as examples the writers of Meiji and himself. He cites the tension between his persona as a naïve young man of provincial Shikoku and his reality as the celebrated darling of Tōkyō's literary elite. As for the Meiji writers, they were torn between western and Japanese culture, and this provided the basic oxymoronic tension in most of their short stories — Mori Ōgai's *Maihime* (*The Dancing Girl*) or *Fushinchū* (*Under Construction*), for example. One should remark that this does not allow for Ōgai's *Sanshō Dayū* (*Sanshō the Steward*), or Kōda Rōhan's *Gojū no tō* (*The Pagoda*) — yet these texts are nevertheless organised by a very strong oxymoronic tension. Ōe goes on to criticise the younger generation, who refuse to subject themselves to this kind of tension and adapt completely to the American subculture: which is why, according to Ōe, there are no great short stories being written today. Ōe Kenzaburō, "Sakka no soba kara", *Bungakkai*, 41-49 (September 1987), 180-83.

Chekhov's *Volodya Bol'shoi i Volodya Malen'kii* (*Big Volodya and Little Volodya*) provides a good example of what I call "secondary tensions".[21] A young woman, Sophia, has just married a colonel much older than herself (Big Volodya) because the man she loves (Little Volodya) does not return her affections. The essential antithetic tension in this story is the clash between Sophia's demonstrative gaiety at the beginning (her "discovery" that she really loves her husband and her happiness in being married) and her despair at the end, when her life seems completely ruined. This is a common theme for Chekhov: the impossibility of leading a pure and joyous life.

Along with this basic tension, a series of others are established: the most important is the opposition between Sophia's exaggerated expressions of deep feelings and the void into which they fall; her husband attaches absolutely no importance to her desire for spiritual purification. She then turns to Little Volodya, who becomes her lover immediately after her marriage, and asks him for guidance — just one word that will help her find a way out of the dreary misery of her life. All he does is to repeat like a refrain, throughout the text, the onomatopoeic "*tararaboumbia*".[22] Similarly it is enough for Chekhov to compare the relationship that binds the two Volodyas with that which bound the great poets Gavrila Derzhavin and Alexander Pushkin in order to illuminate the antinomy between the two worlds in which these relationships exist.[23]

Finally, in keeping with these three oppositions, another contrast plays an important role in our perception of the principal theme: the opposition between Sophia's life of pleasure, and that of her friend Olga, who has just entered a convent as a novice. The contrivance here is obvious: bringing an adulteress and a nun together creates a strong oxymoronic tension, and allows Chekhov to treat the theme very economically. At the end of the story, Sophia visits Olga in the convent almost every day, and her complaints to her pious friend about her all too worldly sufferings totally discredit her

---

21 Anton Chekhov, *Late-Blooming Flowers and Other Stories*, trans. by I. C. Chertok and Jean Gardner (New York: McGraw-Hill, 1964), pp. 127-46 (hereafter Chertok). The Russian text of this story can be found in Anton Pavlovich Chekhov, *Polnoe sobranie sochinenii i pisem*, 30 vols (Moscow: Nauka, 1974-1983), VIII, pp. 214-25 (hereafter Nauka).

22 The beginning of a burlesque song of the time.

23 "[Big Volodya] extolled [Little Volodya], blessing his future just as Derzhavin did for Pushkin". Chertok, pp. 130-31 (Nauka, p. 216). This line comes immediately after a remark that Little Volodya has always had women in his student room. The very lively tradition of the heroic-comic in the preceding century in Russia made readers even more aware of this genre of proceedings: Russian readers are trained by this tradition to detect irony.

character. The global tension gives the story structure while the secondary tensions energise the details: by contrasting Sophia's life with that of Olga's, Chekhov intensifies its emptiness. The recurring use of contrast creates the concrete impression of an abyss, a dead-end situation. Not only does Chekhov show a world closed in on itself, dreary and desperate, but, by presenting its absolute contrast, he "locks in" this world, while making it immediately tangible to the reader.[24]

Vladimir Kataev has shown that the matrix of all Chekhov's work is a series of short stories from his youth that he calls "the short stories of discovery".[25] In these stories, the hero receives at full force the shock of an apparently ordinary event that transforms his entire concept of the world. An evening spent with friends in a street of brothels, an insult inflicted by some merchants on a student whom they paid to play the piano at their wedding, a tooth extraction;[26] these are the "trifling occurrences", but for the hero they provide the occasion for reshaping his whole frame of thought, which he had thought to be stable and definitive.[27] In a great many of these stories, the basic antithesis is emphasised by the contrast of two expressions: *kazalos'/okazalos'* ("it seemed that/it appeared clearly that"). Chekhov always constructs a diptych. He develops first the character's false concept of the world (*kazalos'*), before showing how he becomes aware of its artifice. Only then will he develop the new order of the world as the hero now conceives it (*okazalos'*): confused, complex and in conflict. The oxymoronic tension is thus established and proclaimed, because Chekhov is well aware of the formidable efficacy it gives to his denunciation. We shall see that Chekhov is one of the very few authors of the period who did write stories free from oxymoronic tension, but these texts only constitute

---

24 Goethe's *Novelle* is profoundly structured by the antithesis "strength/gentleness", summarised in the final image: "If it is at all possible to think that, on the features of such a fierce creature, the forest king, the despot of the animal realm, an expression of friendliness, of grateful satisfaction, could be discerned, then here it was so". Johann Wolfgang von Goethe, *Great Writings of Goethe*, ed. by S. Spender, trans. by Christopher Middleton (New York: New American Library, 1958), p. 260. As is often the case, we have here an entire series of secondary tensions: for example, between the princess's vow, out of curiosity, to see the animals on her return, and her anguish at the encounter.

25 V. B. Kataev, *Proza Chekhova: problemy interpretatsii* (Moscow: Izd-vo Moskovskogo universiteta, 1979). For a partial translation see Vladimir Kataev, *If Only We Could Know: An Interpretation of Chekhov*, trans. by Harvey Pitcher (Chicago: Ivan R. Dee, 2002), pp. 11-19.

26 In *Pripadok/The Crisis* (Nauka, VII, pp. 199-221); *Taper/The Pianist* (Nauka, IV, pp. 204-08); and *Znakomyi muzhchina/An Aquaintance of Hers* (Nauka, V, pp. 116-19).

27 Kataev (2002), p. 12.

a handful.[28] Although he is rightly celebrated for the nuances in his plays, when turning to the short story, Chekhov — like Henry James — uses the capacity of the form to the full. He builds oxymoronic tensions out of paroxystic characters, because this is a particularly efficient way to build a story and to create emotion.

Editing antithetic tension: Maupassant and James

By way of conclusion to this chapter, I will examine two examples where writers have reworked material organised by antithetic tension. The first is that of Guy de Maupassant, who reused in the story *La Confession* (*The Confession*) the material he had previously included in the chronicle *Un drame vrai* (*A True Story*).[29] In *A True Story*, the earlier of the two texts, Maupassant declared that the facts he was about to relate were impossible to use in a story, because they were too unlikely, even though they were in fact true. He developed a discussion with the critic Albert Wolff in which he maintained that this material would be fit only for popular novelists.[30] In the latter story, Maupassant removed what he thought to be the most far-fetched details of the story, but he left the deeply improbable antithesis that lay at its core.

In *A True Story*, the following are the "true" but unlikely facts: a man has killed his brother on the eve of the latter's marriage to a young woman whom they both love. The crime is not discovered, and he marries the girl. They have three daughters, one of whom marries the son of the magistrate who had been in charge of the murder investigation. During the wedding feast, the new father-in-law sings a song that the judge recognises, but without remembering the details. Lengthy research enables him to find the song in the midst of the papers on this very old case: it was copied on the torn page that had served to load the gun. He finds the book buried among the father-in-law's possessions, and has him condemned.

---

28 The few examples of Chekhov's stories that are free from oxymoronic tension tend to come later in his career, for example *The Bishop* (1902) and *The Betrothed* (1903). Anton Pavlovich Chekhov, *Anton Chekhov's Short Stories*, ed. by Ralph E. Matlaw (New York: Norton, 1979), pp. 235-63.

29 Guy de Maupassant, *Complete Short Stories of Guy de Maupassant*, trans. by Artine Artinian (Garden City, NY: Hanover House, 1955), pp. 371-74 (*The Confession*) and pp. 491-94 (*A True Story*). For the original French (henceforth cited as Pléiade), see Guy de Maupassant, *Contes et nouvelles*, ed. by Louis Forestier, 2 vols (Paris: Gallimard, collection La Pléiade, 1974), I, pp. 1035-39 (*La Confession*) and I, pp. 495-97 (*Un Drame vrai*).

30 There is a summary of this discussion in Pléiade, I, p. 1448.

The Confession is based on a similar idea of an unsolved murder finally being resolved. It tells the story of two sisters: the youngest, Marguerite, devotes her life to her elder sister Suzanne after Suzanne's fiancé disappeared on the eve of her wedding. Marguerite was obstinate in her refusal to marry, and on her death-bed she reveals the reason: she had killed the fiancé forty years earlier out of jealousy. In this story, Maupassant removed all the fantastic vicissitudes of *A True Story* and substituted the younger sister's remorse for the judge's random finding. She had spent her entire life expiating her crime, and she herself confesses it; there are no clues miraculously discovered in unusual circumstances. The closeness of the two sisters increases the pathos of the situation, and an entire life spent in guilt and atonement collides with the intensity of the jealousy and horror of a confession. The behavioural patterns are what interest Maupassant in the latter story rather than police intrigue.

However, the author retained the first story's eminently rhetorical structure in its entirety. Although his intention was not to write a "popular" novel, he made the details incandescent and let them clash violently with each other within the framework of the short story. He substituted one antithetic tension for another, but without renouncing it, because it is the antithesis that gives the text its compactness and effectiveness. The crime is just as outrageous (to kill a sister's fiancé out of jealousy is on the same scale as killing a brother in order to steal his fiancée).[31] In short, Maupassant did not consider the somewhat forced structure to be contrived; he thought the problem lay in the far-fetched details. For a realist short story writer, improbability depends on the circumstances and not on the organization of the material, no matter how rhetorical. This seems particularly surprising given the theory that, as we saw in the last chapter, short stories must be written simply about simple things.[32]

---

31 Maupassant writes a long passage in which Suzanne, before she grants her sister forgiveness, plunges into a vivid — paroxystic — vision of the life she would have led with the man she loved.

32 It is in this light that I think we must consider Bakhtin's analysis of the *Schwellensituation*, as developed in Mikhail Bakhtin, *Problems of Dostoevsky's Poetics*, ed. and trans. by Caryl Emerson (Minneapolis, MN: University of Minnesota Press, 1984). The classic short story always creates an antithetic tension, which uncouples the elements at their most extreme, contrasts and "distinguishes" them. The "threshold-situation" will then naturally be found there, as it is supremely that of distinctions and reversals, whether narrative or thematic, psychological or symbolic. Because the threshold-situation implies a certain type of mental attitude found in the short story, it often happens that the two are associated.

The second example is of a different order: it is a question of the transformation from a short story into a novel. The initial sketch or "germ" of James's *The Ambassadors*, defined in *The Notebooks* as a short story, was reworked from that shorter version into the novel we know.[33] In this process, an essential element of the concept disappeared.[34] In both the short story and the novel, we see a New England intellectual, Lewis Lambert Strether, delegated by his rich patroness to go to Paris to see her son, Chad Newsome. Mrs Newsome fears that Chad is leading a life of depravity in the French capital, and there are rumours in his hometown of Woollett, Massachusetts that he is living with a "horrible woman".[35] Strether is sent to investigate and deal with the problem.

The story is built around a central scene in which Strether urges one of the young people he befriends in Paris, to *live*, and not to waste his life.[36] When he conceived of the work as a short story, it was crucial for James to diametrically oppose this attitude with another. It was necessary that Strether should have behaved at a different moment *in exactly the opposite way*: "I am supposing him [...] to have 'illustrated', as I say, in the past, by his issue from some *other* situation, the opposite conditions".[37] The first element of the "little drama" that James imagined for his short story was that "[Strether] has sacrificed some one, some friend, some son, some younger brother, to his failure to feel, to understand, all that his new experience causes to come home to him in a wave of reaction, of cumpunction".[38] At the end of the story, Strether was to sacrifice himself to have Chad "live".[39]

However James completely abandoned this crucial element of the short story when he reworked it as a novel.[40] The upheaval experienced by Strether in the short story was sudden;[41] as James puts it he was to "accept

33 This is from James's notebook entry of 31 October 1895. Henry James, *The Notebooks of Henry James*, ed. by F. O. Matthiessen and Kenneth B. Murdock (New York: Oxford University Press, 1947), pp. 225-29 (hereafter *Notebooks*).
34 We have three stages of the text: the "germ" — in the form of a short story (*Notebooks*, pp. 225-29); the project sent to the editor of the review for approval — already in the form of a novel (pp. 370-415); and the final stage of the novel.
35 Ibid, p. 388.
36 This conversation is an indirect response to the situation Strether finds in Paris, and an indication of the way he will behave with Chad himself.
37 *Notebooks*, p. 256 (James's emphasis).
38 Ibid.
39 Ibid, p. 228. By not bringing him back, Strether puts an end to his own engagement to be married to Chad's mother, a marriage that represents for him "rest and security".
40 As stressed by the editors (ibid, p. 371).
41 Ibid, p. 227.

on the spot, with a *volte-face*, a wholly different inspiration".[42] In the novel, instead of being the result of an incident, the change in Strether comes about slowly, and his loyalty to Mrs Newsome and New England values are never lost. At the end of the novel, although Strether's interior world is by now completely separated from that of his rich patroness, he returns to America without marrying his European love interest, filled with a mixture of emotions. Once James conceives of the work as a novel, the subject is no longer "the revolution that takes place in the poor man",[43] but a slow transformation, the creation of complexity, of shades and half-truths (such as the "virtue" of Chad's attachment to Mme de Vionnet). In other words, *the novel has expelled the antithetic structure* in which Strether would have been seen to sacrifice someone close to him, and, for this reason, to sacrifice himself to save someone else. The oxymoronic tension is necessary for the short story but not for the novel.[44]

---

42 Ibid, p. 257.

43 Ibid, p. 227. The word "revolution" is used three times (twice on p. 227 and once on p. 228).

44 We observe the same kind of elaboration and renunciation of antithetic tension in the work which led Verga from his *Padron N'toni, bozzetto marinaresco* (*A Sketch of Sailors*) to the novel *I Malavoglia* (*The House by the Medlar Tree*). Verga wrote to his fellow writer, Luigi Capuana (14 March 1874), that in the short story he wanted to establish a striking contrast between the serenity and freshness of his country hero and the life of the city. The novel, however, abandons this tension as well as the entire mythical and myth-making vision that Verga's other short stories of the same theme carried, for example, *Fantasticheria* (*Caprice*). See Guido Baldi, *L'artificio della regressione: tecnica narrativa e ideologia nel Verga verista* (Naples: Liguori, 1980).

3. Ending with a Twist

A whole body of contemporary criticism is dedicated to the analysis and appraisal of short stories' endings. A story's conclusion has often been thought of as an effective way of grasping the genre's characteristic features, as well as to understand the ways that readers experience the genre.[1] Influenced by the seminal reflexions of Frank Kermode in *The Sense of an Ending*,[2] critics like John Gerlach, Per Winther, David Sheridan and Susan Lohafer have all argued that endings were of key importance in defining the short story.[3] This idea has been present since the very beginnings of the

---

1 To use Rebecca Hernández's words: "the opening and closing markers" are "usually identified as fundamental criteria for triggering the sense of storyness". Rebecca Hernández, "Short Narrations in a Letter Frame: Cases of Genre Hybridity in Postcolonial Literature in Portuguese", in *Short Story Theories: A Twenty-First-Century Perspective*, ed. by Viorica Patea (Amsterdam: Rodopi, 2012), pp. 155-72 (p. 167). See also Susan Lohafer in *Reading for Storyness: Preclosure Theory, Empirical Poetics, and Culture in the Short Story* (Baltimore, MD: Johns Hopkins University Press, 2003). Lohafer notes that there is a "[move] from the analysis of closural features and effects, to a test of the primacy, the necessity, the uniqueness of the short story in the family of genres" (p. 55).

2 Frank Kermode, *The Sense of an Ending: Studies in the Theory of Fiction* (Oxford: Oxford University Press, 2000 [1st ed. 1967]).

3 John C. Gerlach, *Toward the End: Closure and Structure in the American Short Story* (Tuscaloosa, AL: University of Alabama Press, 1985); Per Winther, "Closure and Preclosure as Narrative Grid in Short Story Analysis", in *The Art of Brevity: Excursions in Short Fiction Theory and Analysis*, ed. by Per Winther, Jakob Lothe and Hans H. Skei (Columbia, SC: University of South Carolina Press, 2004), pp. 57-69; David Sheridan, "The End of the World: Closure in the Fantasies of Borges, Calvino and Millhauser", in *Postmodern Approaches to the Short Story*, ed. by Farhat Iftekharrudin, Joseph Boyden,

DOI: 10.11647/OBP.0039.3

genre. In his "Philosophy of Composition" (1846), an essay as famous as his review of Nathaniel Hawthorne's *Twice Told Tales*, Edgar Allan Poe states that the whole short story is a kind of preparation for its ending, and insists that the writer should construct the story with its conclusion constantly in mind.[4] In 1925, the Russian Formalist Viktor Shklovsky also paid particular attention to short stories' endings.[5]

At the end of the nineteenth century, the surprise ending in particular came to epitomise the type of pleasure readers came to expect from the genre. In the newspapers where the bulk of the stories were published at that time, hundreds of stories ended with a "twist-in-the-tail". Lohafer has noted that surprise endings are now in critical disrepute "because they exhibit a simple notion of plot that can easily become simplistic, formulaic, and trivial".[6] And readers and critics are prone to oppose dramatically Guy de Maupassant's classic short stories with the more "modern" stories of Anton Chekhov or Katherine Mansfield, as it seems they represent all the difference between a "closed" and contrived text and an "open", natural one. However, Lohafer also reminds us that one should not condemn these endings too hastily: Ian Reid has showed that the device can be used not only as a mere "gimmick" ("the merely tricky ending"), but also as the "ending which jolts us into perceiving something fundamental about what we have been reading".[7]

Joseph Longo and Mary Rohrberger (Westport, CT: Praeger, 2003), pp. 9-24; and Susan Lohafer, *Coming to Terms with the Short Story* (Baton Rouge, LA: Louisiana State University Press, 1983) and "Preclosure and Story Processing", in *Short Story Theory at a Crossroads*, ed. by Susan Lohafer and Jo Ellyn Clarey (Louisiana State University Press, 1990), pp. 249-75.

4   "It is only with the *dénouement* constantly in view that we can give a plot its indispensable air of consequence, or causation, by making the incidents, and especially the tone at all points, tend to the development of the intention". Edgar Allan Poe, "Poe on Short Fiction", in *The New Short Story Theories*, ed. by Charles E. May (Athens, OH: Ohio University Press, 1994), pp. 59-72 (p. 67).

5   Viktor Shklovsky, *Theory of Prose*, trans. by Benjamin Sher (Elmwood Park, IL: Dalkey Archive Press, 1990), pp. 52-70.

6   Lohafer (1983), p. 97. Valerie Shaw, while discussing famous stories with a surprise ending makes the comment more general: "The main drawback to stories which gain narrative compression by making plot serve a single realization, however ironic in quality, is that like most jokes or anecdotes, they can never arouse the same bafflement and surprise twice over". Valerie Shaw, *The Short Story: A Critical Introduction* (London: Longman, 1983), p. 56.

7   Ian Reid, *The Short Story* (London: Methuen, 1977), pp. 60-62. On the surprise ending, and its more complex variant the "surprise-inversion", see Richard Fusco, *Maupassant and the American Short Story: The Influence of Form at the Turn of the Century* (University Park, PA: Pennsylvania State University Press, 1994). Fusco also talks about the "trick ending" as "a structural dogma", and about the critical disdain towards it (see his introduction, especially p. 4).

Having recognised the crucial importance of paroxystic characterisation and antithetic structure in previous chapters, we will now look at how the short story's ending, be it improbable or "natural", takes its force from the structure at large. The ending is where the forces at play in the narrative come to light. Final twists are one way of unleashing the full power of the antithetical forces, but "open endings" can serve a similar purpose.

The "twist-in-the-tail" and antithetic tension

One of the most famous twist-in-the-tail endings is in Chekhov's *Toska* (*Misery*).[8] It is a story of a sleigh-driver who has lost his son, and tries to tell everyone he meets about his grief. Each person in turn rejects him, including a hunchback whose infirmity should have made him sensitive to the misfortunes of others. Ignored by everyone, and left alone with his distress, his story ends with a twist: he must confide his sorrow to his horse, which is standing in the straw after the night's work. This ending reveals the depth of the sleigh-driver's despair and the terrible abyss separating him from the others. By showing an animal as the only possible confidant for a desperate man, Chekhov emphasises the world's cruel inhumanity.

This of course is a case of a surprise ending adding emotion to the text, as "it brings to the surface the real significance of the foregoing action".[9] The essential point, however, is that the powerful emotional effect of the story is not created at the final moment, but was present in the text from the beginning. It comes from the antithetic structure, which makes us aware of the irreconcilable juxtaposition of two worlds: that of the unfortunate man and that of those who are indifferent to his suffering. Chekhov shows all the steps taken by the old man as a series of useless efforts — each one more desperate than the other — to stress the constant lack of understanding shown to him. The trick ending condenses that unrelenting coexistence into the paradox of the horse alone being gifted with the virtue of humanity. It sharpens our perception of it; it shocks us. But the entirety of the text is

---

8 Anton Chekhov, *Anton Chekhov's Short Stories*, ed. by Ralph E. Matlaw, trans. by Constance Garnett (New York: Norton, 1979), pp. 12-16 (hereafter Matlaw). The Russian text of this story can be found in Anton Pavlovich Chekhov, *Polnoe sobranie sochinenii i pisem*, 30 vols (Moscow: Nauka, 1974-1983), IV, pp. 326-30 (hereafter Nauka). References will be given first to the translation, then to the original text in brackets.

9 Reid (1977), p. 61.

there to create the conditions of that surprise. What happens with the end is that it brings these worlds face to face *in praesentia*.

A most famous and often discussed surprise ending story, Maupassant's *La Parure* (*The Necklace*), is structured in the same way.[10] In this story, a young clerical worker's wife, Matilda Loisel, poor and dreaming of luxury, borrows a diamond necklace from a very rich and worldly school friend to go to the Ministry ball to which her husband is for once invited. She is a great success at the ball, but loses the necklace. She has it copied by a jeweller, and she and her husband spend the next ten years working day and night to pay it off. One day she meets her friend promenading in the Champs-Elysées, and she explains to her why she has grown old and ugly to the point of being unrecognizable. A sudden turn of events: the friend informs her that the original necklace was nothing more than a cheap imitation.

André Vial suggests that the trick ending "balances" and carries equal weight with the rest of the text.[11] This idea can be taken further: the whole story is epitomised by the ending, which brings to the surface the tension that organises the text. Again, it is a question of a radical opposition between two worlds. On the one hand, the ordinary world of the working class — a theme eminently typical of Maupassant — carried to its extreme here in the powerful images of the frantic ten years' work of the Loisels. On the other hand, there is the life of elegance and luxury in the dreams of Mme Loisel — and in the actual world of her friend — which is epitomised by the necklace. The ending lays bare this system by reversing it; it gives the reader a key to this narrative by pushing the process to its paroxysm. By destroying the very idea of the necklace's value, Mme Loisel's dream is reduced to nothing. In a single act, ten years of intense effort — the sacrifice of an entire life — is undermined from within, made even more useless and senseless.

Franck O'Connor notes how remarkable it is that the reader of short stories never thinks about the future of the characters.[12] If we were to take

---

10 Guy de Maupassant, *The Complete Short Stories of Guy de Maupassant*, trans. by Artine Artinian (Garden City, NY: Hanover House, 1955), pp. 172-77 (hereafter Artinian). The French text of this story can be found in Guy de Maupassant, *Contes et nouvelles*, ed. by Louis Forestier, 2 vols (Paris: Gallimard, collection La Pléiade, 1974), I, 1198-1206 (hereafter Pléiade).

11 André Vial, *Guy de Maupassant et l'art du roman* (Paris: Nizet, 1954).

12 Frank O'Connor, *The Lonely Voice: A Study of the Short Story* (Cleveland, OH: World Publishing Company, 1963).

a moment to think about the characters in *The Necklace*, we would see that it would be impossible for no good to result from the efforts of the Loisels. If they have replaced a real jewel with an imitation, they must now own a nice little fortune, equal to the value of the jewels. But our reading never gets that far: we are full of the sight of this misery and these broken dreams, and are unable to escape the magnetic circle which the text draws around us. The basic result of the trick ending is to magnify the already powerful effect of the tension created earlier in the story. And when rereading a story such as this one, our feeling for the drama will be intensified and the antithetic tension will be deepened. Rereading produces the tragic irony: the tension is increased because we know from the outset that all these efforts, described with such force and detail, are in vain. We have in mind the two poles and we see them clash constantly.

The "Twist-in-the-tail" and retroreading

Far from O. Henry's simple trick endings, great stories with a "twist-in-the-tail" force us into some sort of a "retroreading": a reconsideration of the entire text from its beginning.[13] This is the case, for example, in *Poprygun'ya* (*The Grasshopper*), one of the few short stories that the mature Chekhov ended with a twist.[14] Olga Ivanovna — the "Grasshopper", or literally, the "praying mantis" — is an exalted young woman who is passionate about art and artists. She is the wife of a doctor, Osip Stepanich Dymov, whom she finds very dull compared to her seemingly brilliant artistic friends. As the story progresses she becomes increasing disillusioned with these artists. The surprise at the end is that, upon Dymov's death, Olga realises that her husband was, in fact, a scientific genius and the only great man she has ever known.

Behind the apparent neutrality of the narrator's discourse, the reader quickly discerns his condemnation of the heroine and her poor ability to judge her friends. Confronted with the panegyric of men whose false grandeur only she is taken in by, we see clearly that Dymov, in his constant and quiet dedication to medicine, is the only character leading a useful life (something that is always important in Chekhov's universe). The ending vastly strengthens the previous text by concentrating its scattered elements

---

13 The idea of "retroreading" is developed by Michael Riffatterre, *Semiotics of Poetry* (Bloomington, IN: Indiana University Press, 1978).

14 Matlaw, pp. 69-90 (Nauka, VIII, pp. 7-31).

and becoming the catalyst for a more energetic process. Olga's realisation at the moment of her husband's death comes, of course, too late.[15] Here the "twist-in-the-tail" is realised in the mocking commentary she hears from the whole room: "You missed your chance! You missed your chance!".[16] In other words: in your mad chasing of geniuses, you have ignored the one truly great man. As his wife, contributing to his fame, she could have been associated with Dymov's "grandeur"', and, what is more, be truly loved.

In this case the trick ending does more than simply summarise the antithetic tension: it unveils it, making visible a whole aspect of the text that Chekhov had taken pains to conceal from us. Of course we knew from the beginning that Olga's high opinion of her friends was without foundation. From the first page the accumulative repetition of the name "Olga Ivanovna" — unexpected in a stylist as Chekhov — already rouses our suspicion that the tremendous qualities she sees in her friends are in direct proportion to the homage continually paid to her own talents. But the ending reveals the other pole of the tension, the one we could not have entirely foreseen, but which we recognise the moment it is presented: not only has she spent her life believing mediocre people to be great, but — the irony of fate — in her worldly blindness she did not see the one person who was worth noticing, her own husband. This ending creates nothing, but it provides the supplementary turn of the screw, and "clinches" the theme. All the metaphors of confinement are appropriate here: we remain struck by this apparition of destiny, which suddenly imprisons the heroine in an ironic end and leaves her no escape.

On rereading, in the harsh light cast by the ending, we can identify many elements that we underestimated the first time around, if not totally missed: the mention of the painter Ryabovsky's remarkable physical beauty, for example or the worldly tone assumed to judge the value of the drawings of a landowner as "veritable miracles".[17] It is as if the short story were being

---

15 If it were not too late, the forces introduced would not unleash the maximum power they could produce. This is one of the reasons drama is so often mentioned in relation to short stories; see Shaw (1983), pp. 63-66, for example, or the French philosopher Hippolyte Taine on Maupassant's *Le Champ d'oliviers* (*The Olive Grove*), which, he exclaims, is "a piece from Eschyles" (quoted in Pléiade, II, p. 1702). This could very well be an accurate comparison on the level of structure where there is a "twist-in-the-tail": catastrophe brings short stories, like tragedies, to an end because at this point the height is reached and to continue would only weaken or change the subject.

16 Matlaw, p. 89 (Nauka, p. 30). The original Russian is the ironic repetition of a unique word: "*prozevala! prozevala!*" ("missed! missed!").

17 Ibid, p. 70 (p. 8).

read in two different stages: before reading the ending, we were sensitive to the discordances. Some elements perhaps made us uncomfortable, but we were not sure why. On rereading, we discover another landscape in which the contours are clear and defined.

At the end of a story, when a trick ending reveals the truth about the narrative, our mind is settled. Theoretically, there are now two possibilities. Either one meaning replaces the other and eliminates it, or the text plays on the two scenes at the same time and the two meanings become superimposed on one another. Classic short stories generally belong to the former category. One meaning replaces the other: the sense of the first reading is seen to be wrong, and must be replaced by a different truth.[18] This is the case in *The Necklace,* and most definitely in *The Grasshopper.* We certainly cannot go on thinking that the necklace is real (and that the Loisels' efforts are justified), and it is not possible to think that the "great men" around Olga are, in spite of everything, truly important artists. *The Grasshopper* establishes its truth very firmly, and behind the remarks of the artists on the diverse and varied talents of Olga, we read their snobbishness and Ryabvovsky's carnal desire for the heroine.[19]

One specific set of stories, however, retain their ambiguity until the end. Fantastic stories do not generally replace one "truth" with another, but superimpose two interpretations without withdrawing one or the other, as through a stereoscope. This is a feature of fantastic stories at large: generations of readers have discussed the reality of the facts in Henry James's *The Turn of the Screw,* for example. The whole point of the "Modern Fantastic" is to put the reader in a state of uneasiness, where nothing is ever clear or definite,[20] and the surprise ending can be used to strengthen

---

18 This replacement is the origin of the "impossibility" of rereading most of the short stories that rely on a surprise ending. The beginning of the text "falls flat" from the moment the surprise is revealed and the mystery clarified. In the cases where there is no possible "retroreading", the beginning, which was meant to lead us into error, no longer misleads us, and the text loses all its charm.

19 May describes such a "retroreading" of James Joyce's *The Dead.* See Charles E. May, "The Secret Life in the Modern Short Story", in *Contemporary Debates on the Short Story,* ed. by José R. Ibáñez, José Francisco Fernández and Carmen M. Bretones (Bern: Lang, 2007), pp. 207-25 (pp. 216-18). See also Fusco's (1994) analyses of some surprise endings (pp. 22-26 and 107): "these three revelations sharply requalify our comprehension of the story and, hence, of war" — but also of codas (p. 18).

20 See Tzvetan Todorov's definition of the Fantastic as implying the reader's (and often the characters') "hesitation between a natural and a supernatural explanation of the events described". Tzvetan Todorov, *The Fantastic: A Structural Approach to a Literary Genre,* trans. by Richard Howard (Cleveland, OH: Case Western Reserve University Press, 1973), p. 33. See also Maupassant's own reflections, as developed in a famous article

that particular effect.[21] A particularly remarkable example of this is found in Maupassant's *Sur l'eau* (*On The River*), which describes a fisherman's night of anguish when his boat is suddenly stranded in the middle of a river and he falls prey to strange visions.[22] We saw in Chapter One that the structure of this story stems from there being two sets of paroxysms, antithetically opposed to each other: the admiration of the beauty of nature and the anguish which at times replaces it. The narrator claims to be mad about water, and begins his tale with a profession of faith: "Let a fisherman pronounce the word [river]. To him it means mystery, the unknown, a land of mirage and phantasmagoria...".[23] After developing the theme of the beauty of the river, he then in turn describes its danger: it is both seductive and treacherous. Moments of exaltation — the stillness of being at anchor after a long day's fishing, the contemplation of the "phantasmagorias" — alternate rapidly with moments of panic, when the anchor refuses to come up, the fog hides the boat, and the hero becomes prey to nightmares.[24] With daylight his misadventure comes to an end, and two fishermen help him lift the anchor. He is ready to laugh (and we with him) that his evening of terror was the result of his nerves playing an unexpected trick on him. Yet at the precise moment when the story is complete, and we the readers emerge with him from the nightmare, the fishermen manage to raise the anchor; but with it they bring up "the body of an old woman with a big stone tied around her neck".[25]

Here the ending suddenly disturbs the balance which had only just been established: we thought we could laugh at the adventure, we believed it had been an hallucination caused by a mind weakened by solitude and alcohol, and we agreed with the narrator when he considered his feelings somewhat puerile. Then suddenly: "once more I felt the same strange

---

published in *Le Gaulois* (7 October 1883), p. 1: "[Since we entered Modernity], the writer kept roaming on the borders of the realm of the supernatural rather than entering it. He found terrifying effects while staying on the border of the possible, by throwing the [readers'] souls, aghast, into hesitation. The reader, uncertain, lost his footing..." (translation ours).

21 Fusco (1994) does not consider that, in Maupassant's surprise-inversion stories, one meaning replaces the other; he insists to the contrary on the "weav[ing of] competing perspectives" (p. 48). The examples he gives, however, are of fantastic tales or tales of madness — which make a very particular use of the form and, as we will see in this book's epilogue, finally led to its deconstruction.

22 Artinian, pp. 169-72 (Pléiade, I, pp. 54-59).

23 Ibid, p. 169 (p. 54).

24 Ibid, pp. 171-72 (pp. 58-59).

25 Ibid, p. 172 (p. 59).

nervousness creep over me. The anchor remained firm" and, as the body appears, everything is brought into question.[26] It is not that we are ready, consciously, to recognise that the presence of a body blocking the anchor could produce supernatural effects. But at the least expected moment, the apparition of the corpse gives meaning to a whole series of indications of something bizarre that we had observed in passing without being able to give them any precise form or value.

The narrator, trying desperately to "reason with himself", had refused to make the necessary connection between the various bizarre elements. It is the ending that identifies this connection, even though it is only through, and for, our unconscious perception. The rapidity with which it comes upon us is the best guarantee of our accepting this connection, even if only to refute it immediately. It forces us to review all the elements accumulated in our memory and to see how well they are organised. We can therefore no longer ignore either one or the other interpretation; they are no longer exclusive, and we are left with the absolute ambiguity, the very basis of the "Modern Fantastic". What has taken place? The only conclusion would seem to be the one given by the narrator at the beginning: a "singular adventure", which leaves one perplexed.

A traditional comparison associates the short story with the sonnet, because of the intensity of its impressions: in the short story, as in the sonnet, we have in our head all the significant traits which work together to obtain a universal effect. This concept seems to me to be quite accurate from a technical point of view, and I hope to have shown why: in a genre that is so dependent upon antithetic tensions, where the structure is essential, and rests so heavily on the paralleling of elements, the reader is completely accustomed to a work of structural order. We have just seen that if the signs accumulated in the course of the text do not take on meaning immediately, they are organised into a sort of secondary account, half-hidden but perceptible. The elements are, as it were, put on reserve in the memory, and the ending gives them a definitive place in the structure. Whether one rereads it or not, the fullness of meaning of the structure — and of course its brevity — means that it amounts to the same thing. At the end of the text, one's mind runs through the elements stored during the reading and gives them back their hidden meaning, the meaning provided by the general structure and economy of the work.

---

26 Ibid, p. 170 (p. 57).

"Open" texts and tension

One consequence of the structure of the classic short story is that there is no radical difference between "open" texts and those "locked in" by the trick ending; the absence of a twist does not mean that there is no tension, but simply that the tension has not been "unleashed". Sometimes the impact is even more powerful if the tension does not materialise in such an ending. Chekhov's *Dama s sobachkoi* (*Lady with Lapdog*) can be considered the epitome of the "open" text, with its last word: "beginning".[27] This is a particularly important and complex story, with very subtle effects — and one of the very few where the distancing of the characters will be finally supervened. However, I would like to stress here that the structure Chekhov sets up is the same as in the classic stories we have already seen; and that even the ending's effect is very close to what can be observed in texts locked in by the surprise ending, although this effect is reached through the opposite process.

What is built by *Lady with Lapdog* is a dynamic antithesis of the same kind we saw at work in *The Grasshopper* or *The Necklace*. At the beginning of the story, Dmitri Dmitrich Gurov is an apathetic Moscow civil servant and also a libertine; he is a philanderer who constantly deceives his boring wife, only to find in his liaisons an almost greater boredom. In the end, Gurov, in contrast to this past, lives only for his mistress Anna Sergeevna, whom he loves with a prodigious intensity; their love is compared to the natural attachment of two migratory birds, indestructible and with the commitment of a married couple. Gurov is not immediately transformed by the liaison with Anna: at first it is shown to be even more boring than his other adulterous adventures. But from the moment that his life obeys the mandates of his passion, this love becomes as extreme as his boredom had been, the sole principle of his life, the law that governs all of his existence.

This is not to say that *Lady with Lapdog* is confined in the frame of the classic short story. What happens in this story is that, using exactly the usual tools, Chekhov will in fact be moving *beyond* the classic short story; as Charles E. May puts it, he is here "present[ing] spiritual reality in realistic terms".[28] But it is important to recognise that what we have here

---

27 Anton Pavlovich Chekhov, *Lady with Lapdog and Other Stories*, trans. by David Magarshack (London: Penguin, 1964), pp. 264-81 (hereafter Magarshack). For the Russian text, see Nauka, X, pp. 128-43. The story ends with the line: "the most complicated and difficult part was only just beginning" (p. 281 [p. 143]).

28 May (2007), p. 210.

is a transitional form. In a few of the short stories Chekhov produced at the end of his career, such as *The Bishop* (1902) and *The Betrothed* (1903), Chekhov renounced anecdote and freed himself from the classic form — we shall come back to this in the book's conclusion. But *Lady with Lapdog* is a perfectly classic story, based on the usual structure and characterisation process. The remarkable point is that *within* this frame, he has been able to "confront the quintessential problem of the modern short story [...] How is it possible for a realistic narrative to convey meaning and significance," to quote May again.[29]

As we are now used to recognising as typical of the classic short story, Gurov's "conversion" represents the passage from one paroxystic state to another, from the depth of boredom to the height of passion. Chekhov never once justifies Gurov's "conversion". *Mutatis mutandis,* and the same thing happens here as in *Gramigna's Mistress* (see Chapter One): the passage from one pole to the other is sufficient in itself and does not need justification in the eyes of the reader. At no point does Chekhov try to explain Gurov's passion, especially not by means of Anna's own qualities or the quality of their relationship: Anna is remarkably little defined. One single trait is added to that of "the bored young woman": her complete inexperience, the "diffidence and angularity of inexperienced youth".[30] Of course, one could say that it is left to the reader to add the missing links: Gurov, perhaps, was moved by this gaucherie; Anna was, perhaps, an exceptional young woman. But this reading is never supported by the text. What gives the text its structure and builds its basic strength is the tension between the two ways of existence. The absence of a "twist-in-the-tail" does not make it a different kind of text; on the contrary, it ultimately plays the same role; it is the crowning element of the process already at work, the revelation of the force of the antithesis. By finishing with the picture of Gurov searching desperately for a solution to their situation, by indicating that "the most difficult part was only just beginning", Chekhov creates an uncertainty that only deepens the effect of this conversion, albeit subtly.

One of the great characteristics of Chekhov's short stories is that they go beyond the classic use of the form by involving its formal characteristics in the thematic plan. The tension in this story is not established between two narrative elements, but between truth and falsehood, between the life

---

29 Ibid, p. 216. May is again speaking here about Joyce's *The Dead*. The sentence goes on: "It is the same problem that Chekhov had to deal with".

30 Magarshack, p. 268 (Nauka, p. 132).

of a libertine and a first love. Chekhov exploits the tension like a dramatic device, in order to create emotions that owe nothing to the psychological richness of his characters, nor to the complexity of their relationship, but are entirely based on the collision between two worlds established at the outset of the story. The text, however, seems to us neither abstract nor schematic (even though it is based on effects that are both), because of its concreteness and the strength of Chekhov's description. The radical absence of a definitive solution, for which this text is famous, serves just as well as a trick ending to emphasise the clash between the "normal" life of the man who is blasé and the "extraordinary" life where love is the centre of everything. The open ending shows them both to be inescapable.

4. The Tools of Brevity

The short story is almost always praised for its "economy of means". In the classic short story, this restraint is not to be found in the narrative elements that, to the contrary, we have seen to be built on extremes. Nevertheless the short story clearly proceeds towards its goal with a particular speed and effectiveness: within only a few pages, the reader is introduced to a full universe and knows what is at stake in the narrative. The aim of this chapter is to understand how the classic short story achieves this acceleration of comprehension in the reader — its means being drastically different from those of the novel or what I propose to call the "modern" short story. The antithetical structure, as we saw in the previous chapter, is part of the expedition of the readers' understanding. However, there are two other particularly important techniques that we will examine in detail in this chapter: the use of preconstructed material, and the device of focussing exclusively on the subject.

If we are quick to grasp what is at stake in a classic short story, it is because, first and foremost, we are already familiar with the text's characters, situations and values. The classic short story uses what we could call "preconstructed" material: something "ready-to-understand" in the same sense as "ready-made". The reader is introduced to a universe whose elements he or she recognises because she has come across or thought of them previously. These elements can be — and are certainly in the great stories — organised in a new, piquant way. But the fact that they

DOI: 10.11647/OBP.0039.4

are already in some way familiar means that the reader can process them more quickly.

The techniques used in this process are themselves diverse. The short story can use an historical character as the protagonist — someone famous who needs no introduction to the reader; it can re-use a character that is familiar to the reader from another story in the same collection; it can create an "empty" character to be given a personality by the reader; or it can revert to the use of types. The only thing these techniques have in common is the particular role they play in "accelerating" our involvement in the text. This chapter will also review what we could call the "tight focus" on the subject: the classic short story eliminates from consideration everything that is exterior to the precise situation on which it is centred. It concentrates on a partial aspect of the general tableau selected for its subject. However, excluding anything that is not dependent on the precise narrative goal is not a simple "suspension" of the context; it gives a partial — and eventually false — representation of a particular detail.

Preconstructed material

As usual, we shall begin with the simplest case, and look at examples in which the story relies on the use of famous or historical characters. Apart from texts whose sole interest rests in presenting some aspect of a famous person's life,[1] there are many short stories where the reader applies his or her previous knowledge of the hero or of the theme of the story: Nikolai Leskov's *Ledi Makbet mtsesnkogo uezda* (*Lady Macbeth of the Mtsensk District*); Leonid Andreev's *Lazarus* and *Judas Iscariot*; Mori Ōgai's *Hanako*, in which the main character is Auguste Rodin; Gustave Flaubert's *Saint Julien l'Hospitalier*; and Akutagawa's *Karenoshō* (*Withered Fields*) which we have already discussed in Chapter Two.

Clearly *Withered Fields* would lose its essential strength if the heroes were not the well-known disciples of Bashō, revered in Japan since the seventeenth century. If that were not so, the writer would first have to explain at length the disciples' virtues as well as their master's greatness and charisma. The fame of his characters allows Akutagawa to proceed to

---

1   Maupassant's *Auprès d'un mort* (*Beside a Dead Man*), for example, is only interested in describing Schopenhauer's wake. Guy de Maupassant, *The Complete Short Stories of Guy de Maupassant*, trans. by Artine Artinian (Garden City, NY: Hanover House, 1955), pp. 922-25.

the development of the scene. This does not mean, however, that we need to be familiar with each character's individuality in order to appreciate the text: all we need is to grasp the terms of the problem that will be set before us. Western readers who are not familiar with Bashō only have to read the translator's short note indicating their status as good men *par excellence* to be able to enjoy the text. Merely the evocation of these well-known disciples, or of Lady Macbeth, for example, already provides the reader with a complete idea of what might happen in this story, and the writer can begin *in medias res*.

In fact, one might say that *all* characters in the classic short story could be described as in some way famous, or at least (well)-known. My point is not that the short story only provides the reader with traditional literary types or stock characters; on the contrary, everyone insists, and with good reason, on the number and variety of the short story's characters. Henry James and Anton Chekhov have both declared that if their short stories were put end to end they would present a complete picture of the society of their time.[2] This is not inaccurate: an immense panorama of social roles, often overlooked by literature in the past, can be found in the work of short story writers where outlaws, pariahs and marginal people are consecrated by literature.

My point is that all of these social (or psychological) roles are already known to the reader in one way or the other. It could be the first time he or she has read about them in a literary text, but he has already in some way "heard of them". He may not be able to describe their life with the zest of the storyteller, but at least he can place them on society's chessboard; he can recognise their social role. In short, these are "objective types", types found in everyday life, even if they are not literary types. When Ambrose Bierce describes the frontiersmen, when Herman Melville uses seamen in his stories, when Rudyard Kipling mentions the natives of a small town in India, they instantly evoke in the reader's mind clear notions of what an Indian, or a struggling seaman, or a frontiersman is, even if the reader has never met someone like this in the flesh. The story will build on these preconceived notions, without needing to describe the character in detail first.

---

2 James wrote to Robert Louis Stevenson: "I want to leave a multitude of pictures of my time, projecting my small circular frame upon as many different spots as possible". Henry James, *Letters: 1883-1895*, ed. by Leon Edel (Cambridge, MA: Harvard University Press, 1980), III, p. 240.

It is the same with characters not quite so exotic: the ridiculous provincial who haunts the stories of Guy de Maupassant or Chekhov was only too well known to readers of the time, who delighted in his endless misadventures, repeated in after-dinner jokes as well as in stories in the newspapers. This character was also very present in the mind of the readers of intellectual journals, who were concerned with the social misery of the provinces. When the Naturalists describe prostitutes or outlaws, when Giovanni Verga presents his Florentine or Milanese readers with Sicilian fishermen and muleteers, or peasants, they are illustrating a problem that was at the centre of attention in Europe at that time.

In short, this genre — perhaps more than any other form — relies on the readers' own knowledge of the world and its various actors to proceed immediately to the story. The short story will fill one of the sections of the chessboard, giving flesh and blood to the idea the reader already has (which may well have been an abstract and lifeless representation). But at the same time — and this is essential — the short story relies on "ready made" characters. The interest in reverting to such types is obvious: the characters emerge in the reader's mind fully equipped, like Athena from Jove's head, and the reader can follow them in their adventures without losing time in discovering each of their features in detail.

Not only does the short story resort to what is already known, but it also may even repeat the process of "prefabrication". Other characters will be deduced from a character within the text itself. We have already seen quite a few examples of this in Chapter One. Irving Saposnik comments in reference to Robert Louis Stevenson's *Dr Jekyll and Mr Hyde* that Hyde is none other than a "deformed" Jekyll, a Jekyll in reverse; created in our imagination by a simple reversal of the signs for each of Jekyll's traits.[3] Similarly, in O. Henry's *The Gift of the Magi*, Jim is a sort of "male Della", the masculine version of the virtue Della represents; and in Verga's *Gramigna's Mistress*, the rebel Gramigna is the diametric opposite of the heroic "Tallow Candle". These are not, admittedly, the most subtle of short stories, but we have seen that even the more nuanced stories also use the technique: the fiancée of the devoted Corvick in James's *The Figure in the Carpet* is "obtained" simply by splitting Corvick himself in two, and Corvick, by a reduplication of the narrator: he is another admirer of Vereker, only more devoted.

---

3   Irving Saposnik, *Robert Louis Stevenson* (New York: Twayne, 1974), p. 101.

Character types

Here we are touching on a central point: the nature of the enjoyment that is particular to this genre. If the short story is so willing to reproduce its characters from each other or to take them completely formed from society, it is because its interest lies elsewhere. It is hardly feasible to abide by the assertion, though commonly held, that the short story "does not have the time" to build the characters and the universe it presents to us.[4] Brevity has never prevented lyric poetry from elaborating subtle psychological elements, for example. What is more, the constraint of length is not always rigorous; and if magazines have sometimes imposed a precise word count on their authors, it is *because* the short story already existed as a genre, and not the contrary.[5]

The key to this might be that the classic short story favours the effects of structure over the examination and development of characters, over the building of a complex universe. Critics like Boris Eikhenbaum, Tzvetan Todorov or Romano Luperini were not mistaken when they rejected any idea of "psychological depth" in the characters of short stories;[6] Todorov argues that their value is "functional" and Luperini that they are two-dimensional.[7]

---

4   Given as self-evident, the phrase "*la nouvelle n'a pas le temps*" ("the short story does not have the time") is a cliché in French criticism, found everywhere in textbooks. See for example, Jean-Pierre Blin, "Enseigner la nouvelle: perspectives et limites d'une didactique" in *La Nouvelle et d'aujourd'hui*, ed. by Johnnie Gratton and Jean-Philippe Imbert (Paris: Éditions L'Harmattan, 1998), pp. 187-98 (p. 193). It is also used as a statement of definitive truth in educational materials from the Ministère de l'Éducation Nationale: "Contrary to the novel, the short story does not have the time to elaborate the thoughts and feelings of the characters", *Lire une nouvelle réaliste de Maupassant*, available at http://www.academie-en-ligne.fr/Ressources/4/FR41/AL4FR41TEWB0112-Sequence-01.pdf, p. 14 (accessed 22/10/13, translation ours). Even Sean O'Faolain states that in the short story "there is no time for explanation" but for him this means that there must be an allusive power in the short story (as we have seen above). He later remarks that style is in fact often *slower* in the short story: "In a short story one concentrates. Naturally the style is retarded". Later, referring to Stephen Crane's *The Monster*, he says "Compare this slow meticulous style with that of a novelist". Sean O'Faolain, *The Short Story* (Cork: Mercier, 1948), pp. 197, 254 and 255.

5   In Japan, the constraints of length have always been very loose, and for a long period authors had no definition of the form of the short story (the term itself, *taupen shōsetsu*, did not exist before the end of the nineteenth century); many of the short stories of Ōgai, Kunikida Doppo or Akutagawa nevertheless present their characters in exactly the same way, resorting to what the reader already knows.

6   See Boris Eikhenbaum, "How Gogol's 'Overcoat' is Made", in *Gogol's "Overcoat": An Anthology of Critical Essays*, ed. by Elizabeth Trahan (Ann Arbor, MI: Ardis, 1982), pp. 21-36. The original Russian is in *Literatura: teoriya, kritika, polemika* (Leningrad: Priboi, 1927), pp. 149-65.

7   Tzvetan Todorov, *Grammaire du* Décaméron (The Hague: Mouton, 1969); and Romano

The reverse opinion is so common, however, that it must be examined. For a great number of Anglophones and almost all French critics, the short story accelerates the process of perception and entry into the narrative world, but this is attributed to the genre's "allusive power", which would suggest everything it does not say. In their opinion, the genre's value belongs to its characters, which offer great depth and psychological complexity. The length of time spent in elaboration would be replaced by the intensity of the reader's work and by the genre's remarkable ability to create for us an entire character out of a few elements provided by the text. There would be a magic belonging to the text of short stories that could stimulate *something new* in the mind of the reader, and not, as I have suggested something already known or foreseen.

Sean O'Faolain is a typical proponent of this idea, and his remarks on the allusive art of Chekhov are worth pausing to review. O'Faolain states that in *Lady with Lapdog*, the reader is invited "to plumb her [Gurov's wife's] character, to let [the reader's] imagination expand her inward nature from a few outward signs".[8] He also praises the short story's format as being more capable of suggestion than the novel. The examples he gives, however, seem to me to be counter to his thesis. He illustrates his argument with two descriptions of the spouses of the heroes from *Lady with Lapdog*. First, Gurov's wife:

> She was a tall, erect woman with dark eyebrows, staid and dignified, and, as she said of herself intellectual. She read a great deal, used phonetic spelling, called her husband not Dmitri but Dimitri, and he secretly considered her unintelligent, narrow, inelegant, and did not like to be at home.[9]

Then the husband of Anna Sergeevna:

> He bent his head at every step and seemed to be continually bowing. This was the husband whom, in a rush of bitter feeling, she once called a flunkey. And there really was in his long figure, his side-whiskers, and the small bald patch on his head, something of the flunkey's obsequiousness; his smile was

Luperini, *Verga: l'ideologia, le strutture narrative, il "caso" critico* (Lecce: Millela, 1982). See also Giuseppe Lo Castro, *Giovanni Verga: una lettura critica*, Saggi brevi di letteratura antica e moderna, 5 (Soveria Mannelli: Rubbettino, 2001), about types in Verga (p. 23 and p. 63).

8   O'Faolain (1948), p. 190.

9   Here as quoted by O'Faolain, p. 189. The full text of *Lady with Lapdog* can be found in Anton Pavlovich Chekhov, *Lady with Lapdog and Other Stories*, trans. by David Magarshack (London: Penguin, 1964), pp. 264-81 (hereafter Magarshack). For the Russian translation, see Anton Pavlovich Chekhov, *Polnoe sobranie sochinenii i pisem*, 30 vols (Moscow: Nauka, 1974-1983), X, pp. 128-43 (hereafter Nauka).

sugary and in his buttonhole there was some badge of distinction like the number on a waiter.[10]

It seems strange that in reading this we could have the impression of "plumbing her character, letting [our] imagination expand her inward nature from a few outward signs".[11] On one hand, this is true: we do indeed see something appear. We have a vivid picture before our eyes. The power of the description, its effective reliance on hypotyposis, makes the portrait successful. But what we see forming is not a personality in the sense that the novel has taught us to apply this term, but a *type*, and one that is hardly subtle at that.

There is no need to have an in-depth knowledge of Russia at the end of the nineteenth century in order to see that, in the case of Gurov's wife, we are dealing with a Bluestocking. Even for the reader who has not been forewarned, these few "external signs" are enough to figure out the *role* — in the theatrical sense — of the woman who forces her talent, who clumsily imitates the exalted manners of her time. Certainly, for the Russian reader of the period, this description will recall a particular type of pedant, the intellectual woman of the 1860s, so often mocked in literature. The description is indeed effective. However, I do not think that we can go so far as to say that the resulting character is very complex.[12]

The second example is more instructive, because it reveals the essential fact of the variety of these "roles", which, no doubt, prevented the critics from recognising the presence of types in short stories.[13] Anna's husband is

---

10 O'Faolain (1948), p. 190.

11 Ibid.

12 Diana Festa McCormick notes that we know very little about the story's hero Georges d'Estouteville in Honoré de Balzac's *Maître Cornélius*: "What is extraordinary, however, is that each character, despite the limited perspective in which he is presented, appears lively and convincing; it is because Balzac gives *what is essential about each being*, the most striking traits, to allow us readers to *fill in the gaps* left by his pen. Each character is a sketch, an outline which should suggest the complete person". She continues: "And he is defined by his love or the passion which controls him. Georges d'Estouteville is *defined* by his love for Marie de Vallier". McCormick sees clearly that the characters do not emerge from the narrow framework of their definition; yet she does not follow her reasoning to its conclusion: we reconstruct, true, but a two dimensional character, enclosed within a strict definition. See Diana Festa McCormick, *Les Nouvelles de Balzac* (Paris: Nizet, 1973), pp. 134-35 (translation ours; emphases mine).

13 That is certainly the case for French criticism. For the Anglophone critics, however, my feeling is that they are interested essentially in Chekhov's "epiphanic" stories — a few stories at the end of his career that are very near to Hawthorne's or the twentieth century ("modern") short stories. *Lady with Lapdog* is not one of these late stories, but, as we mentioned earlier, it is one of his most complex short stories, which goes beyond this "ready-made" material. In this case, this schematic material is in fact "filled up" by the

also a type, because all the traits converge towards the same concept: that of the ridiculous husband. Here he is *explicitly* confined to his definition: Anna treats him like a "flunkey" and the narrator notes that in truth he fits that definition well.[14] What follows further illustrates the concept: the detailed traits are equally the characteristics of the flunkey. But — and this is the most important point — he does not correspond to a type that is particularly easy to define. He is a servile professor, an important provincial who is, in the larger scheme of things, a non-entity. This type has not been codified in the way the bluestocking of the 1860s has.

But in fact he has the same status in the text, as we see from the assimilation of the "distinguished member of the university" into "just another waiter". This brief description "locks" the character into his role; it is the keystone that eternally supports the building. This light is a little too bright, and the character is without shadow or shade. The fact that the "professor who resembles a flunkey" is not a pre-existing literary type changes nothing: he can immediately be imagined by the reader, because he corresponds in every detail to a definition whose elements are pre-established. The literature of the nineteenth century is full of ridiculous, pompous or pitiful provincial notables, and we recognise one of them immediately when we see him, even if he is of a slightly different species.

Perhaps this process is best delineated by Maupassant. In *Le Rosier de Mme Husson (An Enthusiast)*,[15] the narrator lingers over this rapidity of perception and illuminates for us this process of evoking a character in its entirety, which has been so often called the "work of short story readers".[16]

---

reader, as a result of the richness of the story as a whole. It should not prevent us from seeing that Chekhov uses the same devices as other story-tellers of his time, albeit in a very personal way.

14 "And there really was [...] something of the flunkey's obsequiousness". O'Faolain (1948), p. 180; Nauka, X, p. 139.

15 Guy de Maupassant, *The Complete Short Stories of Guy de Maupassant*, trans. by Artine Artinian (Garden City, NY: Hanover House, 1955), pp. 866-76 (hereafter Artinian). The original French text can be found in Guy de Maupassant, *Contes et nouvelles*, ed. by Louis Forestier, 2 vols (Paris: Gallimard, collection La Pléiade, 1974), II, 950-66 (hereafter Pléiade).

16 Critics speak constantly of the "effort" of a reader who participates much more intensely in the constitution of the text of a short story than in a novel. Helmut Bonheim, however, carried out a survey of a series of readers, and in the short story he found that they rarely added new elements but simply followed the "program" established by the text. See Helmut Bonheim, *The Narrative Modes: Techniques of the Short Story* (Cambridge: D. S. Brewer, 1982). On the short stories of Flaubert and Joyce, see André Topia, "Joyce et Flaubert: les affinités sélectives", in *James Joyce: Scribble 2: Joyce et Flaubert* (Paris, Minard, 1990), pp. 33-63. According to Topia, too, the reader sees the figures vaguely, but invents

The narrator arrives at the home of an old school friend, a provincial doctor, whom he has not seen for twelve years. He introduces him to the reader as he finds him on the doorstep of his house:

> I never should have known him. One would say he was forty-five at least, and, in a second [the] whole [of] provincial life appeared before me, dulling, stupefying and aging him. In a single bound of thought, more rapid than the gesture of extending my hand to him, I knew his whole existence, his manner of life, his bent of mind and his theories of living. I suspected the long repasts which had rounded his body, the little naps after dinner in the torpor of a heavy digestion sprinkled with brandy, and the vague contemplation of the sick, with thoughts of roast fowl waiting before the fire. His conversation on cooking, cider, brandy and wine, upon certain dishes and well-made sauces [were revealed to me just by looking at] the red puffiness of his cheeks, the heaviness of his lips and the dullness of his eyes.[17]

I have quoted this long description because, by its very length, it calls for several comments. First of all, it shows clearly that it is not a question of the short story having or not having the time to make a character complex. Long, detailed, and paroxystic, this description does not differ in length from one found in a novel. However, what is being developed at length here is nothing more than a series of the most worn-out *topoi* of provincial life. This is what makes it different from a description in a (great) novel: the short story's description develops the characteristics one by one until they converge towards a single concept. A "handful of signs" create for us a lively image, yes, but not the manifold facets of a human heart. The combined traits converge to create a stock character: a character whose concept is already in the reader's mind.

The rest of the short story does not challenge this concept of the "provincial" provided at the beginning: the long conversation between the two friends centres on the theme of food, and, as expected, the provincial will appear to be totally absorbed in material life, boasting of the set-up of his farm and the freshness of his produce. In other words, the description *actualises* the abstract idea, using it to the full, relying on the presuppositions it is based upon. When we make quick judgements, we are judging on the basis of well-established pre-existing values.[18] What the short story evokes

---

nothing: his participation is not creative.

17 Artinian, p. 867 (emphasis mine).

18 See Pierre Boulez on improvisation: "what can [the improvising player] do? He can only turn to information he has been given on some earlier occasion, in fact to what he has already played". Pierre Boulez, *Orientations* (London: Faber, 1986), p. 461.

in the mind of the reader are not new ideas. If the reader can put together a total entity, that entity will bear the colours of his presuppositions on the subject; it is similar to the way that a musician, when improvising, makes use of known schemas.

Recurring characters and empty characters

There were two other means that were used in the nineteenth century and developed in the twentieth century to provide the reader with readily understandable material; they were used more in the "modern" as opposed to the classic short story that we have been reviewing here. The first of these is when the writer uses a character that he has introduced to the reader in another story in the same collection. Rudyard Kipling does this a couple of times in *Plain Tales From the Hills*. When he wants to introduce a character of whom the reader, for once, can have no "instinctive knowledge", he proceeds in two steps. In a very descriptive story he introduces Mrs Hauksbee or the policeman Strickland — characters who are almost impossible for his British readers to imagine.[19] Then, in a later story, he makes use of the already formed character whose bizarre traits are now familiar to the reader.[20] It is a technique whose function is akin to the reversion to type or to the use of historical characters: our previous knowledge hastens our comprehension.

This practice is one of the devices that gives cohesion to "cycles" or "sequences" of interrelated short stories.[21] For Forrest Ingram and Susan

---

19 Mrs Hauksbee appears in *Three and — An Extra* and again in *The Rescue of Pluffes*, *Consequences* and *Kidnapped*. Strickland appears in *Miss Youghall Sais* and other stories in *Plain Tales From the Hills*.

20 The French philosopher Alain defines Balzac's short stories, for example, as the "crossroads" at which the characters of the *Comédie humaine* meet. See Alain (Emile-Auguste Chartier), *Avec Balzac*, in *Les Arts et les Dieux* (Paris: Gallimard, 1937), p. 1018. For someone who has not read *Splendeurs et misères des courtisanes*, the Baron Nucingen in the short story *La Maison Nucingen* is perfectly schematic and frightening: he is the "ruthless banker". Readers of the novel will have a slightly different impression: they will be repelled by his buying Esther, and at the same time moved by his love for her. The "substance" of the character therefore comes also from an exterior knowledge that precedes the short story.

21 On the difference between "cycle" and "sequence", see for example James Nagel, *The Contemporary American Short-Story Cycle: The Ethnic Resonance of Genre* (Baton Rouge, MA: Louisiana State University Press, 2004), p. 12. See also the notion of "epi-stories", as a form intermediate between novel and stories, proposed by Andrea O'Reilly Herrera, "Sandra Benitez and the Nomadic Text", in *Postmodern Approaches to the Short Story*, ed. by Farhat Iftekharrudin, Joseph Boyden, Joseph Longo and Mary Rohrberger (Westport, CN: Greenwood Press, Praeger, 2003), pp. 51-62.

Garland Mann, it is precisely the presence of a recurring character that, in most cases, gives a cycle its unity; the reappearance of a hero makes it possible for the reader to remain on familiar territory.[22] Sometimes, a cycle of short stories will make use of this familiarity in order to *rework* the types it presents, showing them in a slightly different light.[23] Although this subgenre is not our topic here, let us note that the story cycle has been one of the subjects attracting most critical attention in the last decade or so. Critics have convincingly argued that it was a genre in its own right, and may very well have been the most innovative form of that period in the United States.[24] This was the genre predominantly written and read by minorities, consequently modifying the relationship between author-reader and the subject addressed.[25] However, one should not assume that the cycles automatically play this role. In James Joyce's *Dubliners*, the inclusion in a gallery of converging portraits accentuates the satirical charge of each. In

---

22 See Susan Garland Mann, *The Short Story Cycle: A Genre Companion and Reference Guide* (New York: Greenwood Press, 1989); see also the classic Forrest L. Ingram, *Representative Short Story Cycles of the Twentieth Century: Studies in a Literary Genre* (The Hague: Mouton, 1971). Recent criticism, however, has emphasised the role in unifying the episodes of the setting. Nagel (2004) argues that a recurrent setting was historically the "most persistent" means of unifying cycles (p. 17), and Gerald Lynch shows this in Canadian story cycles. Gerald Lynch, "The One and the Many: Canadian Short Story Cycles", in *The Tales We Tell: Perspectives on the Short Story*, ed. by Rick Feddersen, Susan Lohafer, Barbara Lounsberry and Mary Rohrberger (Westport, CN: Greenwood Press, Praeger, 1998), pp. 35-46.

23 This would be particularly true when the cycle relies on a plurality of narrators rather than one particular recurring narrator. A good example, outside our time-span, would be Marguerite de Navarre's *Heptameron*: between the stories themselves, the narrators/listeners develop full-length discussions about what they just heard. This allows for a new approach to the stories material, and for reappraisal of the characters. Nagel (2004) describes the genre as having "contrasting point of views", as in Tim O'Brien's *The Things They Carried* and Amy Tan's *The Joy Luck Club* (pp. 128-52 and 188-222). See also Herrera (2003) on the "prism" offered by the "epi-stories". On the sequence as allowing "each apocalypse" to "be served in its own cup; the collision by no means shatter[ing] the vessel of the short story, even if some of the contents spill over", see Robert M. Luscher, "The Short Story Sequence: An Open Book", in *Short Story Theory at a Crossroads*, ed. by Susan Lohafer and Jo Ellyn Clarey (Baton Rouge, LA: Louisiana State University Press, 1990), pp. 148-167 (p. 167).

24 Nagel (2004) stresses the importance of the form, both in quantity and in quality: "By the turn of the century, nearly a hundred volumes of story cycles had appeared in the United States, and the genre was not yet in its most important phase [...] Scores of narrative cycles appeared in each decade of the new century, some of them containing individual works that are among the best ever published in English" (pp. 4-5).

25 "That for the last century many of the most important works of this kind were written by authors from differing ethnic backgrounds suggests that [...] the story sequence offers not only a rich literary legacy but a vital technique for the exploration and depiction of the complex interactions of gender, ethnicity, and individual identity". Ibid, p. 10 (see also p. 17).

Go Down, Moses, John Carlos Rowe shows that the most profound feature of the cycle may well be William Faulkner's "ultimate inability to grant his African-American characters the independent voices he knows they must have in a truly 'New' South".[26]

Finally there is the use of what we could call an "empty" character, a character that is hardly defined at all and can therefore be filled in by the reader. At the end of the nineteenth century, this is even more rare than the reuse of a character. In fact we only come across it in fantastic stories, which exploit the possibilities of the genre along very different lines from most classic short stories. Very near to the "I" used in lyric poetry, this "empty" character is the channel through which emotions are conveyed to the reader. Present in the narrative either as an actor or a witness, he receives no real characterisation, he is left "blank," and our attention is never directed to him as a person: he is our link to the text, a window on the narrative world.

In the fantastic stories of the nineteenth century, the "empty" character helps us to enter the world of the bizarre, because we are invited to share directly in his emotions — as we are in lyric poetry — and to share in his discovery of strange facts and behaviours. The narrator of Maupassant's *Sur l'eau* (*On The River*), discussed in Chapters One and Three, is a good example of this: his only defining trait is his extraordinary love of the river.[27] He is simply a means for conveying to us the strangeness of the adventure, allowing us to share in the excitement and dread of that night's phantasmagoria. He plays the same role of hastening our entry into the narrative; his blankness allows us to take his point of view.[28]

Tight focus

The short story expels everything that is not its subject. At first glance, it seems normal that a text, particularly a short one, should not attempt to talk about everything. But the specific subject of the short story occupies all the narrative space, making itself the sole object, and losing all its connections

---

26 John Carlos Rowe, "The African-American Voice in Faulkner's *Go Down, Moses*", in *Modern American Short Story Sequences: Composite Fictions and Fictive Communities*, ed. by J. Gerald Kennedy (Cambridge: Cambridge University Press, 2011), pp. 76-97 (p. 78).

27 Artinian, pp. 169-72 (Pléiade, I, pp. 54-59).

28 When this character says "I", we are led to feel his experience could be ours. This, however, is not an automatic consequence of the use of the first person narrator, as we shall see in Part III (see especially Chapter Eleven).

with the world. It is only because waiting is shown as John Marcher's *only* activity in James's *The Beast in the Jungle,* that it can be presented in such a paroxystic fashion.[29] The classic short story usually removes its characters from their social ties and the relationships they have to the "real world", and sets them in the sole light of this particular adventure.

Let us think of the social life that a man like Marcher must have led in Victorian England: nothing is said about it, not a single reference is made to his social and cultural surroundings. We are told, incidentally, that both he and his most devoted friend, May Bartram, play their social role very well, but everything ensues as if that role does not exist. They go to the opera together a dozen times a month, but the text gives no hint of the gossip and social reprobation that a relationship such as theirs could not fail to produce in Victorian society. Once May Bartram makes a brief allusion to it ("'I never said,' May Bartram replied, 'that it hadn't made me talked about'"),[30] but it has absolutely no impact on them: they do not change anything in their life.

The descriptions of these conversational currents are not interesting in themselves, and there was certainly no need for James to recreate *Anna Karenina.* But we must recognise that all the terms of the problem are thus falsified: if James had described, or made us feel, the weight of Marcher's social life, if he had restored the real tissue of a man of society's life, he could no longer have presented the waiting for the Beast as prodigious, as the only element of his life. Even the choice of a woman's presence as companion in this wait fits this rarefied atmosphere. Playing on the widespread archetype of the woman who is totally devoted to the man she loves, who weds his values and his destiny, James can extend to her the paroxystic intensity of the waiting without having to justify it. Marcher's friendship with May Bartram is not meant to be a realistic relationship; hers is a duplication of his waiting. Only by blotting out the wider context can *The Beast in the Jungle* develop as a short story. If this tight focus is abandoned, and the exterior world is reintroduced, we are no longer dealing with the "pure bodies" the short story needs. Instead of immediately using simple concepts such as Marcher, the man-who-waits, and May Bartram, the companion-in-waiting, it would have been necessary to establish this waiting as a narrative object, rather than simply presenting it. Comparisons

---

29 Henry James, *The Complete Tales of Henry James*, ed. by Leon Edel, 12 vols (New York: Rupert Hart Davis, 1960), XI, pp. 351-402 (hereafter Edel).

30 Edel, p. 374.

and suggestions of other influences and other preoccupations would have been necessary. The central proof, the reversal of destiny's "visitation" of Marcher, would not have had the same strength; in place of a perfect short story, there would have been the outline of a novel.

We must reject the short story's tame and modest definition of itself: "I am going to show what occurs when X meets Y, when something happens to X in certain circumstances". The idea of a brief and therefore fragmentary text often allows for an unquestioning acceptance of this definition, the short story as a presentation of fragments of existence in a realistic fashion. How could we not acknowledge the right of a short text not to "say everything"? And yet, to remove from the field of attention all that is not the limited subject (the "little action", or the "concetto", in James's terms) does not, by any means, amount to a simple suspension of it.[31] The result is a contrived presentation of this problem; it is now presented in a completely artificial light.[32]

The "complete picture of society" that James or Chekhov suggested one could obtain by putting all their stories end to end is a fraud. Each text is entitled to resolve a unique problem, yes, but the point is that it does so by dealing with only one variable. It refuses to take into consideration all the others and inserts that one chosen variable into a very particular structure, in which everything makes sense. To repeat Marcher's words, enlightened by the discovery of the meaning of his whole history: "Everything fell together [...] the pieces fitted and fitted", but that is only because everything that could not fit in it has been expelled beforehand.[33] It would certainly be rather absurd to accuse James of not having created any real psychological complexity. And if I have chosen an example of his, it is because he cannot be suspected of lacking perfect mastery of such complexities. What should be noted, instead, is that complexity was not his intention in this case: it is never the intention in classic short stories.

---

31 Henry James, *The Notebooks of Henry James*, ed. by F. O. Matthiessen and Kenneth B. Murdock (New York: Oxford University Press, 1947), pp. 148 and 144 (hereafter *Notebooks*).

32 Valerie Shaw says something quite similar about James's stories: "The tightness of the frame actually helps to conceal the author's contrivance of patterns, because within the space marked out the author can appear to investigate the material for its own sake. Inside the frame, looseness can be simulated". Valerie Shaw, *The Short Story: A Critical Introduction* (London: Longman, 1983), p. 75. She does not, however, judge it to be a limitation of the genre: "Framed in a circle, 'The Real Thing' arranges its 'objects' in such a way as to offer us a complete, but not static picture" (p. 74).

33 Ibid, p. 401.

Permanence of types

The short story not only starts with the ready-made, it never departs from it: it does not reshape its material in order to disavow the presupposed simplicity. The descriptions may be very strong and vivid, but they do not challenge either the terms in which the problem is set nor the prejudices of the reader. The characters remain types because they are enclosed in the very simple terms of their original definition. Here again it is important to be precise. The short story does not introduce variations but it may well turn the terms of the problem upside down and reverse the sign that precedes them: present as positive what we perceived to be negative, and vice versa.

Yet the short story almost never does more than present a negation in its purest and simplest form. Consider Maupassant's *Boule de suif* (*Ball of Fat*), a story which shows that it is a prostitute who is a true patriot, rather than the good citizens who scorn her.[34] The setting is the war of 1870 in which France was defeated and invaded by the Prussians. A group of bourgeois residents are fleeing Rouen by coach to protect themselves and their belongings, while proclaiming that they are resolute patriots ready to fight to the end. A prostitute, nicknamed "Ball of Fat" because she is "small, round and fat as lard", is also leaving town by the same coach.[35] Rejected and humiliated, she is nevertheless the only one to show herself capable of greatness of spirit. She refuses to yield to the Prussian officer who is detaining them all, and thinks, speaks and acts with a noble sense of pride. The bourgeois characters, on the other hand, behave basely and finally force her to make love to the Prussian so that they can continue their flight. These characters are vilified by Maupassant for their stupidity, cowardice and hypocrisy. The reader sees before him or her nonentities who are perfectly predictable, even if the extremities to which the text takes them are beyond what the reader would have imagined: pious nuns, for example, draw on biblical quotations to exhort Ball of Fat to give herself to the Prussian. Is it only because these are secondary characters? No, because Ball of Fat herself is treated in the same way: the text simply reverses a prejudice, it turns it upside down. The central antithetical tension contrasts the classic image of the prostitute-pariah with that of the prostitute-patriot.

---

34 Artinian, pp. 1-25 (Pléiade, I, pp. 83-121).
35 Ibid, p. 6.

This inversion is frequently found in short stories, and one of the obvious uses of tension is to "renew" a theme by taking the opposite view of a ready-made image. But it is clear that the battleground for discussion has not changed, that the terms of the problem are pre-determined: is the prostitute a person capable of greatness of soul? Bourgeois prejudice answers: "no"; Maupassant replies: "yes, and much more so than the townsfolk". He thus does not change the usual way of thinking. He contradicts pre-existing presentations, but he is still tied to them. Similarly, at the end of *Dr Jekyll and Mr Hyde,* we are not left with a character from a novel (neither completely good, nor entirely bad), but the coexistence stretched taut between two extremes that never mingle.

In conclusion, we can turn to the problem that Mary Doyle Springer raised without being able to solve: the difficulty of determining with any certainty the main character of James's *The Aspern Papers.*[36] What troubles Springer is that the principal character seems to be the narrator, but, at the same time, James seems to deny him the stature of a hero; for example, in the preface to *The Golden Bowl* he says that this witness is "intelligent, but quite unindividualised".[37] I agree that the essential character is the narrator, but I think that what we just saw makes it clear that what is important to James, here as well as in his other short stories, is not the individual.[38] What interests him is to see the ins and outs of a situation, of a "case", a "problem" confronting a given character.[39] I think "given" should be understood in all its meanings: a precise character, but also a character whom he does not

---

36 Mary Doyle Springer, *Rhetoric of Literary Character: Some Women of Henry James* (Chicago: University of Chicago Press, 1976), pp. 167-248.

37 Henry James, *The Art of the Novel: Critical Prefaces* (New York: Scribner, 1962), p. 329.

38 Although he sees real psychological interest in James's stories (pp. 86-87), Scofield (2006) says of *Julia Bride*: "Its subject is slight but intense (Julia Bride's situation is complex but she is not a morally complex heroine)" (p. 82).

39 As the character in *Broken Wings* exclaims: "We're simply the case" (here: "of having been had enough of"). Edel, XI, p. 232. The "little story" is associated in the *Notebooks* with the "subject": "The great question of the *subject* surges in grey dimness about me. It is everything — it is everything" (*Notebooks*, p. 135). Recurring in the *Notebooks*, are the terms "little drama" (p. 168), "little action" (p. 148), "concetto" (p. 144); and "problem" ("the simple effect that I see in the thing. This effect is that of the almost insoluble problem", ibid, p. 168). See also Clare Hanson: "The subject [of the late nineteenth century tale, as opposed to the "plotless" short fiction] *is* the situation — extraordinary, bizarre, extreme in some way — which is usually referred back to the response of an ordinary, 'typical' human being", Clare Hanson, *Short Stories and Short Fictions, 1880-1980* (New York: St. Martin's Press, 1985), p. 6.

need to build for us to recognise, a character he need only to evoke through some of its characteristics.[40]

As far as *The Aspern Papers* are concerned, these attributes are in fact reduced to their most simple expression; for us to understand and take pleasure in the text, it is enough for the hero to be intelligent, and have a true passion for the memory of the poet Jeffrey Aspern, in whose name he is ready to commit (and will in fact commit) anything vile. To say that the narrator is not individualised is not to say that he is secondary, but only that we are in a *short story*, and that therefore the interest does not lie in a person, a character, but in an event and a structure, from its initial preparation to its realisation.

Finally, it might very well be that Springer's question itself is influenced by the fact that she is dealing with short stories. Short stories do indeed almost always have a main character, and minor parts. Great novels generally don't. Who is the main character in *The Wings of the Dove* or *The Golden Bowl*? Who in Balzac's *La Rabouilleuse*? What distinguishes the character in a novel, as opposed to that in a short story, might well be a tendency to a *fusion* of opposites, no longer experienced as contrasts but as alloys; they are hybrids, resistant to stereotypes. The heroes of short stories, even the main characters, however, embody the coexistence of opposite extremes.

---

40 Springer (1976) is very aware of the supremacy of the situation; she remarks that James "certainly loved character, character in its fullest and subtlest development [...] But he loved one thing more: that the character should be true to the formal requirements of the story in which it appeared" (p. 138).

5. Conclusion to Part I

The techniques we just reviewed combine to make the classic short story's structure an efficient whole. Each of the characters' traits is brought to its ultimate intensity by means of paroxysm; thus making the character an ideal representative of his type. Because this makes the character abstract, the short story can easily and rapidly incorporate him in a strong structure. Similarly, because the structure — the staging of the situation — prevails over the study of individuals, reliance on a type is not a handicap, and the reader's entrance into the story can be accelerated by the use of preconstructed material. Paroxystic characterisation, a structure built on tension, and techniques of acceleration are, therefore, all closely linked. They are not juxtaposed traits, but interlocking folds of a single, unique phenomenon. It is their powerful convergence that makes the classic short story's format so efficient.

Hypotyposis and schematisation

Despite the necessity of these techniques, they can still appear to be somewhat schematic. How is it that the classic short story is rarely criticised for this schematization? Why do readers never see the constantly exaggerated aggrandisement of the characters and why are they never made uneasy by this overwhelming action that sets one extreme inexorably in opposition to another? There would seem to be three reasons for this.

DOI: 10.11647/OBP.0039.5

The first is that, at the end of the nineteenth century as opposed to the beginning, there were few exceptional characters, either very good or very bad. E. T. A. Hoffmann, Théophile Gautier and Edgar Allen Poe were deceased, and the heroes of Goethe's *Novelle* were in the past. The primary character at the end of the century was essentially *mediocre*: an offspring of Gogol's *"mal'enkii chelovek"* ("the little man") who haunts not only Russian literature but also that of the rest of the world. The working man in Maupassant, Verga or O. Henry's short stories, the lacklustre heroes of Akutagawa or Joyce: these are the great battalions of heroes at the end of the century. Regular citizens without any pretence, they are actually men of little substance. It is the ordinariness of their appearance that hides the essential fact: they are *paragons* of mediocrity.

The second reason, perhaps, is that very often the classic short story focuses on a subject that already exists socially and of which the reader already has notions, but which has never been represented in literature. As we have seen, during that period, the character types are not often well-known literary types. On the contrary, the short story explores the social world, and readers and critics alike have been impressed, with reason, by the great variety of characters. This hides the fact that the reader already has preconceived ideas of these "new" characters, and that the classic short story will do no more than develop (along familiar lines) what is already known.

But the main reason seems to me to be that the structure itself is hidden by one of the genre's essential traits: its evocative strength. The sharpness of the antithetical tensions is hidden by descriptions that paint portraits of characters and the setting they are placed in with an extraordinary vividness.[1] What gives the masterpieces of the genre their greatness is the particularly effective use of what ancient rhetoric called "hypotyposis": a lively and striking description, a picture through which the description

---

1 For example, Sean O'Faolain sees in this evocative power the great "charm" or "alchemy" of Alphone Daudet's stories: "Touch upon touch does it. The fine day, his nook in the rocks where he lies like a lizard and listens to the pines, his key put into the cat's hole [...] It is the details that do it". However, he takes pain to distinguish this from mere description: "but is the heart which remembers that really does it". Sean O'Faolain, *The Short Story* (Cork: Mercier, 1948), p. 90. Frank O'Connor argues that "the surface of a great short story is like a sponge; it sucks up hundreds of impressions that have nothing whatever to do with the anecdote". *A contrario*, he judges severely most of Maupassant's stories where "style is sacrificed to anecdote". Frank O'Connor, *The Lonely Voice: A Study of the Short Story* (Cleveland, OH: World Publishing Company, 1963), p. 66.

seems to make us *see* rather than conceive.[2] If we turn to the numerous mediocre short stories found in the newspapers of the late nineteenth and early twentieth centuries, the structure and the exaggerated treatment of material are obvious. It is the evocative power of the great stylists that gives the genre its value.

It is this balance of abstract and concrete, of powerful descriptions and schematic material, which distinguishes the short story from allegory or the mediaeval exemplum.[3] Abstract truths are established through the tangible flesh of the plot and its characters.[4] The lesson is not explicit but rather submerged in the mass of concrete details. In contrast to the ideological novel, the short story usually provides the definition of characters "by extension" — through the enumeration of characteristic traits — and not "by comprehension", through concepts. The strong structure helps the reader's immediate comprehension of what is at stake — and far from impeding his or her pleasure (as it does in the mediocre stories), this schema enhances it.

Short stories, sensational news items and serials

Hypotyposis is also what distinguishes the short story from the genres it rubbed shoulders with in *fin de siècle* newspapers: the serial and the sensational news item (*le fait-divers*). The three genres exist in and through the media, to which they largely contributed, even giving to the European press at the end of the century its specific stamp. Like the short story,

---

2 This is often stressed by readers and critics. See for example Luigi Capuana on Verga's characters: we have the feeling we have "seen them in reality" and not read about them; Luigi Capuana, *Verga e D'Annunzio* (Bologna: Cappelli, 1972), p. 24 and p. 74. Clare Hanson argues that the short story is more concerned with vision than with feeling; Clare Hanson, *Short Stories and Short Fictions, 1880-1980* (New York: St. Martin's Press, 1985), p. 124. O'Faolain (1948) acknowledges that "one does really feel, smell and see the poorhouse " in Ernst Ahlgren's *Mother Malena's Hen* (p. 209).

3 James recalls his own hatred of allegory in his biography of Nathaniel Hawthorne. "[Allegory] is apt to spoil two good things — a story and a moral, a meaning and a form". Henry James, *Hawthorne* (Ithaca, NY: Cornell University Press, 1967), p. 62. For more on the mediaeval exemplum, see André Sempoux, *La Nouvelle*, in *Typologie des sources du moyen âge occidental*, 9 (Turnhout: Brepols, 2009); and Hans-Jörg Neushafer, *Boccaccio und der Beginn der Novelle: Strukturen der Kurzerzählung auf der Schwelle zwischen Mittelalter und Neuzeit* (Munich: Fink, 1983).

4 The necessity of this concrete form is also stressed by Tsutsui Yasutaka (one of the very few Japanese critics to have written on the short story after the lively discussion of the form in the literary journals — especially *Bungakkai* — in the early 1980s). Tsutsui argues that the short story demands an organic adequation to the subject and the invention of new forms. Tsutsui Yasutaka, *Tanpen shōsetsu kōgi* (Tōkyō: Iwanami Shoten, 1990), pp. 157-67.

the sensational news item presents narrative elements carried to their extreme; it deals with events that transgress nature or the normal order of the world.[5] Like the short story, it presents without fail an antithetical tension, in the particularly lucid form of the paradox. *Le fait-divers* always deals with events such as sisters abused by their brother, or children killed by their mother: radical incompatibilities, contrasting in a single structure extremes which should never come into contact.[6] The protagonists — in the short story as in the sensational headline — are reduced to a few sharply defined traits, and never leave their "actantial" role except to embrace the diametrically opposite role, the one which is essentially rendered impossible by definition (the respectable mother who is also a murderer; the love for her son that makes the mother prostitute).[7] Again like the short story, the sensational news item has to anchor its subject matter in the most current daily events: these descriptions take up a great deal of the article, as well as the geographic localization ("In Paris…").

Is, then, the short story a branch of popular literature, functioning along the same lines? To get a clearer idea we must examine another comparison: the serialised novel.[8] Here again, several similarities can be seen. The serial also demands an oxymoronic tension (titles include *Chaste and Sullied* or *Countess and Beggar*). Again, it relies on material already familiar to the reader, on pre-existing formulas and characters, and is sold in more "everyday" places that are passed by the reader on a daily basis (news stands, railway stations and street vendors instead of bookstores). Its value comes from the familiar not the new.[9] However, whereas the serial barely "dresses up" familiar situations and characters, the short

---

5   *Fait-divers* was a genre in its own right at the turn of the century. In every newspaper, the reader was (and still is) sure to find at least one, sometimes two in the tabloids. See Roland Barthes' chapter "Structure of the *Fait-Divers*" in his *Critical Essays*, trans. by Richard Howard (Evanston, IL: Northwestern University Press, 1972), pp. 185-96; and Georges Auclair, *Le Mana quotidien: structures et fonctions de la chronique des faits divers* (Paris: Anthropos, 1982). More recently, see also Anne-Claude Ambroise-Rendu, *Petits récits des désordres ordinaires: les faits divers dans la presse française des débuts de la IIIe République à la Grande Guerre* (Paris: S. Arslan, 2004).

6   Of course, this is as true now as it was in the nineteenth century; see, for example, the recent headline in *Le Figaro* (10 December 2012): "Woman prostitutes herself in order to pay for her autistic son's medical treatment" (translation ours).

7   See Auclair (1982), pp. 19-26 and 90-104.

8   Charles Grivel surveys the history of novels in France between 1870 and 1880, and his study is in a large part made up of popular novels. Charles Grivel, *Production de l'intérêt romanesque* (The Hague: Mouton, 1973). For a general analysis of serials see the excellent Anne-Marie Thiesse, *Le Roman du quotidien* (Paris: Le Seuil, "Points", 2000).

9   See Thiesse (2000), pp. 19-26 and 90-104; and the conclusion to Grivel (1973).

story, on the contrary, gives the impression of something new through the accumulation of striking and concrete details and through the choice of unexpected scenarios. In addition, whereas popular novels deal not only with familiar characters, but also always with the *same* characters, the short story explores the entire social field in order to introduce ordinary people and pariahs, often disdained by previous literature. The short story, like the serial, is dependent on the reader's pre-existent representations; but nonetheless it does not depend on worn-out subjects.

By resorting to the same formulas as serials or sensational news items, the short story can hasten the reader's introduction to the fiction. The antithetical tension is present in the short story because of its powerful ability to create a structure strong enough to satisfy the "occasional" reader, as discussed by Anne-Marie Thiesse, whose reading implies "a certain kind of inattention".[10] The serial gets the attention of readers who may be inadequately prepared for the intellectual exercise of reading. The short story, on the other hand, will give to readers who are used to more complex reading the peculiar pleasure of an immediate entry into the fictional world.

The short story: privileged object of narratology

It is not difficult to see why formalist critics — Gérard Genette, Tzvetan Todorov and Roland Barthes, for example — have been drawn to analysing short stories.[11] Admittedly, the champions of formalism have often declared that they only turned to short stories for reasons of pure and simple convenience: in order to understand how a complete text functions, a short text was thought to be an easier choice.[12] But that choice has been much more successful than expected, or, in other words, the conclusions they drew are subordinate to the form itself. They did not describe the function of "all" narration, as they claimed; what they have described in detail is the

---

10 Thiesse (2000), p. 55.
11 As Lohafer puts it: the short story was "the favorite 'demo' narrative form for New Criticism". Susan Lohafer, Introduction, in *The Tales We Tell: Perspectives on the Short Story*, ed. by Rick Feddersen, Susan Lohafer, Barbara Lounsberry and Mary Rohrberger (Westport, CN: Greenwood Press, 1998), p. ix.
12 Barthes, for example, justifies his choice of text as follows: "I needed a very short text to be able to master entirely the signifying surface..." Roland Barthes, "Textual Analysis of a Tale By Edgar Poe", *Poe Studies*, 10:1 (1977), 1-12. See also Gérard Genot and Paul Larivaille, *Etude du* Novellino (Paris: Presses de l'Université Nanterre, 1985); and Tzvetan Todorov, *Grammaire du* Décaméron (The Hague: Mouton, 1969), pp. 11-13.

structure of the short story. What these critics see as the essential role of isotopisms, for example, is only essential because the texts they are looking at are short stories, which use antithetical tension as their basic frame.[13]

Similar work on a novel is impossible. The reason is not that the length of a novel would overwhelm the signifying oppositions; it is that the effective novel renounces this structure as too simple, rejects the too-clear precision, the light without shade. The novel patiently constructs more complex truths, just as it carefully builds its characters instead of letting them spring fully equipped into the mind of the reader.[14] We have seen an example of this in the work that led Henry James from the short story to his novel *The Ambassadors*.

Indeed, a second reason for the natural attraction of semiotic analysis towards the short story rests in the treatment of character. The short story can be said to belong to what Mikhail Bakhtin calls the "epic" as opposed to the "novelistic" side of literature.[15] The character in a novel is not summed up by his role, he has what Bakhtin calls a "personality" that is more than the sum of his traits; whereas the character in a short story seems to be defined by the few traits attributed to him. This is reminiscent of the "actantial schemas" of semiotic analysis: as Romano Luperini clearly saw, short story characters are not more than their actantial role, and were perfect material for the discovery of this critical tool.[16]

The classic short story always chooses situation over characters.[17] One can certainly defend this, like Genette who cites Aristotle in defence of the

---

13 The "Groupe d'Entrevernes" reveals a series of secondary isotopisms (the "semiotic isotopisms") used within a main isotopism ("semantic isotopism"). This is putting to light the secondary antithetic tensions that, as we have seen, reinforce and stabilise the principal tension.

14 I am of course talking of the great novels here; there is not much interest in comparing successful short stories with mediocre novels. Less successful novels, moreover, have a strong tendency to work with the usual tools of the short story (if we think of Eugene Sue or of the popular novel). Admittedly, Genot tried to apply the principles of narratological analysis to a novel. But that novel was *Pinocchio*, which cannot be considered far from popular literature, nor of very great complexity. Gérard Genot, *Analyse structurelle de 'Pinocchio'* (Pescia: Fondazione Nazionale Carlo Collodi, 1970).

15 M. M. Bakhtin, "Epic and Novel", in *The Dialogic Imagination: Four Essays*, trans. by Michael Holquist and Caryl Emerson (Austin, TX: University of Texas Press, 1981), pp. 4-40.

16 Romano Luperini, *Verga: l'ideologia, le strutture narrative, il "caso" critico* (Lecce: Millela, 1982).

17 This is perhaps the essential difference between the classic short story and what I have called the "modern" short story, practiced from 1900 onwards, or the "epiphanic" short story, as discussed by Mary Rohrberger and other Anglophone critics. See Mary Rohrberger, *Hawthorne and the Modern Short Story* (The Hague: Mouton, 1966); also

absence of the character.[18] I do not wish to discuss this position here, but want simply to note that such an analysis is particularly suited to short stories. When she was teaching creative writing, Flannery O'Connor demanded of her students a very detailed study of the summaries of short stories: for one whole year her students were only permitted a maximum of four lines in which to draw their characters. The emotion of the classic short story is contained in the idea and the situation, not in the characters or the shades of meaning.

Structure has often appeared to be the tangible point at which one could hope to define the genre of the short story. Poe's famous comments on Nathaniel Hawthorne tried to characterise the short story through this expedient: the singleness of effect, obtained by the convergence of absolutely all the effects.[19] The Russian Formalists also defined the short story by way of its composition (contradictions, parallels, contrasts, etc), while, as we saw in Chapter Two, Ludwig Tieck defined the genre by the presence of a narrative reversal, the *Wendepunkt*.[20]

However, even if we can bring to light an in-depth series of constants, that does not necessarily mean that they contain the key to the genre. It seems to me that the main thing we should keep in mind is the congruence of means, and the adequation to an *effect*. The features we have described in this section are not "laws"; it could be that a particular short story may not characterise its material in any extreme fashion, that it may not have a strong structure, nor rely on the reader's preconceptions. Yet, during the period

---

"Origins, Development, Substance, and Design of the Short Story: How I Got Hooked on the Short Story and Where It Led Me", in *The Art of Brevity: Excursions in Short Fiction Theory and Analysis*, ed. by Per Winther, Jakob Lothe, and Hans H. Skei (Columbia, SC: University of South Carolina Press, 2004), pp. 1-13. The latter abandons the anecdote, and, with it, that very precise organization and the somewhat stifling effectiveness of the genre.

18 Gérard Genette, *Narrative Discourse: An Essay in Method*, trans. by Jane E. Lewin (Ithaca, NY: Cornell University Press, 1980). Vincent Descombes clearly defines the limits of narratology. Among others, he shows that Genette's analyses of Proust were not able to account for the novelistic character of *À la recherche du temps perdu*. See in particular the analysis of Genette's summary of the novel, a summary which Descombes (who is also relying on Aristotle) sees as far too simple, schematic and ultimately wrong. Vincent Descombes, *Proust: Philosophy of a Novel* (Stanford, CA: Stanford University Press, 1992).

19 See Poe's review of *Hawthorne's Twice-Told Tales*, in Charles E. May, *The New Short Story Theories* (Athens, OH: Ohio University Press, 1994), pp. 59-64, and his essay "The Philosophy of Composition", pp. 67-69.

20 See Viktor Shklovsky, *Theory of Prose*, trans. by Benjamin Sher (Elmwood Park, IL: Dalkey Archive Press, 1990), pp. 52-70; and Ludwig Tieck, *Ludwig Tieck's Schriften* (Berlin: G. Reimer, 1828-55), XI, p. lxxxvi.

we are studying, almost all the short stories are constructed in this way. Even for writers as subtle as James or Chekhov, this structure guarantees that effective economy of means that is so often praised in the genre. But these techniques are no more than means, technical solutions, and we need to go further, and analyse their effect. Our task in Part III will be to show how the use of these means changes the fundamental relationship between the reader and the author on the one hand, and between the reader and the characters on the other. But first, we must examine the media through which these texts were conveyed to their readers.

PART II: MEDIA

6. Exoticism in the Classic Short Story

> *Stevenson's short stories were written originally for periodicals. For the sake of acceptance, Stevenson had to study the market; as he understood it, that market flourished when the literary commodity sold by the periodical was escapist, highly colored, and unobtrusively moral in its implications.*[1]

Harold Orel's remark about Robert Louis Stevenson does not apply to all short story writers at the turn of the century, but his three essential points can be given a general application. Almost all short stories were written for periodicals at the end of the nineteenth century; as such, the author needed to adapt to a market and a pre-existing public (the readership of the periodical in which he published). Moreover, Orel points to the great law of the classic short story: exoticism. This may be surprising or shocking considering that exoticism — so overused in the preceding era — was known to be rejected by the Naturalists and, indeed, there are fewer texts that are exotic in the strict sense of the word in the end of the nineteenth century. But the term can be used to indicate in general the essential *distance* between readers and characters in the classic short story.

Almost everywhere in the world the "golden age" of the classic short story is intimately connected with that of the press. The periodical — grand purveyor of fiction — enthusiastically welcomed short narratives, along

---

1 Harold Orel, *The Victorian Short Story* (Cambridge: Cambridge University Press, 1986), p. 127. On the extent of the influence of publication in periodicals, see too John Hellmann, *Fables of Fact: The New Journalism as New Fiction* (Urbana, IL: University of Illinois Press, 1981).

DOI: 10.11647/OBP.0039.6

with serials and sensational news items[2]. The genre developed within this privileged framework, and Orel's remark reminds us that such symbiosis between periodical and short story is heavy with implications for how stories were written at this time.

The role of the press

The rise of the press at the end of the nineteenth century profoundly transformed the literary landscape.[3] The arrival of the "penny papers" made it possible for everyone to buy one or more newspapers a day; the number of titles and the print-runs were enormous.[4] Writing for the newspapers

---

2   This is one of the great differences between the end of the nineteenth century and the beginning of the twenty-first. Charles E. May calculates that "the total number of stories in wide-circulation magazines per year in America is less than a hundred"; the rest of the very many stories appear in reviews or journals of which the "subscription lists are largely limited to university and college libraries, so they often go unread". Charles E. May, "The American Short Story in the Twenty-first Century", in *Short Story Theories: A Twenty-First-Century Perspective*, ed. by Viorica Patea (Amsterdam: Rodopi, 2012), pp. 299-324 (p. 299).

3   Among the features that are associated with this rise: the growth of general education, technical inventions (the rotative printer, the invention of "half tone" which reduced the cost of printing colours); the rise of publicity; changes to American copyright laws; and a new European law that abolished the need to present the texts to a censor *before* publishing. In Europe, these changes all happened around 1880. See Andrew Levy, *The Culture and Commerce of the American Short Story* (Cambridge: Cambridge University Press, 1993), pp. 31-35 and Laurel Brake and Marysa Demoor (eds.), *Dictionary of Nineteenth-century Journalism in Great Britain and Ireland* (Gent: Academia Press and London: British Library, 2009).

4   The Library in Florence subscribed to 1,360 titles in 1891 and, in a call for papers in an exhibition in Italy, 1,800 periodicals are mentioned (*Nuova rivista*, 12 December 1882). See Orazio Buonvino, *Il giornalismo contemporaneo* (Milan: R. Sandron, 1906); Valerio Castronovo and Nicola Tranfaglia, *Storia della stampa italiana* (Rome: Laterza, 1976); and Franco Nasi, *100 [i.e. Cento] anni di quotidiani milanesi* (Milan: Comune di Milano, 1958). In France, *Le Petit Journal* ("*le plus grand des petits*" — "the largest of the small press" — as it calls itself proudly) reached a print-run of 220,000 copies in 1872, 825,000 in 1884 and exceeded one million in 1890. This enormous figure does not mean that it reigned alone: *Le Petit Parisien* had print-runs that varied from 350,000 to 700,000 copies between 1890 and 1900. See Francine Amaury, *Histoire du plus grand quotidien de la IIIe République, Le Petit Parisien, 1876-1944* (Paris: Presses Universitaires de France, 1972). See also Pierre Albert and Christine Leteinturier, *La Presse française* (Paris: Secrétariat général du gouvernement, La Documentation française, 1978); Claude Bellanger, *Histoire générale de la presse française. 3, De 1871 à 1940* (Paris: Presses Universitaires de France, 1972). For detailed data, see Florence Goyet, *La Nouvelle au tournant du siècle en France, Italie, Japon, Russie, pays anglo-saxons. Maupassant, Verga, Mori Ōgai, Akutagawa Ryūnosuke, Tchekhov et James* (doctoral thesis, Université Paris 4-Sorbonne, 1990). Part II of the thesis, which is on the short story and the press, is available at http://w3.u-grenoble3.fr/rare/spip/spip. php?article341 (accessed 7/11/13).

became an important part of an author's income: from France to the United States to Japan, authors — particularly those of short stories — more or less lived off their earnings from newspapers.[5] Anton Chekhov is known to have supported his whole family in Moscow thanks to his contributions to the press. Luigi Pirandello was able to supplement his meager professor's salary with his short stories, and he found himself in deep financial trouble when this outlet was no longer available to him. As a young man, Henry James responded with some acrimony when his father suggested that he publish his first works at his own expense, and James instead turned to the periodicals. In the beginning he obtained contracts for travelogues, and his first short stories were published soon after. Later, around 1887, James found himself in financial trouble when some periodical editors were slow to publish his manuscripts. Leon Edel shows that the problem went deep: for James, losing the press as an outlet for his work virtually meant losing his status as an author, or at least as an author who was read.[6]

---

5   For details of Chekhov's income from newspapers, see Boris Esin, *Chekhov Jurnalist* (Moscow: Izd-vo Moskovskogo universiteta, 1977). More generally on Chekhov and the press, see Vladimir Kataev, *Sputniki Chekhova* (Moscow: Izd-vo Moskovskogo universiteta, 1982) and *Literaturnye sviazi Chekhova* (Moscow: Izd-vo Moskovskogo universiteta, 1989). For Henry James, see Leon Edel, *Henry James: A Life* (New York: Harper & Row, 1965). For Maupassant, see Gérard Delaisement, *Maupassant, journaliste et chroniqueur; suivi d'une bibliographie générale de l'oeuvre de Guy de Maupassant* (Paris: A. Michel, 1956); André Vial, *Guy de Maupassant et l'art du roman* (Paris: Nizet, 1954); and Florence Goyet, "L'exotisme du quotidien: Maupassant et la presse", in *Maupassant multiple*, Actes du colloque de Toulouse, Presses de l'Université de Toulouse-Le Mirail, 1995, pp. 17-28, available at http://w3.u-grenoble3.fr/rare/spip/IMG/pdf/Maupassant_et_la_presse_-M-_multiple-_Toulouse-.pdf (accessed 22/10/13). For the new conception of authorship in the Naturalist period in general, see Yves Chevrel, *Le Naturalisme* (Paris: Presses Universitaires de France, 1993), ch. 9, and more recently Dominique Kalifa, Philippe Régnier et Marie-Ève Thérenty (eds.), *La Civilisation du journal: histoire culturelle et littéraire de la presse française au XIXe siècle* (Paris: Nouveau Monde éditions, 2012), and Marie-Françoise Melmoux-Montaubin, *L'écrivain-journaliste au XIXe siècle: un mutant des lettres* (Saint-Etienne: Editions des Cahiers intempestifs, 2003). In Japan, at the beginning of the twentieth century, the big newspapers hired authors to whom they could guarantee sufficient revenues that they need not work elsewhere: Akutagawa was contracted to *Mainichi* in the 1920s.

6   Edel (1965). See also Anne T. Margolis, *Henry James and the Problem of Audience: An International Act* (Ann Arbor, MI: University of Michigan Press, 1985); and Michael Anesko, *Friction with the Market: Henry James and the Profession of Authorship* (New York: Oxford University Press, 1986). Anesko makes short work of the myth that would have James confined to his ivory tower, writing for the "happy few": the entire beginning of his career was that of a very successful author. Even when he was having difficulty publishing his novels, he continued to publish his short stories. The regular income from periodicals was higher than all the earnings that James and the majority of authors ever received for their books.

Not only did the press provide the money that allowed writers to make a living, it also provided them with most of their readers. The numbers speak for themselves: 3,000 copies in one or two years would be considered excellent sales for a collection of short stories, whereas 30,000 copies was normal for any periodical of the time. Giovanni Verga's collection *Vita dei campi* (*Life in the Fields*), constantly cited in articles as a bestseller, sold around 5,000 copies in ten years.[7] Guy de Maupassant's *Les Contes de la Bécasse* (*The Deaf Mute*), considered a huge success, sold 4,000 copies between September 1882 and February 1884. This represents seven successive editions. Which means that for each of the additional editions, the publisher decided not to publish more than 300 copies. Clearly, even best-selling authors such as Maupassant (together with Zola the author with the highest print run of the time) was not expected to sell more than a few thousands copies of his stories.

On the other hand, when Verga published his short stories in the newspaper Fanfulla, 23,000 copies were sold; and when Maupassant published in *Le Gaulois* or *Gil Blas*, the print run was in the order of 30,000 copies.[8] Thus, without even mentioning the giants of the small press and their hundreds of thousands of copies, the newspapers of average circulation represented an infinitely larger audience than the readership of collections.

Exotic subjects

The thousand or so stories I have surveyed for this study have exotic subjects at their core, with only a handful of exceptions. There is almost always a radical difference between the characters in classic short stories and the readers for which they were written. Sometimes what we find is exoticism in the strict sense: although there was a movement away from

---

7   Verga wrote this in a letter to Luigi Capuana, *Lettere a Luigi Capuana*, ed. by Gino Raya (Florence: Le Monnier, 1975), p. 77. Verga advised his friend to follow the same custom as he had of issuing a small print-run of the first edition: 2,000 copies, which made it possible, if it were a success, to print a second edition within the year; this means that a successful book might achieve a circulation of 4,000. Even for *Life in the Fields* he had to wait ten years for a third edition. See Carla Ricciardi, Introduction to Giovanni Verga, *Tutte le novelle*, ed. by Carla Ricciardi, 2 vols (Milan: Mondadori, 1983), vol I.

8   It was the same in Russia: when giving a story to the journal *Novoe vremya*, Chekhov was addressing about 35,000 readers, and *Novoe Vremya* was far from being the periodical with the biggest circulation. See F. A. Brockhaus and I. A. Efron (eds.), *Entsiklopedicheskii slovar'*, 82 vols and 4 supplements (St. Petersburg: Granat, 1890-1907), sub loc.

locating stories in exotic locations at the end of the nineteenth century, it was not completely abandoned, and the short story is one place where foreign settings persisted.[9] Stevenson was not the only one to set his work in distant countries: Joseph Conrad and Herman Melville developed the dramatic potential of a sailor's life; Ambrose Bierce dedicated himself to describing the unfamiliar world of the American frontier; while Jack London wrote of the Great North. Meanwhile, Maupassant provided vignettes of life in Northern Africa in short stories such as *Allouma* or *Un soir* (*One Evening*).

Rudyard Kipling, who became instantly famous with his Indian tales, continued to produce exotic short stories throughout his life, from his early Indian accounts, to his tales of South Africa, and other stories of soldiers, sailors or animals.[10] His short stories were first published for the ex-pat community in Lahore, for whom they represented a more immediate record of an exotic life. But it was the English who made Kipling's success. In his autobiography, the author explains that the exoticism of his subjects was what made Mowbray Morris, the editor of *Macmillan's Magazine*, pursue him enthusiastically on his return from India.[11] Even James's stories of the "international theme" were drawing on exoticism, giving to his American readers the spectacle of the seemingly great differences of life in Europe, and vice versa.

As for the Japanese, they often chose as their subject the world of the West: there are innumerable stories, beginning with Mori Ōgai and Nagai Kafū, that reference Germany, France or America. Temporal exoticism was also popular: a great many of Ōgai's stories were "historical" and Akutagawa Ryūnosuke set most of his tales in the distant past. Frequently the latter would take his inspiration from mediaeval chronicles, amplifying traditional tales of gods and famous men of history, but also of the Brigands or the petty nobles of the Heian court. Fantastic short stories could also

---

9   Scofield notes in relation to American short stories: "The short story was frequently the form chosen by writers introducing such new areas to a still predominantly East Coast reading public: it could give brief and vivid glimpses of new and 'exotic' places and ways of life". Martin Scofield, *The Cambridge Introduction to the American Short Story* (Cambridge: Cambridge University Press, 2006), p. 8. Scofield demonstrates this in some detail using the examples of Stephen Crane and Ambrose Bierce.

10 David Trotter is very clear on the topic of Kipling's English perspective on India following his school years in England. See his introduction to Rudyard Kipling, *Plain Tales From the Hills* (London: Penguin, 1995).

11 Rudyard Kipling, *Something of Myself: For My Friends Known and Unknown* (Rockville, MD: Wildside Press, 2008), p. 78.

be described as exotic in their description of the "other"; they play on the sometimes infinitesimal but always crucial distance between the normal and the strange world. Similarly, James often focussed on the character of the "Great Writer", in all his difference from "ordinary" men.

But the principal form of exoticism at the end of the nineteenth century is what might be called "social exoticism". The majority of Maupassant's stories, as well as those of Verga or Pirandello, and of the young Chekhov or Joyce, focus on the lower middle class. Their subjects are often prostitutes or other pariahs of society, but also "average" working men, petty bureaucrats or peasants. I conducted a survey of the forty or so periodicals in which most of the short stories of Verga, Maupassant and Chekhov appeared, and found that they each had a specific audience, of which the characters in the short stories were almost never members.[12] The short stories about working people and peasants appeared in newspapers intended for high society (Maupassant, Verga) or satirical papers (the young Chekhov). Stories about provincials were appearing in the newspapers of the capital cities: Milan, Rome, St Petersburg and Moscow. The point here can be summed up in one word, the epithet Benedetto Croce used for Maupassant: "*pariginissimo*".[13] When Maupassant was writing about the provinces, he was a Parisian speaking to Parisians.

Maupassant was bound by contract to *Le Gaulois* and *Gil Blas* for the exclusive rights to all his future work. The difference between these two periodicals has often been stressed: *Gil Blas* was a light newspaper, somewhat licentious, to which Maupassant gave the short stories and chronicles that he could not have offered to *Le Gaulois* because they would shock its readers, especially women. But the two newspapers shared a great deal in common: both were accessible only to members of high society because of their price (15 and 13 centimes) and their subjects. *Le Gaulois* contained worldly gossip and high-society news only of interest to those who knew the people alluded to, news from abroad, and accounts of official receptions. *Gil Blas* offered political news side by side with pieces of scandal,

---

12 Details of this survey can be found in Goyet (1990), available at http://w3.u-grenoble3.fr/rare/spip/spip.php?article157 (accessed 7/11/13).

13 "[...] *pariginissimo, libero, malizioso, beffardo, sarcastico novellatore* Guy de Maupassant". Benedetto Croce, *Poesia e non poesia* (Bari: Laterza, 1923), p. 307. See also Fusco: "To the cosmopolitan Parisian [ie Maupassant], the Norman peasant and world probably appeared as a distant and alien being and place". Richard Fusco, *Maupassant and the American Short Story: The Influence of Form at the Turn of the Century* (University Park, PA: Pennsylvania State University Press, 1994), p. 16.

and the publications of the *Official Journal*; it also gave weather reports for chic resorts and foreign cities. Regular topics included: "Chronicle from the [Parliament] Chamber", "Behind the Scenes in Finance", and "Paris Affairs: From the Council [of Ministers]". The paper offered some financial news and a little culture: on the whole nothing of any great intellectual breadth but very worldly. Advertisements in *Gil Blas* are very similar to those in *Le Gaulois* — sometimes even the same.[14] They both included notices for hotels and expensive houses for sale, for example, a "Unique mansion, Opera quarter, 20,000 fr. a year", or a "Factory, in Aubervilliers [a suburb near Paris] with mansion", as well as mortgage and investment funds, period furniture, etc.[15] It was these two elegant periodicals that published short stories about urban employees who "worked for eighteen hundred francs a *year*", and about provincials in Normandy who were shown as simple, coarse and greedy.

Verga published most frequently in the supplement of the *Fanfulla*.[16] This was a very expensive periodical (24 lire per year), published in Rome, and considered fashionable enough for the Princess of Savoy-Aosta to be photographed holding it.[17] French was quoted without translation and there were daily reports from the stock exchange, foreign book announcements and reviews, and advertisements for expensive products. Literary and theatrical reviews appear side by side with society clippings on "the fox-hunting season" (using the English term), or Princess Marguerite's visit to San Remo. It was here, or in even more sophisticated periodicals, that Verga

---

14 On 17 March 1886, for example, both newspapers ran the same advertisement for period furniture.

15 The archives of *Le Gaulois* and *Gil Blas* are accessible via the website of the Bibliothèque Nationale de France. The issues described here are at: http://gallica.bnf.fr/ark:/12148/bpt6k7523230x/f3.image.r=gil%20blas.langFR, and http://gallica.bnf.fr/ark:/12148/bpt6k525695q/f4.image.r=Le%20Gaulois.langFR (accessed 07/07/2013). The contrast is great with advertisements in the "small press": there, instead of reports of the stock market, we find reports of the wholesale prices of one particular product (meat, material, corn, etc). The ads have little in common with those of *Le Gaulois* or *Gil Blas* (except the universally advertised cough lozenges "pastilles Géraudel"). Watches are advertised at 5, 12.5 and 18 francs; furs from 3 to 50 francs. There are session reports from the Paris Municipal Council — not the Council of Ministers. *Le Petit Journal* (1 January 1887), available at http://gallica.bnf.fr/ark:/12148/bpt6k609266n (accessed 22/10/13). These (leftist) popular periodicals would often include rants against Paris Municipal Council members who "indulge in *dîners fins* at 30 francs per person". *L'Intransigeant* (1 January 1891), translation ours.

16 Verga published 29 short stories (out of 70) in the *Fanfulla della Domenica*.

17 The photograph of the princess with *Fanfulla* is in the private collection of the Villa Torrigiani at Camigliano near Lucca.

published his stories about the peasants of far-away Sicily, the opposite end of the reader's world.[18]

The key to this contrast and this distance is given by the beginning of Verga's short story *Pentolaccia*: "Let's do as if we were at the *cosmorama* [...] There's 'Pentolaccia', he's quite a type in himself".[19] Pentolaccia is a jealous provincial, who is all the more striking for having long accepted his wife's infidelities. "La Venera" has been the mistress of Don Liborio for years; an affair which, by the way, made Pentolaccia a rich man. The entire story is told in the colloquial language of peasants, and the text is full of comparisons between these people and animals (hens, mules and a bull). The gulf separating high society readers from the jealous "country bumpkin" is central to this text. The mention of the "cosmorama" — a typical feature of working-class amusement parks at the end of the nineteenth century — indicates that we will be looking at a fixed and distant image. There, as Verga himself describes in the text: "during a country fete, if we put our eye to the glass, we can see everything pass before us from Garibaldi to Victor-Emmanuel" (where the narrator who says "we" is a Sicilian peasant).[20] The cosmorama signifies the naive pleasure of country people as they discover the beauties of a wider world. They are happy and content to see "as if real" their king or heroes. For the readers of *Fanfulla* the perspective is, of course, reversed: they *were* living in the world of Victor Emmanuel, and it was the provinces and the working people, the Pentolaccias and the "Lupas", the poor Sicilian muleteers and fishermen, whom they were looking at in this way.[21]

Chekhov provides another symbol of this kind of distance. On his return from a trip to Sakhalin, Chekhov published a landmark study of the convict

---

18 *L'Illustrazione italiana* (eleven stories), *La Fiametta* (*Gli Orfani*); *La Domenica letteraria* (*Libertà*; *Il Canarino del n. 15*; *La Chiave d'oro*). *La Cronaca bizantina* (which published *Conforti*, a particularly sordid affair) was perhaps the most famous review of the time, the very symbol of the elegant periodical: titles, layout, advertising style, graphics, tail-pieces, quality of texts and signatures were all of an extreme refinement.

19 Giovanni Verga, *Tutte le novelle*, ed. by Carla Ricciardi, 2 vols (Milan: Mondadori, 1983), I, p. 208.

20 Ibid, p. 209.

21 The same gulf existed between Verga's readers and his characters from the urban working population of Milan. Franco Ferrucci shows Verga in these stories as the "occasional visitor", "the passer-by who was gathering impressions from the streets, looking for the daily pathos": "The working class world is seen through the eye of the philanthropist, as Russo stated, or, what is ultimately the same thing, of the sociologist in search of typical examples". Franco Ferrucci, "I Racconti milanesi del Verga", *Italica*, 2 (1967), 124 (translation ours).

prison, as well as two stories whose heroes were Siberian convicts or exiles. His story *V ssylke* (*In Exile*) paints the terrifying and hopeless picture he had seen on his way there. What is of interest to us is that the story appeared in *Vsemirnaya illustratsiya*, a Russian review homologous to the French or Italian *Illustration*: twenty well-illustrated pages, with plates and polished presentation. It contained the obituaries of famous Russians, but also Polish, English and French personalities, which appeared side by side with society news items, and long articles on topical events like the Panama affair. It was a beautiful and expensive publication at 15 roubles a year.[22] For the readers of *Vsemirnaya illustratsiya*, an account of the desperately hard life of the exiles in Siberia was as exotic as a story of another country.

Chekhov gave many of his early short stories about provincials to the satirical papers of the two cities which played the role of capital in Russia: Moscow and St Petersburg. For the readers of these two metropolises, he repeatedly returned to the eternally popular theme of the shortcomings of the provincials — characters who appeared ridiculous to his readers simply because they lacked urban "sophistication". The tone of Chekhov's short stories in the satirical press was direct, and the characters are caricatured to such an extent that they would have been deeply offensive to those who were the subject of the ridicule. But the people living in the provinces had no opportunity to read these papers, nor did they have access to them if they had wanted to. Similarly the poor peasants of Normandy could hardly enjoy reading the short stories of Maupassant in which they are portrayed — as we shall see later in some detail. The point is that the authors could be as satirical as they liked, because the papers in which these stories were published would in no way lose a sale from an angry or offended customer.[23]

Verga and Chekhov also frequently published in the intellectual journals — the "thick journals" (*tolstye zhurnaly*), as they were called in Russia.[24]

---

22 I have only seen the "regular" edition of *Vsemirnaya illustratsiya*; there was also a deluxe edition, which cost twenty roubles.

23 Although subscriptions to all the great daily newspapers were sold throughout the country, as well as abroad, these periodicals were only ever accessible to the same rich and worldly people. Yes, nobles living on their estates in Normandy read *Le Gaulois*. But *Le Gaulois* was precisely a link with the capital, a sign of belonging to the elegant circle, like the outfits ordered from Paris. Reading it gave them the pleasure of belonging to the Parisian world, and separated them from their provincial surroundings. As Levy (1993) puts it in describing the *New Yorker* of Poe's time: "designed to appeal to those social elites in each town and city that considered themselves 'honorary New Yorkers' — representatives of a wealthy, cosmopolitan class" (p. 20).

24 Verga published eighteen out of his seventy stories in them. Chekhov, from 1888 on, was a regular contributor, especially to *Russkaya Mysl'* and *Severny Vestnik*. This is not true of

These played a great role in the intellectual life of the time. Naturalism, as is well known, was the expression of a period when artists felt deeply concerned with the social and political state of their countries. This was also true of the educated public at large, especially in Italy and Russia: they were ready to read serious and demanding publications. The *Rivista nuova di scienze, lettere e arti, Rassegna settimanale di politica scienze, lettere e arti* and *Nuova rivista* in Italy, and *Russkaya mysl', Severny vestnik* and *Zhizn'* in Russia were austere periodicals, of more than two hundred pages. They offered regular articles on military affairs, geography, moral philosophy, political analysis, descriptions of and reflections on political institutions, and many reviews of books, both scientific and literary.

The short stories in these publications were on quite a different footing from those published in the worldly newspapers. Appearing side by side with statistical studies, reflexions on the administration of the provinces or reviews of books on philosophy or agronomy, they illustrated with all the force of pathos the horrifying state of the nation. There was just as much distance between the reader and subjects of short stories in these journals as in the daily newspapers, but the gap was of a different kind: it was the intellectual's distance from his object of observation and reflection in what was a quasi-ethnographic document. For the readers of these intellectual publications, short stories offered a kind of scientific reflection; the ultimate aim being to transform reality.

The constraints of the newspapers

Newspapers imposed restrictions on authors, the most obvious being that of length: Kipling, in the *Civil and Military Gazette* of Lahore, was allowed exactly a column and a quarter for each of his *Plain Tales From the Hills*; James, throughout his career, never ceased to complain of the 5,000 word limitation imposed on him. But let us remember that the short story sometimes continued through two or even three issues of the paper, so the restriction on length was not absolute. Another constraint was adamantly imposed on the author: since he was publishing in a periodical, he had to adapt to his public. As we know, newspaper editors were particularly

---

Maupassant. His only contribution to intellectual publications was, to my knowledge, a few stories reprinted in *La Revue bleue*, the newspaper of the French Sorbonne, which did not play the same role as the many and admirable intellectual journals used by Verga and Chekhov.

attentive to the reactions of their readers. Gabriel Tarde insisted on the importance of the barometer provided by the number of subscriptions, and all the studies of the press show a good editor to be a constant observer of his public's taste.[25]

As we have seen, classic short stories were mostly published in newspapers that their provincial or popular objects of satire did not read. There are, however, a few counter-examples, all of which seem to prove the rule that the most successful classic short stories relied on some form of exoticism. Joyce, Proust, James and Maupassant each tried to publish stories in which the readers could recognise themselves. These are arguably among their greatest failures. Joyce's misfortunes in publishing *Dubliners*, for example, are well known: the editor of the *The Irish Homestead* only published three of the ten or so stories he had ordered, and it took almost ten years and the intervention of Ezra Pound for the collection to see the light of day.[26] Critics tend to see this as the result of the crude work of a "complex and extended censorship (judicial, social and psychological)" to quote Etienne Sarkany.[27]

It seems to me, however, that the problems with *Dubliners* essentially came down to Joyce rejecting the conventions of short story publishing at the time, by trying to have his stories read by those who were most involved.[28]

---

25 Gabriel Tarde, *L'Opinion et la foule* (Paris: Presses Universitaires de France, 1989 [1901]).

26 See Richard Ellmann, *James Joyce* (New York: Oxford University Press, 1959); Robert Scholes, "Some Observations on the Text of Dubliners: 'The Dead'", *Studies in Bibliography*, 15 (1962), 191-205; Hans Walter Gabler, Introduction to *Dubliners*, by James Joyce, ed. by Hans Walter Gabler and Walter Hettche (New York: Garland, 1993), pp. 1-24. A summary of the text's publishing history is also given in Jeri Johnson, Introduction to *Dubliners*, by James Joyce, ed. by Jeri Johnson (Oxford: Oxford University Press, 2001), pp. xlii-xlvi.

27 Etienne Sarkany, *Forme, socialité et processus d'information: l'exemple du récit court à l'aube du XXe siècle* (doctoral thesis, Diffusion Université Lille III, 1982), pp. 354-73 (p. 357, translation ours). Sarkany dedicated a whole section of his thesis to Joyce's difficulties in publishing the stories from *Dubliners* (with conclusions radically different from mine). Johnson (2001) also sees the origin of the negative judgements on Joyce in the fact that he described what had almost never been described: "Readers have more than once responded to *Dubliners* by feeling that the stories were cold, unsympathetic, distanced, clinically dissective, mocking. [...] They have described it as 'naturalistic' (that 'odour of ashpits and old weeds and offal', the pervasive air of 'disillusionment', its 'detachment'). Such criticisms make sense of one aspect of *Dubliners*, that through which Joyce calmly addresses matters which in the first decade of the last century were seldom mentioned in literature: poverty, drunkenness, bullying, child-beating [...]" (p. xii). Which does not prevent her from seeing that it was indeed on the part of Joyce "defamation" (see p. xi and note 10).

28 Levy (1993) observes the way in which institutions preside over short story writing today: "By agreeing to enter a creative writing workshop, we implicitly agreed to write, or learn to write, literature that would be socially sanctioned" (p. 5; see also pp. 11-26). The idea

Joyce was unable to achieve publication for a broad Irish public because the stories lacked the usual distance between readers and characters. When George Russell wrote to Joyce suggesting that he send short stories dealing with Ireland to *The Irish Homestead*, he defined for him a formula for his reader's expectations: it was a question of writing "something simple, rural, livemaking, pathos".[29] We should not look on these as idle words from Russell — he knew the Irish intellectual and literary world well, in an Ireland at the height of its Gaelic euphoria, when folklore and national traditions were elevated to the level of myth.

It is Joyce's concept that is in question here, and a concept of which he himself was very conscious. In *Dubliners* he made an accusation of the "hemiplegia" which he saw as paralyzing his country; he envisaged his texts as an opportunity of educating his fellow citizens.[30] The saying is famous: the *Dubliners* would be a "nicely polished looking-glass", which he would hold up to the people of Dublin to see themselves as they are, so that they could improve. It was a case of wanting deliberately to confront the Irish with his stories, and he refused to follow the advice of his brother to try to publish them in the French papers instead of the Irish.[31] *The Irish Homestead* refused to continue the publication after the third story, telling Joyce too many readers were complaining.[32] Joyce, then abroad, nevertheless wrote the ten stories he had intended to send to the magazine, and more, and looked for a publisher. At first, the editor Grant Richards accepted Joyce's

---

that institutions of writing play a crucial role in shaping the genre is widely recognised. See for example, in Japan, Tsutsui Yasutaka, who stresses the role of prize-contests in the development of the Japanese short story. Tsutsui Yasutaka, *Tanpen shōsetsu kōgi* (Tōkyō: Iwanami Shoten, 1990). See also Hashimoto Kenji on the importance of the nineteenth-century American short story as mass entertainment. Hashimoto Kenji, *Amerika tanpen shōsetsu no kōzō* (Ōsaka: Ōsaka Kyōiku Tosho, 2009).

29 The letter reads: "Could you write anything simple, rural?, livemaking?, pathos?, which could be inserted so as not to shock the readers". Quoted in Johnson (2001), p. xli. On the press in Ireland at that time see, for example, Karen Steele, *Women, Press and Politics During the Irish Revival* (Syracuse, NY: Syracuse University Press, 2007). Steele describes Russell as one of the great men in the Gaelic Renaissance movement, with its philosophy of a "redemptive rural civilization" (p. 189). He was editor from 1905 of *The Irish Homestead*, weekly organ of the Irish Agricultural Organisation, which supported young Irish authors.

30 See Joyce's well-known letter to Constantine Curran: "I am writing a series of epicleti — ten — for a paper; I call the series *Dubliners* to betray the soul of that hemiplegia or paralysis which many consider a city". James Joyce, *Letters*, ed. by Stuart Gilbert and Richard Ellmann, 3 vols (New York: Viking Press, 1957-1966), I, p. 55.

31 Similarly, Joyce distributed his pamphlet entitled "The Holy Office" amongst the intellectuals of Dublin, with the intention of their self-improvement.

32 See Sarkany (1982), p. 360.

manuscript, but after the printer refused to print the texts, retracted his offer. The reason given was that coarse language was used. But even when Joyce finally submitted and made *all* the demanded substitutions, Richards refused to publish the book — as did no less than fifteen other publishers.[33]

If we think of the publishing conditions of short stories in that period, things are quite clear. In a famous letter to Richards, Joyce himself outlined the problem very precisely, stressing that the portraits he had drawn were unacceptable to the readers, who for once were the very "models": "The printer denounces *Two Gallants* and *Counterparts*. The more subtle inquisitor will denounce *An Encounter* [...]. The Irish priest will denounce *The Sisters*. The Irish boarding-house keeper will denounce *The Boarding-House*. [...]". And in the same letter: "I have come to the conclusion that I cannot write without offending people".[34] Joyce's eventual success in publishing the book points in the same direction: Joyce owed the publication of *Dubliners* to an external intervention, that of a foreign literary "institution", in the person of Pound.[35] It was the "international reader" that made the book finally publishable, but even then only 1250 copies were printed. This was very far from the large readership of a magazine like *The Irish Homestead*, and it meant that very few of the intended readers got a chance to see it. Joyce's desire to educate the middle-class people of Ireland was frustrated.

Marcel Proust's first volume, *Les Plaisirs et les Jours*, a collection of short stories and poetry, encountered similar difficulties.[36] Proust published some poetry from this future collection in *Le Gaulois*, but his attempts to publish the short stories were thwarted.[37] His letters at the time show him asking his friends to help him convince *Le Gaulois*'s director, Arthur Meyer, as well as other newspapers directors, to take them; other letters show him

---

33 Johnson (2001), p xliii.
34 Letter of 5 May 1906 (Joyce, *Letters*, II, p. 134).
35 Although "success" is perhaps not the right word. See Johnson (2001), calling it a "disheartening process" (p. xliii).
36 Marcel Proust, *Pleasures and Days: And Other Writings* (Garden City, NY: Doubleday, 1957).
37 An example of Proust's poetry can be found in *Le Gaulois* (21 June 1895), p. 2. It was accompanied by a laudative comment from the editor: "We are happy to give our readers a front seat preview of some delicate verses by a charming young poet, Mr Marcel Proust, of whom *Le Gaulois* has already published a few articles. These lines have been orated recently at Mme Madeline Lemaire's by Mlle Bartet, together with very pleasant music by Mr Rinaldo Hahn" (translation ours). I quote *in extenso* this comment: it shows we are in a society circle in which "nice" verses were welcome, but harsh satire was not. For a more detailed account of this publication, see Florence Goyet, "*Les Plaisirs et les Jours* entre nouvelle classique et nouvelle moderne", *Bulletin d'Informations proustiennes*, 44 (2014).

offering the stories directly, but without success.[38] Most Proustian scholars tend to feel that these stories are not very good, and therefore they do not question or explore the author's initial failure to have them published.[39] Of course, these stories compare unfavourably with À la recherche du temps perdu but, compared to the other short stories that were being published in the newspapers at the time, they do not appear bad at all.

The problem for editors, once again, seems to be not so much the quality of the work as the relationship between readers and characters. Proust tried to publish his stories depicting high society and its shortcomings in society papers. These papers did not want to present their readers with their own caricature. The one exception seems to confirm the rule: *La Mort de Baldassare Silvande* (*The Death of Baldassare Silvande*) was pre-published in *La Revue hebdomadaire*.[40] Yet this story was very different from the rest of the collection (some of which were a direct attack on recognisable socialites of the time, and all of which are harsh satires of fashionable urban life) — it was more of a metaphysical reflection on life and death, and only very mildly satirical.

With this in mind, the case of James, the young American writer traveling and living in Europe, becomes exemplary and emblematic: for years, he published his short stories about America in Europe, and his short stories about Europe in America. This yet again confirms his inspired intuition concerning the genre. Michael Anesko shows that James obtained, for nearly all his stories, a quadruple publication — prepublication in journals in the United States and in England, followed by publication in volume in both countries.[41] Among the few short stories that were not reprinted were the

---

38 Proust not only wrote to Meyer, but also to the director of *La Revue Hebdomadaire*, who refused all but one very particular text (see note 40), and to other editors as well. In a letter to Suzette Lemaire, he says "I have tried with *La Patrie*, but failed, and at *La Presse* too". Marcel Proust, *Correspondance*, ed. by Philip Kolb (Paris: Plon, 1970-1993), I, p. 388 (translation ours; hereafter *Correspondance*). I am speaking here of *newspapers* — *not* intellectual journals. Proust had good access to intellectual journals — among them the famous *La Revue Blanche*. As we have mentioned, the "gap" between reader and subject is very different in these journals — one can mock socialites in a journal of the avant-garde, especially in *La Revue Blanche*, which was then associated with anarchist authors. See Paul-Henri Bourrelier, *La Revue blanche: une génération dans l'engagement 1890-1905* (Paris: Fayard, 2007).

39 Albert Thibaudet wrote in the 1920s that Proust's short stories were "*médiocres*" (see *Correspondance*, XIX, p. 331). More recently, Thierry Laget has even given a precise analysis of their shortcomings. Thierry Laget, Introduction to *Les Plaisirs et les Jours*, by Marcel Proust, ed. by Thierry Laget (Paris: Gallimard, 1993), pp. 27-28.

40 *La Revue hebdomadaire* (29 October 1895), pp. 584-606.

41 Anesko (1986).

ones about the country in which he was trying to get them published; stories that would have shown the readers their own image were not accepted.

Similarly Maupassant's short stories about the working class were never reprinted in the popular newspapers, although they did publish most of his other stories. Maupassant was under contract to *Le Gaulois* and *Gil Blas* for the original publication of his texts, but it was possible for other periodicals to pick them up later. He became hugely popular in his lifetime, and the reprints of his short stories were extremely numerous, especially in the popular papers like *Le Petit Journal, Le Petit Parisien, La Lanterne* and *L'Intransigeant,* all of which were big publishers of fiction. But these periodicals did not automatically reprint any text he produced. From the long list of Maupassant's short stories about the "working class", only *four* texts were reprinted in *Le Petit Journal* and *Le Petit Parisien.* One of them was *Boitelle,* whose hero, admittedly, is a young peasant from Normandy; however the heroine is of African descent, and she is described in the spirit of the purest exoticism.[42] As for the rest, none of the most famous of the Normandy stories were reprinted, nor those which depicted the life of the "employees at 1800 francs a year". Maupassant was also rejected by the provincial papers. Only three of his stories, to my knowledge, appeared in the provincial illustrated press between their publication and World War I, compared with hundreds of reprints in the Parisian papers.[43] His treatment of provincials in his short stories, of which we shall explore at length later, might very well explain their lack of enthusiasm.

These are rare cases of authors who tried to have their short stories read by the very characters they portrayed, and failed. Short story writing was a flourishing business when it met the absolute conditions of its medium. It was up to the writer to adapt to the public for whom he was writing, not the other way round. The people of Dublin were not fond of *Dubliners*

---

42 We shall return to Boitelle in Chapter Eight. *Mon oncle Jules* (*My Uncle Jules*) is equally somewhat special: the uncle is one of the poor unfortunates who sought his fortune in America, an "exotic" story for those who have never ventured far. The case of *Fermier* (*The Farmer's Wife*) and *Petit soldat* (*Two Little Soldiers*) are more open to discussion; but even if we were to conclude that they are not exotic, there would still be only two exceptions among the three hundred stories published by Maupassant. These stories can be found in Guy de Maupassant, *The Complete Short Stories of Guy de Maupassant*, trans. by Artine Artinian (Garden City, NY: Hanover House, 1955), pp. 1308-12, 917-22 and 755-59 respectively.

43 With personal thanks to Jean Watelet for helping me to clarify this point. See Jean Watelet, *La Presse illustrée en France 1814-1914* (Villeneuve d'Ascq: Presses Universitaires du Septentrion, 2000).

any more than the peasants would have been of Maupassant's Normandy stories or the Russian provincials of Chekhov's satires. A condition for a classic short story's success was to choose an unfamiliar or remote subject.[44] One cannot publish just any short story in the periodicals: success depends on a respect for the medium's own constraints. Editors selected the "right" stories so effectively that one could fail to notice that it was impossible to write anything else.

Exceptions to the rule

In all of the one thousand or so classic short stories I have surveyed, I have found only one unambiguous exception to the "law" of exoticism: in contrast to the other short story writers, Chekhov used his readers as characters in many stories later in his career, from *Dama s sobachkoi* (*Lady with Lapdog*) to *Strakh* (*Fear*) or *Nevest'* (*The Bride*). These are what we might call "transition stories" between the classic and modern form (which we will examine in detail in Part III). There are, in addition, two more exceptions, but here again these are exceptions that prove rather than challenge the rule.

The first is that of the narrators of frame-stories. Some stories, like James's *The Turn of the Screw,* follow a structure inherited from Giovanni Boccaccio: we are first introduced to a narrator who then proceeds to tell us a story within the story. This narrator generally belongs to the same world as the reader. He sets the mood before the real story unfolds. This narrator is one of a small group (hunters, guests in a country house, etc), who gently brings his readers into the warm intimacy of the circle around the fire or the relaxed after-dinner atmosphere of a group of friends. He will then let us hear the story as he heard it: because he has created a sense of familiarity, we are ready to enter the world of the unusual. As we shall see in regard to travelogues in the next chapter, this narrator is the intermediary who puts the reader in contact with a foreign world.

---

44 This may not be a feature only of nineteenth-century short stories. Even if authors generally moved away from the exotic in the twentieth century, readers in a few countries at least retained their former taste for exotic short stories. It has become common in France to complain of the public's disaffection for the short story. But on closer examination, this disaffection only concerns French texts; foreign short stories — from Isaac Bashevis Singer to Jorge Luis Borges to Katherine Mansfield — are widely read. French short story writers today generally write about the immediate and topical; the public would seem to prefer, as in earlier times, stories about the other side of the world.

The second exception in our corpus involves the few stories, published in the society newspapers, in which Verga and Maupassant talk about high society. First we should note that, in these stories, the attitude towards the characters is very different from the attitude towards workers or peasants. Members of the upper class are not shown to have certain types of behaviour that define them as a social group. The heroes are frenzied hunters, busybodies, coquettes, adulterous women who cling desperately to their lover: they are seen as unique individuals, and it is not likely that the reader will identify with them. He will not feel challenged by the story's ridiculing of them, and neither will their abusive or ridiculous behaviour compromise the upper class as a whole.

These types of stories are very similar to *anecdote*, and the reader's involvement in them is quite different from the stories discussed earlier in this chapter. Like the serialised novel or the sensational news items, anecdote is a journalistic genre of its own: all the newspapers of the time published anecdotes, including those of good repute. These short stories are on the border of that genre, of the kind that is told at a dinner party: the "tall tale". The tension they are built upon usually relies on paradox, with an end which brings an unexpected answer, one that introduces narrative elements in an unusual combination, or at least is perceived that way. Examples include Maupassant's *La Bûche* (*The Log*), *Le Gâteau* (*The Cake*), *Le Verrou* (*The Lock*), *Mon oncle Sosthène* (*My Uncle Sosthenes*), *Sauvée* (*Saved*); and Verga's *Giuramenti di marinaio* (*Sailor's Oaths*), *Carmen* and *Commedia da salotto* (*Drawing-room Comedy*). These "high society" short stories are usually published in men's magazines like *Gil Blas,* and are close relatives of the misogynist after-dinner tale. Here, too, the reader's identification with the character is unlikely. Distance is not brought by the difference in social status, but in the amusement or irony with which the subject is treated.[45]

Despite these few exceptions, the overwhelming fact about the publication of short stories in newspapers at the turn of the century was that the characters in these stories could not overlap with their readers. Tales of peasants and workers appeared in fashionable periodicals that were available to neither of these groups; short stories about the provinces

---

45 This is also the case in many of James's stories, where the characters are admittedly of the same social circle as the author, but thrown by the author into eccentric, quasi-fantastic stories (*The Private Life, Fordham Castle, Broken Wings*). I will discuss this further in Chapter Eight.

appeared in the newspapers of the capitals. There is always distance, and this distance was largely a result of the commercial constraints of the press.

7. Short Stories and the Travelogue

At the beginning of their careers, Henry James and Guy de Maupassant wrote as many travelogues as they did short stories. The travelogue — by which I mean a "factual" article describing a journey to a foreign place — became another important item in the newspapers of the late nineteenth century. We shall see in this chapter that short stories of that time shared many characteristics with the travelogue, and that this had a direct and important bearing on the short story as a genre. Authors in general — and these two authors in particular — very often wrote travelogues and short stories at the same time, and set them in the same countries. They also sometimes published them both in the same periodicals.[1] In the stories as in the travelogues, the characterisation of the foreign world emphasised the differences with the readers' world.

Characteristically the writer of a travelogue plays the role of intermediary. He belongs to the same world as the reader, and, during his

---

1   For example James's first published items were chronicles of a journey within the United States. Then he went to Europe and returned with his first short stories. From then on, and for several years, he published alternately and sometimes for the same periodical, travelogues and short stories in which the action takes place in the same country. In the case of Maupassant, there is a series of short stories set in North Africa, *Afrique* (*The Africans*), *Au soleil* (*In the Sun*), *La Vie errante* (*The Life of Wandering*) and several texts about the south of France and Corsica, published together with travelogues about the same places. Chekhov's scientific description of a Sakhalin penal colony was in the same way accompanied by the story *V Ssylke* (*In Exile*) published after his trip to Sakhalin.

DOI: 10.11647/OBP.0039.7

stays abroad, he gathers knowledge and impressions of a foreign country that he will share with them. The important point is that he perceives the foreigner with the eye of his own civilization; ideally he is an "expert" of that country, but one who never forgets his origins. In this way, he can describe the foreigner in terms that the people at home understand. Almost always this involved the author adopting a sharply critical and, as we shall see, superior tone.

For both authors — Maupassant and James — there is a striking continuity between their travelogues and short stories: in the tales set in exotic countries we shall find descriptions, judgements and explanations that would not be out of place in the corresponding travelogues. We can also find identical sentences in both the "factual" chronicle and the short story.[2] Sometimes a text begins as a travelogue and then goes on to narrate a story: in Maupassant's *Un bandit corse* (*The Corsican Bandit*), for instance, the initial descriptions are like a travelogue, and then the transition is made with the request, "'Tell me about your bandits'", which introduces the anecdote.[3] The exact nature of the text is not always clear, something which has proved difficult for editors. Louis Forestier, for example, included in the body of his edition of Maupassant's short stories many texts that verged on the travelogue, but then relegates to his appendix one text which has all the characteristics of a short story even though it describes effusively the nature of Switzerland.[4] This story is in the form of a letter written by the author to someone staying in Paris — a classic device of the travelogue — in which descriptions of the countryside and the customs are presented as if the author were writing familiarly to the reader.

Praise of nature, criticism of culture

The essential feature of travelogues and the corresponding short stories is something we also find in the genre of the "exotic novel": the foreign

---

2   Louis Forestier draws many such parallels between Maupassant's travelogues and short stories. See the notes in his edition of Guy de Maupassant, *Contes et nouvelles*, ed. by Louis Forestier, 2 vols (Paris: Gallimard, collection La Pléiade, 1974), II, for example pp. 1673 and 1680 (hereafter Pléiade).

3   Guy de Maupassant, *Complete Short Stories of Guy de Maupassant*, trans. by Artine Artinian (Garden City, NY: Hanover House, 1955), pp. 902-04 (p. 903, hereafter Artinian). The French text can be found in Pléiade, I, pp. 436-39. Hereafter, the references are given first to the translation, then to the original text.

4   Pléiade, II, pp. 1261-70.

landscape is seen as delightfully picturesque and praised unreservedly, while its inhabitants, their customs and their institutions are shown as strange, bizarre and inferior.[5] The narrators of short stories are almost invariably dazzled by the astonishing beauty of a foreign land. Whether it is James striding through the Old World, or Maupassant passing through North Africa, the discovery of a different landscape is at times breath-taking: tourist attractions in Italy, the gorges of Chabet, or the Algerian coast, all give rise to long emotional outpourings.

James, for example, presented the spectacle of America to the British readers of the London magazine *Cornhill*. His description of Broadway in *An International Episode* begins with these words:

> Nothing could well resemble less a typical English street than the interminable avenue, rich in incongruities, through which our two travelers advanced — looking out on each side of them at the comfortable animation of the sidewalks, the high-coloured heterogeneous architecture, the huge white marble facades, glittering in the strong, crude light and bedizened with gilded lettering, the multifarious awnings, banners and streamers, the extraordinary number of omnibuses, horse-cars and other democratic vehicles [...] the white trousers and big straw-hats of the policemen.[6]

We have here a long list of things that might astonish two Englishmen on landing in America, and James, as a good chronicler, does not forget a single "picturesque" element: the enormity of everything ("huge", "heterogeneous", "extraordinary number"), the white trousers of the policemen, the "democratic" transportation. He emphasises the confusion of the English, and their conviction that it must be impossible to find a bath in such a country. And then "they found that a bath was not unattainable, and were indeed struck with the facilities for prolonged and reiterated immersion with which their apartment was supplied".[7] What is clear in each of these cases is the desire to make a different reality visible: to be the

5   There are many well-known texts on exoticism, for example, Edward W. Said, *Orientalism* (New York: Vintage Books, 1979); Homi K. Bhabha, *The Location of Culture* (London: Routledge, 2004); and Albert Wendt, Introduction to *Nuanua: Pacific Writing in English Since 1980* (Honolulu: University of Hawaii Press, 1995), ed. by Albert Wendt, pp. i-ix. For a study focussed specifically on the short story, see Catherine Ramsdell, "Homi K. Bhabha and the Postcolonial Short Story", in *Postmodern Approaches to the Short Story*, ed. by Farhat Iftekharrudin, Joseph Boyden, Joseph Longo and Mary Rohrberger (Westport, CN: Praeger, 2003), pp. 97-106.

6   Henry James, *The Complete Tales of Henry James*, ed. by Leon Edel, 12 vols (New York: Rupert Hart Davis, 1960), IV, pp. 243 (hereafter Edel).

7   Ibid, p. 244.

cicerone for readers to whom one explains an unfamiliar reality, often in enthusiastic terms.

But when it comes to describing the people, or their way of life, the tone is dramatically different. From the moment that the topic is no longer the landscape, judgements in both the short story and the travelogue are almost always in favour of the readers' country.[8] Anton Chekhov's *V ssylke* (*In Exile*), discussed in the previous chapter, is an obvious example: the very aim of the story was to bring the public's attention to the horrors of a world where there is neither hope nor values.[9] Nature is depicted as extraordinary: not as breathtakingly beautiful, as it is in James's or Maupassant's chronicles, but as unfathomably harsh, a country where, at Easter, the earth is still solidly frozen, where rivers are disastrously swollen. Of course, in this terrible world, where the customs are as horrifying as the living conditions, there is no common ground with the world of the readers of the expensive *Vsemirnaya illustratsiya*.

James also emphasised the moral superiority of his own country and the disagreeableness of some foreign customs. Despite the emotion roused by the beauty of Europe, institutions and customs compare unfavourably to those of America. The status of women is the source of an entire series of comparative commentaries. *Travelling Companions* explicitly states the difference between the Old and the New World when it comes to gender roles. The narrator is an American raised in Germany who is traveling through Italy. He is, of course, enthusiastic about the beauties of Milan. But he meets there an American girl, and he is just as thrilled by the discovery of a more liberated femininity in his own far-away home country that he has grown up barely knowing. He bows to the moral superiority of his original nation: "there was a different quality of womanhood from any that

---

8   The exceptions are not very convincing. Maupassant's comment in *Allouma* is typical in its facile misanthropy. The author finds himself in the middle of the desert and feels like a different man, better for not participating in the mediocre life of his fellow Parisians: "how far I was from everything and everybody connected with a town-dweller's life". Artinian, p. 1250 (Pléiade, II, 1096). The story consists of raptures over the "purity" and the "naturalness" of the wilderness, but without really threatening the character's deep attachments to home. We will return to this story in Part III.

9   Anton Pavlovich Chekhov, *The Oxford Chekhov*, trans. and ed. by Ronald Hingley, 9 vols (London: Oxford University Press, 1971), VI, pp. 89-96. The Russian text can be found in Anton Pavlovich Chekhov, *Polnoe sobranie sochinenii i pisem*, 30 vols (Moscow: Nauka, 1974-1983), VIII, pp. 42-50. Nature is described in the same way as before, although this time the style is horror; Chekhov insists that nature in Siberia is profoundly different from that familiar to the Russian reader.

I had recently known; a keenness, a maturity, a conscience , which deeply stirred my curiosity".[10]

Similarly, *At Isella*, also written for an American readership, is on first glance a celebration of Italy's irresistible attractions for the young American narrator.[11] At the first inn after the border, the American meets a young *marchesina* who is running away from her husband to join the man she loves in Geneva. She is the embodiment of the concept of "the Italian woman": rich complexion and sombre eyes, consuming passion and nobility. James makes this representation of a national type explicit: "The Signora seemed to me an incorporate image of her native land".[12] Yet the young *marchesina* discovers the freedom of American women, and this becomes a subject of astonishment and reflection that takes a good deal of our attention in a supposedly "European" tale:

> 'What is said in your country of a woman who travels alone at night without even a servant?'
> 'Nothing is said. It's very common.'
> 'Ah! women must be very happy there, or very unhappy. Is it never supposed of a woman that she has a lover? That is worst of all.'
> 'Fewer things are "supposed" of women there than here. They live more in the broad daylight of life. They make their own law'.[13]

The author's comparison between European and American customs leaves no room for doubt: America is the advanced country, the country with the moral ingenuity and maturity to allow women equal freedom.

James's characterisation of foreigners as inferior is not always portrayed as an explicit comparison: very often, his "portraits" speak for themselves. His stories include a whole gallery of strange and "unacceptable" foreign characters. The Italians are ingratiating and ready to profit from the generosity of passing Americans (Giovanelli in *Daisy Miller*; the archaeologist in *The Last of the Valerii*). The French are without conscience: in *Madame de Mauves*, Monsieur de Mauves is the nobleman absorbed in his own high birth and debauched like the unscrupulous aristocrats in *The American*. *Théodolinde* is based entirely on the idea that Parisians are void of any moral sense, and that their example can corrupt *even* an American. In

---

10 Edel, II, p. 178.

11 Edel, II, pp. 307-40.

12 Ibid, p. 327. Then, when the narrator suggests returning with her to Switzerland to help her join her friend, he says: "'To go with you [...] will be to remain in Italy, I assure you'". Ibid, p. 332.

13 Ibid, p. 330.

the preface to the New York edition of *A London Life*, James regrets having made his morally bankrupt heroine an American when, on reflection in his later life, he now sees her depravity as typical of an English woman of the Prince of Wales "set".[14] But the young adulteress, while certainly of American origin, is nevertheless living in London and driven "into the mire" by an English husband, who is presented as a sort of monster. An oxymoronic tension results from the opposition of customs: the story is told from the sister's point of view, who has just arrived from America, and cannot bear the sight of these European excesses.[15]

Perhaps it is Maupassant, though, who provides the most interesting perspective on the subject of "foreignness". *Allouma* explicitly develops the world vision that underlies all these short stories.[16] The central device here is to have the story told by a colonial, M. Auballe. His long familiarity with the Arabian world and his happiness to be living in the region give the narrator and the reader confidence in him. He presents himself as having knowledge of Algeria and he provides his public with descriptions to help them understand — the framework is the same as in a travelogue. What is remarkable is that the speech in which he poses as "the person with knowledge" is a sharp and definitive judgement of the people of that country, as he develops the stereotype of the "lying Arab":

> The habit of lying is one of the most surprising and incomprehensible features of the native character. These people [...] are liars to the backbone, to such an extent that one can never believe what they say. Do they owe it to their religion? I cannot say. One must have lived among them to understand to what a degree falsehood forms a part of their whole existence and becomes a kind of second nature, a necessity of life.[17]

This very same narrator makes clear that the French can never truly understand the Arabs, but this does not prevent him, in the same sentence, from characterising them in six adjectives: unknown, mysterious, sly,

---

14 Henry James, *The Notebooks of Henry James*, ed. by F. O. Matthiessen and Kenneth B. Murdock (New York: Oxford University Press, 1947), p. 38.

15 At the end of his life, James no longer understood why he made it an "international" story but in this context, things become clear: at this stage of his career, he used American characters in sharp contrast to Europeans, to heighten the latter's depravity and then again, by contrast, to enhance the moral superiority of the Americans. The great novels, however, brought about an evolution: this kind of caricature is not to be found after *What Maisie Knew* (1897).

16 Artinian, pp. 1249-63 (Pléiade, II, pp. 1095-1117).

17 Ibid, p. 1254 (p. 1103).

untrustworthy, smiling and impenetrable.[18] He continues his stereotype of the Arab with categorical judgements: "An Arab, where women are concerned, has the most rigorous standards coupled with the most inexplicable tolerance".[19] He then describes his paradoxical love of the girl Allouma as being impossible because of her race:

> [...] one does not love the young women of this primitive continent [...] They are too primitive, their feelings are insufficiently refined to arouse in our souls that sentimental exaltation which is the poetry of love. [20]

Maupassant had expressed almost the same opinion in the same terms in one of his travelogues, *The Wandering Life*.[21] His decision in *Allouma* to have what could be regarded as highly biased opinions about Algeria "endorsed" by a character presented as an expert, with the self-assured tone of a guide, makes the judgement final. Foreign men are mostly demonised in Maupassant's "African" short stories, whereas women, like nature, are seen as exotically beautiful, if still backwards and morally questionable. He often talks about love with native women, following a well-worn topos of exotic literature:[22] the women are depicted as being all the more beautiful for being some sort of wild animal.[23] In effect, the praise of the women's beauty must always be linked with that of nature; and the desirable if animalistic allure of their bodies is set in contrast to their negative behaviour. In *Allouma* the narrator's lover is described in terms that are the hallmark of the exotic sublime:

> Her white body, gleaming in the light admitted through the raised flap, seemed to me to be one of the most perfect specimens I had ever seen [...] She had an unusual face: with regular, refined features with a slightly animal expression, but mystical like that of a Buddha".[24]

---

18 Ibid, p. 1255 (p. 1104).
19 Ibid, p. 1255 (p. 1105).
20 Ibid, p. 1256 (p. 1107).
21 See Forestier's comparisons (Pléiade, II, p. 1680).
22 To his fictive addressee of the story *Marocca*, Maupassant had indeed promised amusing love stories: "You ask me, dear friend, to send you my impressions of Africa and an account of my adventures, especially of my love affairs in this seductive land. You laughed a great deal beforehand at my dusky sweethearts, as you called them". Artinian, p. 577 (Pléiade, I, 367). On this topos, see, for example, Frantz Fanon on the hoax *Je suis Martiniquaise* (1948) in *Black Skin, White Masks* (New York: Grove Press, 1967), where Fanon criticises the vision of herself that is given by the narrator, and pretended author, a young mulatresse.
23 "She was a wonderful, a delightful animal, but no more, in the form of a woman". Artinian, p. 1261 (Pléiade, II, p. 1114).
24 Ibid, pp. 1251-53 (p. 1101).

Does this mixture of bestial imagery and mysticism define a beauty that is "equal" to that of the French? Not at all. What follows does not elaborate on this feature of "local colour" (a Buddha in Africa!) but goes on to emphasise only the absence of thought in the native woman:

> I told you a little while ago that Africa, this bare artless country [sic], devoid of all intellectual attraction, gradually overcomes us by an indefinable and unfailing charm, by the breath of its atmosphere, by the constant mildness of the early mornings and the evenings, by its delightful sunlight and by the feeling of well-being that it instills in us. Well, Allouma attracted me in the same way by numberless hidden and fascinating enticements.[25]

Maupassant then provides the key to Allouma's character by defining her as the ultimate "other": "this creature of another race, who seemed to me to be almost of another species, born on a *neighboring planet*".[26]

The end of *Allouma* is especially interesting: Maupassant manages the transition from pure exoticism — the setting of the Algerian desert — to social exoticism. Allouma occasionally leaves her white lover to return to live for a while among the nomads. The Frenchman, bound to her by powerful carnal ties, gives permission for these absences — but he does not *understand* them. He sees them as an imperious necessity for his mistress, and he is even touched by the woman's words: "She pictured this to me so simply, so forcibly and so reasonably that I was convinced of the truth of it, and feeling sorry for her...".[27] The important point is that he does not see her reasons as reasons, the product of a brain like his own. He sees them as childish, animal-like caprices. Every time he speaks of her spirit, he recognises in it "a picture of nomadic life from the brain of a squirrel leaping from tent to tent".[28] The final departure of the young Arab woman with a paroxystically "repugnant" shepherd leads to a meditation on women in general, those of France, the "finest and most complicated", as well as the "creatures" of the desert.[29] All of them seem strangers and strange to the colonial man:

> Why had she disappeared with that repulsive brute? Why, indeed? It may have been because for practically a whole month the wind had been blowing from the South. A breath of wind! That was reason enough! Did she know,

---

25 Ibid, p. 1256 (p. 1107).

26 Ibid (emphasis mine).

27 Ibid, p. 1260 (p. 1113).

28 Ibid, p. 1254 (p. 1103).

29 The shepherd is described paroxystically as the antithesis of the Occidental "upright" man; he is a "repulsive brute". Ibid, p. 1262 (p. 1116).

do any of them, even the most introspective of them, know in most cases why they do certain things? No more than a weathercock swinging in the wind. The slightest breeze sways the light vane of copper, iron, or wood, in the same way that some imperceptible influence, some fleeting impression, stirs and guides the fickle fancy of a woman, whether she be from town or country, from a suburb or from the desert.[30]

There has been an attempt to give a little nobility to this type of judgement by calling it a "meditation on the changing heart of women".[31] It is important, however, to note that the two essential features of this concept of feminine character — foreign and unacceptable — are developed through the many comparisons to animals.[32] This type of discourse is perfectly in tune with what was generally written about women in the "light and somewhat licentious" newspaper that the *Echo de Paris* was at that time.[33]

It would be easy to be malicious about Maupassant's misogyny and racial stereotypes. This is not my intention here. On the contrary, what is important to note is that, *in spite of this*, Maupassant is one of the great short story writers, for whom love and women are a privileged subject. The short story permits this use of simple and simplistic concepts, and it can build on dismissive character types that would be unacceptable elsewhere; it uses them when the great novel could not. What would be quite unbearable in another context has not prevented him from being appreciated by generations of readers, including women. We are facing a crucial feature of the genre, which can make powerful use of extremely simple, and at times almost base, features. In these short stories, as in travelogues, the narrator is a guide who is "one of us", an intermediary who speaks the same language and possesses a knowledge that he bestows on us.[34] But this knowledge does not allow the reader to understand *from within* the logic of the world the narrator is describing. The reader can taste all the sensual joys of African life and the countryside, but he or she cannot enter into the inhabitants' vision of the world.

---

30 Ibid.

31 See for example Pléiade, II, p. 1684 (Forestier's note to *Le Rendez-vous*).

32 On this topic, see Part III, especially Chapter Eight.

33 On the magazine *Écho de Paris*, see Pierre Albert and Christine Leteinturier, *La Presse française* (Paris: Secrétariat général du gouvernement, La Documentation française, 1978).

34 Scofield says of Bret Harte: "Perhaps part of the novelty was the treatment of this rough new world by a writer who was clearly educated and literate [...] but who also knew the mining camp world at first hand", while earlier he speaks of the reading public as being "still predominantly [of the] East Coast". Martin Scofield, *The Cambridge Introduction to the American Short Story* (Cambridge: Cambridge University Press, 2006), pp. 54 and 8.

From vision to judgement: guidelines for description

As we have seen, the classic short story usually depicts worlds that are socially or culturally unfamiliar. We might expect, therefore, to find an abundance of descriptions whose aim would be to inform us, to teach us the characteristics of the unknown object. But such descriptions are extremely rare. There are a few examples, as in Maupassant's *Le Colporteur* (*The Peddler*): "As he approached I saw he was a hawker, one of those wandering peddlers who sell from door to door throughout the countryside";[35] or as in Mori Ōgai, when he describes Berlin for his Japanese compatriots: "It was one of those rooms called 'garrets' which overhang the street and have no ceiling".[36]

However, among the hundreds of short stories I have studied, there are only a few instances of these potentially useful explanations. Instead, there is an abundance of descriptions that develop all the details of objects already known which create a distance between the reader and the subject. As we saw in Part I, it is a question of beginning with a pre-existing idea and developing this "type" in ways that do not necessarily challenge it. It is not — as in the case of the peddler or the garret — to teach the reader something he or she knows nothing about, but rather to replace an abstract concept with a vivid concrete image.

In the classic short story we may learn *in detail* about the life of Sicilian peasants and wandering comedians (Verga's collection *Don Candeloro e Ci* [*Don Candeloro and Company*]), how one chops down an entire wood (Maupassant's *La petite Roque* [*Little Louise Roque*]), the nature of a vendetta (Maupassant's *Un bandit corse* [*The Corsican Bandit*]), life aboard a trawler (Maupassant's *En mer* [*At Sea*]), or the life of brigands in the Middle Ages (Akutagawa's *Chūtō* [*The Brigands*]).What these stories give us are the precise, picturesque and moving details of the scene. However, they do not

---

35 Artinian, p. 538 (Pléiade, II, p. 1253).
36 The quote is from *The Dancing Girl* (*Maihime*). See Mori Ōgai, *Youth and Other Stories*, ed. and trans. by J. Thomas Rimer (Honolulu: University of Hawaii Press, 1994), pp. 12-24; this is our translation, as the phrase in Rimer's version is translated only as "in a room lit by an open skylight" (p. 16). The Japanese text can be found in Mori Ōgai, *Mori Ōgai zenshū*, 38 vols (Tōkyō: Iwanami Shoten, 1971-1975), I, pp. 425-47 (p. 432). *Maihime* is often described as "the very first authentic short story [in the western sense of the term] written by a Japanese" (as opposed to the many kinds of short fictional genres, from *setsuwa* to *otogisōshi* to *gōkan* or *kokkeibon*). J. Thomas Rimer, "Three Stories by Mori Ōgai", in *Approaches to the Modern Japanese Short Story*, ed. by Thomas E. Swann and Tsuruta Kin'ya (Tōkyō: Waseda University Press, 1982), pp. 201-09.

change the abstract conception we already had of it. We were well aware that the life of itinerant traveling comedians is an inextricable mixture of grandeur and poverty. The short story is based on what is already known. It may take its time to detail the contours, and give life to a scene, but it can do this precisely because it does not need to create the essential concepts from scratch.

The problem is that these are not pure concepts in the reader's mind — they come with connotations and values. When one relies on the reader's knowledge of the objects, what is evoked is his preconception of them: the "atmosphere" surrounding them, the value judgements with which they are imbued. Descriptions in short stories are usually a "point of view" rather than an explanatory analysis. Thus Maupassant describes the peasant woman from Normandy explicitly as an archetype: "the true type of robust peasantry, half animal and half woman".[37]

These descriptions remind us of the approach taken by Gustave Flaubert in his famous "lesson of description". He gave Maupassant the exercise of describing a taxicab from the point of view of what is absolutely unique about it, in such a way that it "differs from fifty others before or behind it".[38] This is generally thought to have endowed Maupassant with evocative power of the kind that is evident in the classic short story in, for example, its particularly effective use of hypotyposis that we saw in Part I. But such an approach presupposes that the reader knows what a cab is, and has the same notion of it from the outset. To separate out the individuality of a particular specimen presupposes a notion of the cab that is common to the author and all readers. However precisely, violently or sharply the cab is described as being different from others, this description is based on a generic notion, to which its individuality is only secondary. The reader will never learn from Maupassant what a taxicab is.

We should remember that Flaubert first asked Maupassant not to describe an object, but "a grocer sitting in his doorway, a porter smoking his pipe".[39] Which means that, for people as well as taxicabs, he was relying on what was generally evoked in the mind of the nineteenth-century reader: in this case, a strong feeling of the pettiness of the *petit-bourgeois*.[40]

---

37 The quote is from *The Mother of Monsters* in Artinian, pp. 378-81 (p. 379); *La Mère aux monstres* in Pléiade, I, pp. 842-47 (p. 843).

38 Guy de Maupassant, *Pierre and Jean: And Other Stories* (New York: French Library Syndicate, 1925), p. xvi.

39 Ibid.

40 We remember with somewhat of a shudder the vision given by a Jean Richepin of

By relying on the reader's own concepts and immediately proceeding to the highly coloured descriptions of the details, the writer never raises questions about the underlying foundation of his scenes and characters. One cannot question what has never been stated, but only presupposed. The description recommended by Flaubert, and used so well by short story writers, gives the story's archetypes "life". Very logically in this context, one of the most common remarks of admiring readers is that "finally, this is a portrait that's true to life!". One vividly "sees" Maupassant's comical peasants in their rustic farmhouse. But these images are, in fact, something that has always been there.[41]

The prejudice that enters these archetypical descriptions is reserved for the human rather than the natural realm.[42] There are many moving descriptions of the countryside, but never praise for the houses or familiar objects.[43] Nature does not offer any real challenge, it does not call into question our values, because it does not bear the human mark. Admiration of foreign nature is an easy way to praise oneself for one's curiosity and tolerance. It does not involve absorbing what is different from us. Together with travelogues, short stories indicate and explicitly emphasise the difference separating "us" and "them", through descriptions and judgements of exotic people and customs. The result of this type of presentation of the world is always the same: it gives both the author and the reader a feeling of agreeable superiority over those who are different from them. To use Chinua Achebe's words about Joseph Conrad's *Heart*

---

different social classes in *Les Assis* (*The Penpushers*), a famous piece that was often reprinted in the newspapers of the time: "Because for the penpushers, there is neither spring, nor breezes, nor butterflies. The only greenery they know is the green of the register covers. And they don't complain! So is it for us to pity these poor, bleary-eyed, miserable creatures who have no desire to provide their shrivelled lungs with something other than the thick, heavy, confined air stewing with the disgusting, mouldy odour of old volumes, shabby clothes, leather cushions and seats of pants". Jean Richepin, *Le Pavé* (Paris: Dreyfous, 1883), pp. 290-91 (translation ours).

41 See Helmut Bonheim, *The Narrative Modes: Techniques of the Short Story* (Cambridge: D. S. Brewer, 1982).

42 The same dichotomy is found in the exotic genre par excellence: the colonial novel, which is not known for its deep understanding of foreign people.

43 There are a couple of exceptions: Maupassant's beauteous descriptions of the farmyards of Normandy (although it could be argued that farmyards — with their vineyards, apple trees, poplars and arbours — belong just as much to nature as to humans); and Verga's *Fantasticheria*, which is a reverie not a tale, and more especially an indictment of the "worldly" world of the listener through the intermediary of the "simple" life of the peasants. However, even then, the praise of the peasant world is extremely vague: it is about the beauty of place rather than of people.

of Darkness: the short story "projects the image of Africa [we could add: of Norman peasants or petty office workers] as 'the other world', the antithesis of Europe and therefore of civilization".[44]

44 Chinua Achebe, *Hopes and Impediments: Selected Essays* (New York: Doubleday, 1989), p. 3. *Heart of Darkness* is a complex story, in which, as Achebe himself is well aware, the main concern is with the hero Marlow's own psychological journey. However, it also exhibits much of the same distancing we see in the classic short story. Achebe's famous lecture of 1977, "An Image of Africa: Racism in Conrad's *Heart of Darkness*" (pp. 1-20), offers analyses of the same type I lead here and many of the quotations about "savages" from *Heart of Darkness* could be taken from Maupassant's *Allouma*.

PART III: READER, CHARACTER AND AUTHOR

8. A Foreign World

If we were to define the classic short story in one word, it would certainly be "distance". This distance is very often recognised for individual stories, but critics never, to my knowledge, see it as a characteristic feature of the genre per se.[1] There are two possible reasons for this. The first one is that we share with the readers of the periodicals of the time the objectifying distance from the characters. Nineteenth-century workers, provincials or peasants are as far — or rather further — from twenty-first century readers as they were from the readers of Milan's *Fanfulla* or Paris's *Le Gaulois*. For this reason, perhaps, we do not notice their ridiculing as acutely as

---

1 With the exception of Clare Hanson who sees the "short story" (as opposed to "short fiction") as having "characters [that] tend to be viewed externally". Clare Hanson, *Short Stories and Short Fictions, 1880-1980* (New York: St. Martin's Press, 1985), p. 6. And of Andrew Levy, who even thinks this distance has not disappeared in the twentieth century. Andrew Levy, *The Culture and Commerce of the American Short Story* (Cambridge: Cambridge University Press, 1993), pp. 108-25. When analysing individual works, critics often recognise this distance, very often in the form of irony. On the "ironic detachment" of Chekhov, see Sean O'Faolain, *The Short Story* (Cork: Mercier, 1948), p. 97. For Maupassant's pervading irony, see Richard Fusco, *Maupassant and the American Short Story: The Influence of Form at the Turn of the Century* (University Park, PA: Pennsylvania State University Press, 1994), especially pp. 17-18. Postcolonial criticism, however, usually does acknowledge the distancing of characters. We saw in Chapter Seven the example of Chinua Achebe on *Heart of Darkness*: Chinua Achebe, *Hopes and Impediments: Selected Essays* (New York: Doubleday 1989), pp. 1-20. See also, for example, Bill Mullen, "Marking Race/Marketing Race: African American Short Fiction and the Politics of Genre, 1933-1946", in *Ethnicity and the American Short Story*, ed. by Julie Brown (New York: Garland, 1997), pp. 25-46.

DOI: 10.11647/OBP.0039.8

we might. For example, *we* can see each of the stories in *Dubliners* as an epiphany, and be sensible to their "radiance";[2] the Dubliners of the turn of the century saw in them instead a powerful attack on their very essence.

The second reason is that critics tend to see the classic short story as different in essence from the "modern" short stories that have been at the centre of critical attention since Mary Rohrberger's and Charles E. May's influential studies of the 1960s and 70s.[3] Critics tend to think that classic stories represent a very limited "naturalistic" corpus that was practiced only by minor writers. We have begun to see, however, that great authors like Henry James, Anton Chekhov, Luigi Pirandello and Mori Ōgai all wrote classic short stories prolifically and were masters of the very specific "laws" of the form that we have already seen. Critics tend to think that these great authors are "above" the often simplistic and simplifying characterisation that is inherent to this form. In fact, their greatness came from using the somewhat limited features of the genre — such as distance — in a way that generated masterpieces.

In this chapter, I shall attempt to show that distance is a defining trait of the genre at the end of nineteenth century, not only in the so-called "naturalistic" story, but also as it was used by great authors of the time. This distance is put to use in many widely different ways: it can be used in anecdotes, satire, stories of the fantastic, social commentaries and tales of the countryside. One of the most interesting features of the short story is that its generic conventions have the potential to be actualised in rich and varied ways. However, at the time we are considering, the most important form "distancing" takes is through a discrediting of the characters: they are shown to be different *in essence* from the reader and the author. In other words, the classic short story is a "monologic" genre, to use Mikhail Bakhtin's term, the diametric opposite of "polyphonic": the character does not have a consciousness "with equal rights" as the author's and the reader's; he does not have a full "voice".[4] Prostitutes in Maupassant — as well as women from the colonies — are always seen as bizarre and

---

2   A commonly held critical view, from Hanson (1985), p. 7, to Rust Hills, *Writing in General and the Short Story in Particular* (Boston: Houghton Mifflin, 2000), pp. 19-22.

3   See Mary Rohrberger, *Hawthorne and the Modern Short Story: A Study in Genre* (The Hague: Mouton, 1966); and Charles E. May (ed.), *Short Story Theories* (Athens, OH: Ohio University Press, 1977).

4   Mikhail Bakhtin, *Problems of Dostoevsky's Poetics*, ed. and trans. by Caryl Emerson (Minneapolis, MN: University of Minnesota Press, 1984), p. 6.

picturesque; their feelings, ways of life and opinions are all part of an exotic spectacle.[5]

What we just saw in the last chapter makes this of no little consequence. When discrediting a character, the short story is in fact discrediting the *other* — which, when it comes to the readership of the stories we are looking at, mostly means the colonised, peasants, office workers, provincials or the urban poor. The judgements the short story invites us to pass are not just judgements on literary characters — as different from persons — which would be of no great importance. These judgements are part of a broader social attitude. Like the exotic novel in the colonial era, they are comforting readers in the feeling of their superiority, by showing them how delightfully strange, but ultimately inferior, these "other" people are.

In this third part of the book, we will begin by looking at the often explicit and radical difference authors created between their readers and their characters. The short story is much too subtle an art always to rely on the obvious, however, so we shall then analyse the use of more indirect rhetorical techniques. We shall dedicate a complete chapter to two of those techniques that are generally associated with a characters' proximity: dialect — the reproduction of ways of speaking that are specific to a linguistic group — and the relations between author, narrator and reader.

An explicit distance

The classic short story does not shrink from caricaturing its characters in the most extreme ways. Even the greatest authors — Chekhov, Maupassant, Akutagawa, Verga and James — all at times explicitly indicate how we should consider the character, rather than relying on more subtle portraits. We will not be surprised, of course, to find this in most satires, where the ridiculing of characters is expected. In Chekhov's *Smert' chinovnika* (*The Death of a Civil Servant*) — published in the humorous journal *Oskolki* (*Splinters*) and widely republished in anthologies — the hero is presented throughout the story, paroxystically, as the incarnation of the type of pitiful minor civil servant familiar to readers since Gogol. The whole story is a development of this character type, and the narrative is based on the

---

5   Compare this to a novel like *Crime and Punishment*, which is all about Sonya being "just like us", with her "voice" of equal value to that of Raskol'nikov, the judge Porfiry, or the reader. Her ways of living and thinking act as a powerful source of reflection for characters and readers alike.

grotesque bad luck that comes with it.[6] As a kind of summing up of all these elements, he is called "*Cherviakov*" ("worm").

But such caricature is not to be found only in stories written for the "small press". In the beginning of *En famille* (*A Family Affair*), Maupassant describes the people that can be found in the tramway:[7] "The few inside consisted of stout women in strange toilettes, shopkeepers' wives from the suburbs, who made up for the distinguished looks which they did not possess by ill-assumed dignity".[8] And later:

> In the suburbs of Paris, which are full of people from the provinces, one meets with the indifference toward death, even of a father or a mother, which all peasants show; a want of respect, an unconscious callousness which is common in the country, and rare in Paris.[9]

The suburb where the characters live is described as "the garbage district", and the hero, on his mother's death, is described as "revolving in his mind those apparently profound thoughts, those religious and philosophical commonplaces, which trouble people of mediocre minds in the face of death".[10] The situation is very clear: on the one hand there are the Parisian readers of a high society journal, and on the other the people who live in the suburbs, "provincials" who have not been civilized by city life, and who have brought with them their brutish country ways. Let us note that *A Family Affair* is not one of Maupassant's minor short stories, but a text which has been hailed by critics; not an anecdote for *Gil Blas*, but an "adorable short story [...] a fine study of the dregs of the lower middle class", to use

---

6 At a theatre, a petty civil servant sneezes. No big deal. But he has sneezed on the head of the person in front of him. Learning this person is a general, he apologises once, twice, five times — until the official is so irritated he quite harshly sends him away. Desperate, the civil servant returns home and dies.

7 Guy de Maupassant, *The Complete Short Stories of Guy de Maupassant*, trans. by Artine Artinian (Garden City, NY: Hanover House, 1955), pp. 1025-42 (hereafter Artinian). The French text of this story can be found in Guy de Maupassant, *Contes et nouvelles*, ed. by Louis Forestier, 2 vols (Paris: Gallimard, collection La Pléiade, 1974), I, pp. 195-218 (hereafter Pléiade). A working-class family, the Caravans, learn of the death of their grandmother, who lived in an apartment above them; they rush up to take possession of the most precious objects before the other heirs arrive, planning to pretend that they had been given to them by their grandmother, directly, in gratitude for what they had done for her. An antithetic tension is created between the excessive efforts made by the Caravans to ensure their possession of these objects, and the futility of these efforts. On the one hand, the objects are hideous; on the other, the old lady is not dead: she wakes up and solemnly gives them to the other members of the family.

8 Ibid, p. 1025 (p. 195).

9 Ibid, p. 1032 (p. 203).

10 Ibid, p. 1037 (p. 211).

an expression of the critic Albert Wolff:[11] such methods of distancing did not in any way bother the critics of the time.

Ridiculing the character does not destroy the short story; in fact it is almost a defining feature, very similar to the prevalence of paroxystic extremes. Endless numbers of heroes of short stories are described as "ridiculous" by the narrators, from Maupassant's Miss Harriet ("ridiculous and lamentable"), to Pirandello's Donna Mimma ("a ridiculous and pitiful spectacle"), to Akutagawa's Goi in *Yam Gruel* (ugly to the point of "strangeness"). What we have here is exactly the attitude that we saw in Maupassant's *Allouma* in the previous chapter: the judgement of the narrator is assured, and is founded on the comfortable feeling of the white man's/high society member's superiority.

Maupassant's characterisation of Allouma as an animal was not limited to the native woman: it was also the standard way in which he described peasants. I have listed at length the cases in which Maupassant uses animal vocabulary to represent people.[12] It ranges from descriptions of their physicality (the old peasant "just like a rat"; "What was it that opened it? I could not tell at the first glance. A woman or an ape?"; [she was] "the true type of robust peasantry, half brute and half woman [...]; [...] the brutal sound of her voice, a sort of moan, or rather a mew"),[13] to descriptions of their customs ("in the country the useless are obnoxious and the peasants would be glad, like hens, to kill the infirm of their species"),[14] and to their domestic situation ("the brats were crawling all over [...] The two mothers could barely distinguish their products in the heap [...] the housewives gathered their offspring to give them their mash, like gooseherds gathering their creatures [...] the mother [...] fattening her calf").[15] What Maupassant suggests here is a radical difference: peasants belong to a "different species" (to use his own phrase from *Allouma*). It is not that the peasants are simply different from us; they are expelled from the circle of human beings.

---

11 See Forestier's note in Pléiade, II, p. 1343 (translation ours).

12 Florence Goyet, *La Nouvelle, 1870-1925: description d'un genre à son apogée* (Paris: Presses Universitaires de France, 1993), pp. 140-44.

13 *Autres temps* in Pléiade, I, p. 455 (translation ours); *Old Mongilet* in Artinian, p. 940 (*Le Père Mongilet* in Pléiade, II, p. 468); *The Mother of Monsters* in Artinian, p. 380 (*La Mère aux monstres* in Pléiade, I, pp. 842).

14 *The Blind Man* in Artinian, p. 900 (*L'Aveugle* in Pléiade, I, p. 402).

15 *The Adopted Son* in Guy de Maupassant, *The Entire Original Maupassant Short Stories*, trans. by Albert M. C. McMaster, A. E. Henderson and Mme Quesada (Project Gutenburg, 2004), available at http://ia600204.us.archive.org/9/items/completeoriginal03090gut/3090-h/3090-h.htm#2H_4_0137 (accessed 7/11/13) (*Aux champs* in Pléiade, I, p. 607).

Again, this did not bother the critics of the time any more than the characterisation of women — especially exotic women — as inferior. This last example, *Aux champs*, is no more a minor story than *A Family Affair*. It is even today often republished — quite a favourite of short story collections of Maupassant, in fact — and at the time it had been selected by the magazines of quite good repute: *La Vie populaire*, and *Le Voleur*, which presented the story to its readers as "a living study of the heart of peasants".[16] My point is not that these stories shouldn't be republished, but that it seems odd that few critics, even today, comment on the brutal "othering" of these characters. This type of extreme and unflattering characterisation is so typical of the short story that it somehow goes unnoticed.

The classic short story did not shrink from stating explicitly that its heroes are of a resolutely different humanity from its readers, but given the subtlety of many short stories, it is not surprising that this effect is often achieved through indirect, implicit means. Most frequently readers will be left to draw their own conclusions about characters and events. As in ironic texts, the reader has no need to be told that the characters are in error; he knows it from seeing them believe in things that are clearly wrong ("known error proclaimed", as Wayne C. Booth calls it), or holding values inferior to his or the author's (Booth calls this "conflicts of belief").[17] In *Une aventure parisienne (An Adventure in Paris)*, for example, Maupassant tells the story of a chaste provincial woman, the wife of a notary, who comes to Paris in order to see for herself the extremes of luxury and corruption she is sure are hidden in the capital.[18] Purely by chance, she meets one of the great men of the day, and has the opportunity to spend a full day, and even a night, with him. The whole point of the story is her disillusionment at discovering that the man's famous and cherished reputation hides a very unpleasant personality. The structuring antithesis is between what she has imagined from reading the daily papers and the reality of Paris. In the end, she plainly acknowledges her "provincial" error.

---

16 *La Vie populaire* was a weekly publication founded by the author Catulle Mendès, with long articles and well-known authors. *Aux champs* was first published in *Le Gaulois* on 31 October 1882; it was then republished in *Le Voleur* — a well-respected publication that specialised in the republishing of texts — on 10 November 1883, and in *La Vie populaire* on 1 October 1884.

17 Wayne C. Booth, *A Rhetoric of Irony* (Chicago: University of Chicago Press, 1974), pp. 57-60 and 73-75.

18 Artinian, pp. 1008-12 (Pléiade, I, pp. 329-35).

However, the Parisian readers of *Gil Blas* or *La Vie populaire* — where the story was republished[19] — had no need of this explicit denunciation to enjoy the spectacle of her error. From the very beginning, they knew from their own experience how much she erred, just from the description of her thoughts. Sentences like "she saw Paris in an apotheosis of magnificent and corrupt luxury" and "there could be no doubt that the houses there [on the boulevards] concealed mysteries of prodigious love" make her error as clear to them as any explicit statement.[20] Similarly, there is no need to state explicitly, as Maupassant does in *En famille* (*A Family Affair*), that the clock coveted by the Caravans is ridiculous: "one of those grotesque objects that were produced so plentifully under the [Second] Empire".[21] Readers of the elegant *Nouvelle Revue* would inevitably feel disgust for such artistic atrocities as suggested here: the clock's apparatus is in the shape of a young woman, and the pendulum is a ball with which she plays cup-and-ball. This design was generally recognised in the 1880s as a contrived and rather crude sexual symbol, and considered to be the height of bad taste by anyone in intellectual or elegant circles. Here the characters are as effectively discredited by Booth's "conflict of values" as they would be through direct characterisation.

The objective social distance which we have identified between the readers of short stories and their characters is galvanized in the *feeling* of that distance. In their ferocious and ludicrous struggle for a grotesque object, the characters establish their distance from the reader who would not for the world have it cluttering his room. Wolff, in the article where he described Maupassant's story as "an excellent study of the dregs of the lower middle class", stigmatised the Caravans' "rapacity" and praised the author for being a "thinker". It is definitely an affair of the suburbs — the "district where rubbish is deposited".[22] This section of society has little to do with him or his readers.

---

19 *La Vie populaire*, 14 August 1884.

20 Artinian, p. 1008 and p. 1009 (Pléiade, I, p. 329 and p. 330).

21 Ibid, p. 1037 (p. 210).

22 Wolff describes the story as "beautiful from beginning to end, beautiful in its general conception, in its study of the characters, in its wholesome and powerful truth". The article, originally published in *Le Figaro*, was reprinted by *Le Voleur*, along with the first instalment of *A Family Affair*, in its issues of 1, 8 and 15 September 1882. It can now be found in Pléiade, I, p. 1343 (translation ours).

The use of types: subversion or immersion?

We have seen that the short story does not hesitate to use types — social if not traditional literary types — in order to facilitate the reader's rapid entry into the story (see Chapter Four). Instead of being reworked, the type is usually developed along expected lines. When Akutagawa, for instance, describes the life of brigands in the Middle Ages in *Chūtō* (*The Brigands*), he relies on all the reader's preconceived ideas of what constitutes a "brigand".[23] With little surprise — but with all the power of the topos — we see the development of life outside the law, with its train of evil deeds perpetrated with the greatest indifference, and encounters endured with the greatest *sangfroid*. Similarly, Maupassant's *La Maison Tellier* (*Madame Tellier's Establishment*) plays on the stereotype of the prostitute, while Pirandello's *Lumie di Sicilia* (*Sicilian Limetrees*) builds for our pleasure an antithesis between the immoral urban female singer, and the poor and virtuous provincial musician in love with her.[24]

Rarely will a narrative short story bypass the opportunity offered by exoticism of this kind, even when the author appears as the "defender" of a type known to be ridiculous. From this point of view, Maupassant's *Miss Harriet* is a particularly interesting story, because critics have seen in it the symbol of the author's "compassion" for his characters.[25] As we become aware of the many signs of distancing, such a conclusion becomes surprising. From her first appearance, Miss Harriet is characterised as having the "face of a mummy"; she is "a sour herring adorned with curling papers", a "singular apparition" which makes the narrator "laugh".[26] This

23 Akutagawa Ryūnosuke, *Akutagawa Ryūnosuke zenshū*, 19 vols (Tōkyō: Iwanami Shoten, 1954-1955), I, pp. 207-75.

24 Artinian, pp. 43-58 (Pléiade, I, pp. 256-83); Luigi Pirandello, *Il vecchio Dio* (Milan: Mondadori, 1979), pp. 133-44.

25 Artinian, pp. 328-41 (Pléiade, I, pp. 876-95). In a letter to Maupassant, the editor Victor Havard describes *Miss Harriet* as having "accents of tenderness and of a supreme emotion" (quoted in Pléiade, I, p. 1546, translation ours); Louis Forestier himself argues that Maupassant shows in this story "a sensibility and a sensuality that are not absent from the rest of the works, but are here particularly visible" (ibid, translation ours). Denise Brahimi, in a book dedicated to the denunciation of the clichés of the criticism on Maupassant, uses the word compassion dozens of times, for example: "he sometimes reveals without mask his infinite compassion". Denise Brahimi, *Quelques idées reçues sur Maupassant* (Paris: Editions L'Harmattan, 2012), p. 62 (translation ours). Fusco (1994), while not calling it "empathy", feels nevertheless that Maupassant had "sympathy" for his characters, even the Norman peasants (p. 27). But he puts to light the central role of irony (especially pp. 17, 21, 67-70).

26 Artinian, p. 331 (Pléiade, I, p. 880).

narrator, a "strolling painter" who collects sketches and favours from the farm girls on his walks through Normandy, does not subscribe to the peasants' judgement of her as a "demoniac". But he goes on to develop at length what she *truly is*:

> She was, *in fact*, one of those people of exalted principles, one of those opinionated puritans of *whom England produces so many*, one of those good and insupportable old women who haunt the tables d'hôte of every hotel in Europe, who spoil Italy, poison Switzerland, render the charming cities of the Mediterranean uninhabitable, carry everywhere their fantastic manias, their petrified vestal manners, their indescribable toilets and a certain odor of India rubber, which makes one believe that at night they slip themselves into a case of that material. When I meet one of these people in a hotel I act like birds which see a manikin in a field.[27]

This time the type is well documented: this particular kind of elderly lady, typified by the "English Old Maid", haunted the literature of the time, just as she haunted the tourist hotels. True, Maupassant embellishes the worn-out topos: his narrator makes friends with her. But we should not forget under what conditions: it is because she is so pitifully bizarre that she interests him, and then she expresses her admiration for one of his sketches.[28] He never refrains from characterising her as ridiculous:

> Wrapped up in her square shawl, inspired by the balmy air and with teeth firmly set [...] She now accepted these with the vacant smile of a mummy.
> [...] She was a caricature of ecstasy.
> I turned my face away from her so as to be able to laugh.[29]

And this at the precise moment when he says that both of them are "as satisfied as any two persons could be who have just learned to understand and penetrate each other's motives and feelings".[30] I do not see how the narrator's representation of a caricature permits talk of "compassion", or of a touching and emotional understanding of a being whom the rest of society despised. He feels the same interest in her as he did in "the little bell which struck midday". The narrator admits that he felt for her "something besides curiosity" which even makes him say: "I wanted [...] to learn what passes in the solitary souls of those wandering old English

---

27 Ibid, pp. 331-32 (emphases mine) (p. 881).

28 "This woman appeared so singular that she did not displease me". Ibid, p. 332 (p. 881).

29 Ibid, p. 334 (p. 885). I take the liberty to modify Artinian's translation, which reads "It would have been an ecstatic caricature". (Maupassant: "*la caricature de l'extase*").

30 Ibid. Note the two juxtaposed sentences: "And we became firm friends immediately. / She was a brave creature with an elastic sort of a soul [...]".

dames".[31] However, that is what short story narrators never do. And when, in the end, he meditates on the "secrets of suffering and despair" borne by Miss Harriet, he still talks of her "disagreeable" and "ridiculous" body, with the same mixture of pity and ridicule, as when he met her ("Poor solitary beings [...] poor beings, ridiculous and lamentable") or when he discovered that she loved him ("feeling that I could just as soon weep as laugh").[32] Of course he wants to weep, and this is what strikes the critics when they speak of compassion and understanding; but nevertheless he still wants to laugh.[33]

We are prevented from seeing this distancing because this type is considered to be obvious by both readers of the time and modern critics. It clearly relies on the traditional image of the English spinster who evoked in every late nineteenth century reader the same sentiments Maupassant ascribed to his painter. The English Old Maid is thought to be laughable and *Miss Harriet* will certainly not change our opinion. The story merely succeeds in showing that it is possible to have pity, *even within the heart of ridicule*.[34]

When pretending to rework a type, the classic short story will generally be establishing another. Maupassant will provide us with a quick example. In *La Rempailleuse* (*A Strange Fancy*), published in *Gil Blas*, the heroine is a poor and elderly chair-mender.[35] The narrator is a worldly Parisian doctor who has retired to the provinces. To contribute to the inevitable, endless

---

31 Ibid, p. 333 (p. 883).

32 Ibid, pp. 335 and 337 (pp. 886 and 890).

33 Admittedly, the narrator calls himself, in the same sentence, "ridiculous"; but he only describes in this way his behaviour as a philanderer who had not, for once, anticipated his success, finding the adventure as "both comic and deplorable", feeling "ridiculous" and thinking her nearly crazy with unhappiness. He thinks his own departure should take care of everything. In the meanwhile he continues to expound: "that grotesque and passionate attachment for me" and finally these thoughts "put [him] now in an excited bodily state" (ibid, p. 338): he will go on to kiss the servant.

34 The examples I have come across all show that short stories were more abrupt when published in the press, and much of the violence of the short stories were softened before publication in a collection. In the original version of *Miss Harriet* published in *Le Gaulois* (9 July 1883), the caricature is more extreme. Firstly, it lacks the great description of nature at the beginning that unites the "principled fanatic" and the painter. Secondly, the definition of the activity of the "strolling painter" is much more trivial ("studies of servants and memorable nonsense"). The adventure with Miss Harriet thus is in violent contrast to the lesser loves which are the only background. Finally, the "portrait" of the Englishwoman is much shorter: "sour herring", "she never spoke at table" [...] [but read] a small book of some Protestant propaganda" (the original version can be found in Pléiade, I, pp. 1546-52).

35 Artinian, pp. 651-55 (Pléiade, I, pp. 546-52).

after-dinner discussion of love and passion, he announces the story of a "love which lasted fifty years", and his audience of women of the province's "good society" immediately break into lyrical couplets about life-long love.[36] When he tells them that the protagonists are the village pharmacist and the chair-mender, however, the ladies now express violent disgust — the chair-mender is considered to be part of the dregs of society, even lower on the social scale than peasants. When the narrator asserts forcefully that her love is no more ridiculous than any other, we are ready to believe that he is free from the prejudices usually expressed by the short story. However, his characterisation of the girl is paroxistically pejorative: she is "ragged, flea-ridden, sordid".[37] She is also shown as being taken in by all the spectacles of society — exactly those that the Parisian readers of *Gil Blas* would *not* be taken in by. She is enamoured by the pharmacist's son — who becomes her idol and accepts repeatedly all her money — and enchanted by the pharmacy window, before which she stays "charmed, aroused to ecstasy by this glory of coloured water, this apotheosis of shining crystal".[38]

Yet the characters who are ultimately "distanced" in this story are the narrow-minded women to whom the doctor tells the story. *Gil Blas* published hundreds of stories about love told by similar narrators, and the chair-mender's love is shown to be *no more* ridiculous than that of the provincial women. Readers are in agreement with the doctor in their contempt for the silly, romantic notions seemingly found in every bourgeois woman.

"Deceptive representations" of reality

Chekhov may very well have been the most subtle of all this period's short story writers. Even his early satires are capable of complex representations, and the stories of his later career extend the territory of the genre, creating texts that break with some of the rules we have thus far seen at work; perhaps more than any other author he paved the way to the "modern" short story, with its new perspective on self and society. Chekhov is the one author who really challenges the reader's existing conceptions of the world. Perhaps surprisingly, I would argue that this too is achieved

---

36 Ibid, p. 651 (p. 546).

37 Our translation from Pléiade, I, p. 547 ("[...] *haillonneuse, vermineuse, sordide*"). Artinian's translation is very tame: "ragged and dirty" (p. 652).

38 Artinian, pp. 652-53 (Pléiade, I, p. 549).

through distancing. Chekhov takes full advantage of the short story's "laws" and his difference from other writers is not in abandoning distance but in putting at a distance *all* the positions he observes.

Vladimir Kataev has shown that the seeds of all Chekhov's work are to be found in the early "stories of discovery".[39] In Chapter Two we saw Chekhov's powerful use of antithesis in these stories, where the simple and deluded concept of the world that his character entertained was violently opposed to the new and rightful concept he came to have: "*kazalos'/okazalos'*" ("it seemed that/it appeared clearly that"). What Kataev makes apparent is that from then on, Chekhov continued to denunciate his characters' "hallucinations" ("*lozhnye predstavleniya*", or more literally "deceptive representations") of the world.[40] The phrase is Chekhov's, and is used in a story that makes the technique particularly clear: *Spat' khochetsya* (*Sleepy*).[41] The heroine is a young girl, Varka, who works as a servant in a rich farmer's house. She does all the normal household chores as well as baby-sitting at night. The baby cries all the time so that she can never get to sleep, and then at dawn she must begin a new day's work. Overcome with exhaustion, and in the grip of a semi-conscious dream, she finally kills the baby so that she can get some rest.

It is a powerful story, and one in which the reader had the opportunity to be immersed in a world of which he or she was most likely ignorant. Our pity for the girl is intense, and we feel vividly Chekhov's often discussed interest in the plight of the poor. My point here is that this interest takes advantage of the genre's specific features. Varka, like nearly all Chekhov's characters, is seen to be trapped by her false concept of the world; she is incapable of judging her situation correctly, of understanding the real (and social) causes of her exhaustion. This is why she identifies the baby as the source of her misery and strangles it: "the hallucination takes hold of Varka".[42] What is important is that Chekhov shows vividly *both* her

39 V. B. Kataev, *Proza Chekhova: problemy interpretatsii* (Moscow: Izd-vo Moskovskogo universiteta, 1979). For a partial translation, see Vladimir Kataev, *If Only We Could Know: An Interpretation of Chekhov*, trans. by Harvey Pitcher (Chicago: Ivan R. Dee, 2002), here pp. 11-19; see also, pp. 53-55. Given that this translation is much abridged, I shall give future references to the Russian edition.

40 Anton Pavlovich Chekhov, *Polnoe sobranie sochinenii i pisem*, 30 vols (Moscow: Nauka, 1974-1983), VII, p. 12 (hereafter Nauka).

41 Anton Pavlovich Chekhov, *Anton Chekhov's Short Stories*, ed. by Ralph E. Matlaw, trans. by Constance Garnett (New York: Norton, 1979), pp. 64-69 (hereafter Matlaw). The Russian text can be found in Nauka, pp. 7-12.

42 Ibid, p. 69 (p. 12)

misery and her inability to analyse the situation. Through the powerful hypotyposis of the abuse and exploitation of the girl by her masters, he makes sure that the reader, on the other hand, will not mistake the reason for her suffering.

Throughout his career, Chekhov forcefully depicted his characters' objectively terrible situations — moral or physical — and at the same time made it clear that the reason for their predicament lay in their inability to understand "correctly" the world around them. This is an important point, especially since western critics have generally insisted, to the contrary, on Chekhov's so-called refusal to take a position in relation to political problems. In his often-quoted declaration to Alexei Suvorin, Chekhov said that one should not ask a writer for solutions to the problems of his time.[43] But there are two steps to Chekhov's declaration, as Kataev most opportunely reminds us: "You are right to demand from the artist a conscious relationship with his work but you confuse two ideas: *resolving the question, and asking the correct question*; only the latter is obligatory for the artist" (the emphasis is Chekhov's).[44] Chekhov is in no way a "relativist" for whom all positions would be equal. He refuses to give practical answers, but thinks his responsibility as a writer is to "ask the correct question". By doing this, he occupies a position from which he can state what is correct and what is not. In the terms we have been using, he occupies a position of superiority to his characters, and his goal is to make his readers understand "correctly" what is happening to them.

In *Sleepy*, the satire that is applied to everyone except the heroine is quite blatant. Chekhov's later stories were more subtle, but the "distancing" of certain characters only gained in strength. *Kryzhovnik* (*Gooseberries*), written towards the end of Chekhov's life, relates the pitiful story of a bureaucrat whose only dream is to grow gooseberries in a garden of his own.[45] The hero is denounced along lines that are now already familiar to us: Chekhov draws a paroxystic portrait of the despicable traits of the lower middle class. The hero wears himself out working all his life to obtain money; for that purpose he marries a rich woman whom he does not love. Sordid avarice (which deprives him and his wife of any degree of comfort), the niggardliness of the "dream" (summarised by the pitiful and haunting

---

43 Suvorin was a major intellectual, and the director of the journal *Novoe vremya*. The letter, dated 27 October 1888, is in Nauka, III, p. 46.

44 Kataev (1979), p. 40.

45 Matlaw, pp. 185-94 (Nauka, X, pp. 55-65).

image of the scarcely edible gooseberries), the ludicrous presumption and vanity of someone who thinks he is a gentleman because he possesses a shabby house, and the animal satisfaction of eating inedible gooseberries — the author does not spare his hero one iota. The conclusion of the story takes the form of a judgement delivered by the narrator against the hero. This is one of the most famous moments in Chekhov's work, always quoted by Soviet critics who saw in this and a few other similar stories the proof that the author was, at heart, ready for the advent of the Revolution:

> There is no such thing as happiness, nor ought there to be, but if there is any sense or purpose in life, this sense and purpose are to be found not in our own happiness, but in something greater and more rational. Do good![46]

In fact, as Kataev clearly shows, this is by no means a direct and personal expression of Chekhov's "real" thoughts.[47] It is that of a *character,* in this case the narrator, who is in fact distanced and discredited by the "frame" of the story.

Gooseberries is not presented on its own, but as part of what is generally known as the "little trilogy": three different stories told by three companions.[48] All the rhetorical techniques in these three stories contribute to the discrediting of their heroes. But the "framing" provided by the trilogy itself is used to distance each one of the narrators in turn. The characters inside the stories are mocked by their objective presentation as well as by the comments of the narrators, but the narrators themselves are also mocked in the "frame". For example, Ivan Ivanich, the narrator of *Gooseberries,* is discredited by Chekhov's insistence that the story has bored its listeners, but also by the fact that he is incapable of feeling nature's beauty. This is one of the techniques that Chekhov used to show a character's limitations (his soul *cannot* feel it). The "frame" presents us with one of Chekhov's famous descriptions of nature: the pure beauty of the river where the characters are bathing in the rain is one of the moments deeply felt and

---

46 Ibid, p. 193 (p. 64).
47 Kataev (1979), pp. 238-50.
48 See ibid, pp. 211-21. The "little trilogy" comprises *The Man in a Case, Gooseberries* and *About Love* (1898). All three can be found in Anton Pavlovich Chekhov, *The Kiss and Other Stories,* trans. by Ronald Wilks (Harmondsworth: Penguin, 1982). At the beginning of *The Man in a Case,* we see two men, Burkin and Ivan Ivanich, who take to telling stories while on a hunting trip together. Burkin tells the first story, while Ivan Ivanich follows with *Gooseberries.* The third story is told the next day, when they have come to a landowner in the district, who offers drinks and conversation after a bath in the river.

well remembered by generations of readers. But the character is shown to be unable to perceive it.

All the characters in both the stories and the "frame" of the trilogy are discredited because they hold to their "truths": fragmented, inadequate concepts of reality that prevent them from seeing the world's complex and contradictory facets and inherent natural beauty. Even when it is not a question of pure material interest (as was the case of the rich farmers of *Sleepy*), even when it is a "truth" that can be taken for capital-T truth by generations of critics (as in the indictment against petty individual happiness), Chekhov shows its insufficiency. He challenges the image of all his characters, and also the pre-revolutionary expressions in their mouths. Refusing to believe in ready-made "truths" — refusing, of course, to give ready-made practical answers to the problems of his time — Chekhov fulfils in his stories what he feels is the true duty of the writer: showing *all* the shortcomings, he denounces the falseness of his contemporaries' values.

The great man

Distance does not necessarily imply a negative discreditation. It is just as possible to imagine that it can, on the contrary, help to raise a character to the status of a hero. Although there were many stories that did this in the newspapers of the time, they are very rare in my corpus of classic short stories by great authors. However, one extremely good example is Mori Ōgai's *Hanako*.[49] Published in a Japanese review, this short story is essentially an *homage* to Auguste Rodin. The narrator is a young Japanese student, Kubota, who relates an interview between the sculptor and his fellow countrywoman, the dancer Hanako, for which he acted as interpreter. In it we find reversed the same processes of distancing as in the stories that show their heroes in an extremely negative light. For example, Ōgai emphasises the radical difference between Rodin's concept of beauty and that of the narrator and his readers. Kubota insists at length on the fact that Hanako is only a variety dancer, with no particular beauty according to the Japanese canon. Rodin, on the contrary, from the moment he enters the studio, expresses his admiration for the young woman, and the end of the

49 Mori Ōgai, *Youth and Other Stories*, ed. by J. Thomas Rimer (Honolulu: University of Hawaii Press, 1994), pp. 274-79. The Japanese text can be found in Mori Ōgai, *Mori Ōgai zenshū*, 38 vols (Tōkyō: Iwanami Shoten, 1971-1975), VII, pp. 189-97.

text consists of a translation of the sculptor's remarks on Japanese beauty.[50] Rodin's vision is radically different from that of the typical Japanese reader at the turn of the century, but his view is shown to be superior.

The aesthete Ōgai gives his contemporaries a glimpse of the intellectual world of the great man, and the account is merely a pretext for this portrayal. In the same way that short stories about peasants and working people accumulate the traits of their characters which make them "other", so Ōgai reviews here the attributes which make the sculptor a different person from us: his powers of concentration, his memory of forms, the breadth of his reading, and his idea of a concept of beauty according to each race. The character is as distant as Maupassant's peasants, but for the purpose of praising not dismissing him.

"We are simply the case": James and abstract entities

In James's work, the distance is made and used slightly differently. A whole section of James's stories are social dramas, in which the characters, for once, belong to the same world as the readers. The distance here is born of the very construction of the short story, which is another instance of what Booth calls "known error proclaimed": the text presents as real facts that we know are false. The effect is, however, very different from what we saw in Maupassant's *An Adventure in Paris*. In *The Great Good Place*, James shows an author devoured by worldly life — social calls, reviews and articles — who suddenly finds himself "saved"; he wakes up one day in a sort of sunny Thélème, a marvellous world in which there is nothing but intellectual work.[51] The fiction of this magical retreat is never denounced; it simply gives this obvious unreality something of the strength of allegory.

In *The Private Life*, James again uses parallel universes to articulate the status of the artist in society. He depicts a lord who literally has no existence outside the presence of others, whose body and soul disappear when he is alone. Parallel to this, he develops the idea that the artist only has value through his work, and that the worldly life can only overwhelm the true creator. In order to demonstrate this fact, he gives a writer, Clare

---

50 We know that Hanako was a model much loved by Rodin. These remarks were published by a Parisian journal from which Ōgai made his translation. The story itself was published in July 1910, a few months before the special issue, dedicated to Rodin, of the great journal *Shirakaba* (December 1910).

51 Edel, XI, pp. 13-42.

Vawdrey, *two* bodies. One inhabits the salons, dines and gossips in town; the other remains cloistered in his room, writing his celebrated novels. The casual way in which James unites both proofs in one text is part of his particular tone: he masters better than anyone the constraints and resources of the short story format, and will often make of it quasi-abstract narratives, playing with the structural traits — paroxysms and distancing — that are the rule in the genre at that time. As one of his characters state of themselves, they represent only the abstract law of the narrative: "We're simply the case [...] of having been had enough of".[52]

Another example of James's characters as "cases" can be found in *Fordham Castle*, a story from the final phase of his career.[53] The narrator, Abel F. Taker, is an unpolished American whose wife has sent him to Switzerland, and told him to pretend to be dead, while she attempts to conquer London's social scene. James is not content to insist amusingly on the literalness of Taker's wife's command.[54] He brings Taker face to face with an American woman whose daughter has also sent her into exile so that she can work on her ascendancy of the social ladder without being embarrassed by the presence of her provincial mother. Those of us who have read enough short stories of James will suspect very quickly that the two aspirational women will also find themselves in the same site of worldly success: Fordham Castle, an estate belonging to English gentry, to which each has succeeded in getting an invitation once they have unloaded their unwanted relation. They even become friends, like the two exiles. James then heaps on the coincidences, and emphasises the incredible aspect of his stage-setting. It is surprising to think that this is the same author who led us through the wanderings of Kate Croy's thoughts in *Wings of the Dove*. James does not try to bring us close to the heroes of his short stories. He develops a narrative line that supposes, on the contrary, absolute detachment on our part, even if this detachment is accompanied by real pleasure in watching the hero's progress.

---

52 In *Broken Wings*, two artists love each other at a distance and do not dare admit their love, each being (falsely) convinced that the other is enormously successful, and so could not be interested in him/her. The hero thus defines their adventure as the incarnation of a law that they only illustrate. Edel, XI, pp. 217-38 (p. 232).

53 Edel, IX, pp. 125-49.

54 The narrator repeats that he is not allowed to use his name, and that he is ready to die if that would help his wife in her career, etc.

Reading at face value: the double distance

To conclude and prepare the way to our next chapter on dialect, I will turn to an apparent counter-example — Maupassant's *Boitelle*, one of the extremely rare stories that were published in the penny papers that presented lower class readers with an image of themselves — in order to understand how these readers might have responded to seeing themselves "distanced" in this way. To my mind, the short story as a genre works in the same way as an ironic text. As with irony, the author can choose never to make explicit how we are to interpret the text — never to signal what he is doing through "straightforward warnings in the author's own voice".[55] The author can use the characters' own words and values to discredit them, without ever saying that they are ridiculous. It is then possible for the readers not to see the indirect indications scattered through the story and therefore to read it at face value. In irony, the result is well known: we are returned to the hell of "bad readers", we do not experience the euphoria of values shared with the author.[56] In the short story, the essential result is that, for once, these stories can be read by the very people they represent. What interests me here is that, in the cases I know of, *another* — a second — distance is present in the text, which serves to make it exotic to these unexpected readers.

Boitelle was republished by the *Supplément du Petit Parisien,* a popular and very inexpensive newspaper, and a number of other cheap newspapers.[57] When first published in the society paper *L'Echo de Paris*, it functioned exactly as all the stories we have seen. Boitelle is a young peasant, who falls in love with a black servant-girl while fulfilling his military service in the large town of Le Havre. The story's zest is in the description of his vain efforts to get his parents to accept her as their daughter-in-law. The elderly peasants express their anxiety in phrases that must have seemed droll to the society readers: "she's too black", says the mother; before asking silly questions, from "It doesn't soil linen more than other skins?", to "Are there more black people besides her in her country?". The hero himself is distanced from the society reader by all the usual devices: Boitelle is presented as a "night cartman" (he cleans the drains and cesspools), as naive as his parents. When waiting for his sweetheart, his attention is divided between the girl and the parrots of a shop nearby, and for him she

---

55 Booth (1974), pp. 53-56.
56 Ibid, pp. 73-89.
57 Artinian, pp. 1121-26 (Pléiade, II, pp. 1086-94).

is just as exotic as the birds: "he really could not tell which of these two beings he contemplated with the greater astonishment and delight".[58]

But in this story, Maupassant relies completely on his readers' capacity to perceive the implied ridicule of his characters: he never explicitly states that the parents are silly or the girl has bad taste, he simply gives examples that his readers will recognise. *Echo de Paris* readers were not at risk of being in the "hell of bad readers": they were accustomed to these types of subjects and jokes. But lower class readers *could* ignore their own distancing, which is only indirect, and be interested in the second exotic spectacle, that of the girl. The African woman was the epitome of the exotic subject at the time, and Maupassant depicts this girl departing for her parents' village: "She had put on, for this journey to the house of her lover's parents, her most beautiful and most gaudy clothes, in which yellow, red and blue were the prevailing colors, so that she had the appearance of one adorned for a national fete".[59] Against this background, the tragedy of the lovers' fate can expand and interest the readers, as would one of the serials in the newspaper — which often play on the same subject of virtuous and unfortunate love. The parents' refusal of the marriage is, for a respectful son, a condemnation of fate: the lovers can only weep, and the readers with them.[60]

Given the examples in this chapter, I cannot share Richard Fusco's judgement of the relationship between reader and author in Maupassant's short stories. He does not deny the distance that occurs between the two groups.[61] However, for him, as for many critics, distance in the short story is equally distributed to everyone. The main effect of this would be to distance the readers themselves from their own prejudices. For Fusco,

---

58 Ibid, p. 1122 (p. 1087).

59 Ibid, p. 1123 (p. 1088).

60 A somewhat similar case is that of Simone de Beauvoir's *La Femme rompue*, in which the distancing of the heroine is very strong, but the irony is never made explicit. To Beauvoir's dismay, the readers of the popular women's magazine *Elle* felt sympathy for the girl, not paying attention to the strong condemnation of her petty bourgeois conception of love — a constant target of Beauvoir here as elsewhere. The condemning is that of a woman who "has allowed herself to be removed from the world of productive work, of earning power and independent self-definition". Ray Davison, "Simone de Beauvoir: 'La Femme rompue'", in *Short French Fiction: Essays on the Short Story in France in the Twentieth Century*, ed. by J. E. Flower (Exeter: University of Exeter Press, 1998), pp. 71-88 (pp. 79 and 77).

61 See the already quoted: "To the cosmopolitan Parisian [ie Maupassant], the Norman peasant and world probably appeared as a distant and alien being and place". Fusco (1994), p. 16.

the essential point would be in the "battle" the author is leading against the reader, in the "attack" he would launch and then "escalate", inducing the reader to "self-doubt in his intellectual confidence".[62] In the "surprise-inversion" stories, for example, by revealing at the end that the reader has misconstrued the tale, he would reveal to the reader his or her own prejudices.

However, compared to the attacks on the foreign and strange characters that occur in these stories, this attack seems to me to be quite mild; the stereotype is confirmed rather than truly undermined.[63] Indeed, in 1945, the Writers' War Board issued a pamphlet entitled "How Writers Perpetuate Stereotypes" that ranked the short story — even below radio, comics and advertising — as the medium that is "the most heinous of race offenders".[64] To my mind, the crucial point is to consider these stories in the place where they appeared: the society newspapers. If we look at all the other articles, reports and advertisements that appeared alongside the short stories, it is clear that these papers were not prone to question the existing values of the readers, but rather to affirm them. That is not to say that a "transformation" of sorts does not take place: to take again the example of the "surprise-inversion" stories, the readers of Maupassant in *Gil Blas* or *Le Gaulois* relished the pleasure of discovering a new, unexpected way of rearranging the narrative elements so that their meaning would change dramatically. Fusco insightfully compares this to the pleasure of the Sherlock Homes stories.[65] The baffled reader and Watson himself are certainly in awe of Holmes's genius. However, this does not mean they fustigate themselves for *not* seeing what the great mind, against all odds, has been able to see.

---

62 Ibid, pp. 22-23, 29, 30, 33 and 34.
63 With the important exception of fantastic stories and stories of madness, which we have seen — and will see again — to be historically, at the end of nineteenth century, the place of the disintegration of the self-assured, positivist "self".
64 Mullen (1997), p. 25.
65 Fusco (1994), p. 34.

9. Dialogue and Character Discreditation

It is clearly not part of Conrad's purpose to confer language on the 'rudimentary souls' of Africa. In place of speech they made 'a violent babble of uncouth sounds.' They 'exchanged short grunting phrases' even among themselves. At first sight these instances [of quoting the characters] might be mistaken for unexpected acts of generosity from Conrad. In reality they constitute some of his best assaults.[1]

So far we have looked at some of the most common techniques that create a sense of distance between reader and character in the short story. There are, however, two devices that are rather more subtle and deserve a longer look. In this chapter we shall analyse the first of these: what happens when the story makes room for the character's "actual" words. Then, in the next chapter, we will pause to look at the interaction among the various participants in the narrative process: author, narrator, reader and character. The short story is at its most exquisitely subtle and complex in both of these cases. The result, however, is once again the distancing and "discrediting" of a character, even though these techniques are usually thought to have the automatic effect of creating a sense of intimacy with the reader.

The analysis of speech is of crucial importance to us, because any discussion of it is intimately bound up with the problem of polyphony. By making room for his characters' words, by retiring from the scene in order to let them speak, the author, in fact, reveals his concept of them;

---

1   Chinua Achebe, *Hopes and Impediments: Selected Essays* (New York: Doubleday 1989), pp. 8-9.

DOI: 10.11647/OBP.0039.9

the degree of validity of the speech permitted them will be a touchstone for their status in the story. But before analysing the short stories in our corpus to see how these techniques are used, we shall first take a look at the criticism surrounding them, especially since one of our authors, Giovanni Verga, has been at the centre of a rich and complex discussion in Italy.

More often than not critics agree, *a priori* and without discussion, that the use of direct speech provides proximity to the character.[2] This systematic belief, however, is often undermined by the theorists themselves when they take time to analyse the contexts in which direct speech occurs: we shall see that they then often come to reverse their previous assertions. When critics as far apart as Luigi Russo and Valentin Voloshinov approach the issue of direct speech, they do so in a remarkably similar fashion: their first assertions are to say that quoting someone's own terms, reproducing not only the "what?" of a discourse but also the "how?" is a guarantee of "immediacy" (in the case of Russo), or of "tolerance [...] a positive and intuitive understanding of all the individual linguistic nuances of thought" (in the case of Voloshinov).[3] To use Chinua Achebe's words in this chapter's epigraph, this corresponds, in their mind, to an "act of generosity", of letting a foreign character express himself in his own words.

Reported discourse, on the contrary, for Voloshinov is the sign of a rational, reductive understanding: the character's thoughts are filtered through the narrator. This, for both Voloshinov and Russo, means that the author refuses to make room for the character's own idiosyncrasies, that he digests his character's being and allows it no expression of its own. Reported speech is reduction, where direct speech indicates freedom and respect for the character. The two critics thus adhere to what seems to be

---

2   Even Helmut Bonheim, who is known for questioning the reader's immediate feelings, argues that "*Direct speech* suggests the closest possible nexus between character and reader, as the term *direct* suggests. *Indirect* and *reported speech* by contrast blur the impression and distance us from the character". Helmut Bonheim, *The Narrative Modes: Techniques of the Short Story* (Cambridge: D. S. Brewer, 1986), p. 52. We all know, however, that repeating someone's words and intonations is a classic device of satire. According to Bakhtin, this is even the essence of parody, which can "expose to destroy". Mikhail Bakhtin, *The Dialogic Imagination: Four Essays*, trans. by Michael Holquist and Caryl Emerson (Austin, TX: University of Texas Press, 1981), p. 364.

3   Luigi Russo, *Giovanni Verga* (Bari: Laterza, 1941); and V. N. Voloshinov, *Marxism and the Philosophy of Language*, trans. by Ladislav Matejka and I. R. Titunik (Cambridge, MA: Harvard University Press, 1973). *Marxism and the Philosophy of Language* has been attributed to Mikhail Bakhtin, although I am going to follow Emerson and Morson's belief that it is indeed by Voloshinov. See Gary Saul Morson and Caryl Emerson, *Mikhail Bakhtin: Creation of a Prosaics* (Stanford, CA: Stanford University Press, 1990).

the credo of criticism since the nineteenth century, from Verga himself to twentieth-century critics such as Helmut Bonheim and Gérard Genette:[4] the use of direct speech would indicate being "with" the character.

What is interesting in Voloshinov and Russo is that, when they submit this abstract statement to textual proof, both end up renouncing it. Voloshinov, for example, very quickly tempers the abstract proclamation that "tolerance" is inherent in direct speech. He recognises at once that quoting the character's own words is essentially a question of "coloration", of something "picturesque": this is very different from the theory of giving the character his own space through "all the linguistic nuances of his thought". He then states something which is a truism, although generally not recognised: "The authorial context [...] is so constructed that the traits the author used to define a character cast *heavy shadows on his directly reported speech*".[5]

The image of the character that has already been built conditions our perception of his words, giving us in advance his essential tone. Voloshinov describes it as being of the same order as the make-up and costume of a comic actor — we are prepared to laugh before he even opens his mouth. Direct speech provides the character's words but "at the same time the author's own nuances are added: irony, humour, etc".[6] This challenges Voloshinov's initial idea about the direct relationship between mimesis of conversation and "immediacy". By the end of his work, Voloshinov swings to a diametrically opposite position from where he began. Talking of Pushkin, he shows that it is only in reported discourse that it is possible to achieve immediacy:

> Such a substitution [of the author 'speaking for' the character] presupposes a *parallelism of intonation*, the intonations of the author's speech and the substituted speech of the hero (what he might or should have said), both running in the same direction.[7]

---

4   Verga expresses the theory of "impersonality" in *Gramigna's Mistress*; the author must efface himself, and leave the reader face to face with the "bare fact", with the characters who express themselves in their own terms. Giovanni Verga, *The She-Wolf and Other Stories*, trans. by Giovanni Cecchetti (Berkeley: University of California Press, 1973), pp. 86-88. See also Bonheim (1986) and Gérard Genette, *Figures III* (Paris: Le Seuil, 1972), pp. 189-93.

5   Voloshinov (1973), p. 134 (emphasis mine).

6   Ibid, p. 133.

7   Ibid, p. 138 (emphasis Voloshinov's).

In other words, it is the reported discourse that is "with" the character; critical distance or judgement is best obtained by using the character's actual words. Voloshinov is even clearer on this when he writes about Jean de La Bruyère: "He invested quasi-direct discourse with his animosity toward [the characters] [...] He recoils from the creatures he depicts".[8] And later: "All of La Bruyère's figures come out ironically refracted through the medium of his *mock objectivism*".[9] We are far from the initial validation of "tolerance", and much nearer to Achebe's vision of the character's language as an "assault" on him. Interestingly, Russo, who also changes his opinion on direct speech, sees this as a matter of genre. As we shall see, this is the case of a rift not so much between two *techniques* (direct speech and reported speech), but between two *ways of using* speech: in the best novels, direct speech creates immediacy, while in short stories, it results in distancing the character.

Direct and indirect speech: Verga's novel versus short stories

To get a clearer view, we can turn to Verga, whose work has always been at the heart of Italian discussions of direct speech. For Italians critics, Verga's stature is almost the equal of Alessandro Manzoni's because he represented the absolute success of the use of free indirect speech and dialect.[10] He portrayed the life of peasants in the then newly-created Kingdom of Italy with a unique warmth using what some critics have called "regression".[11] In many of his works, particularly in his great novel, *I Malavoglia* (*The House by the Medlar Tree*), the point of view of the author "regresses" to one of his characters: even the narration is both from the point of view and in the style of the peasants introduced in the scene.[12]

---

8   Ibid, p. 151.
9   Ibid (emphasis mine).
10 By "dialect" I mean all speech that reproduces distortions of the language that denote the social or geographic origin of the character. Verga's work on dialect represents an original contribution, in tune with the work of the folklorists of his time, always stressed by critics. See for example Giuseppe Lo Castro, *Giovanni Verga: una lettura critica*, Saggi brevi di letteratura antica e moderna, 5 (Soveria Mannelli: Rubbettino, 2001), p. 5, pp. 45-56 and 49-70.
11 See Guido Baldi, *L'Artificio della regressione. Tecnica narrativa e ideologia nel Verga verista* (Naples: Liguori, 1980).
12 Giovanni Verga, *The House by the Medlar Tree* (Berkeley, CA: University of California Press, 1983). The novel describes the efforts of the Malavoglias, an essentially honest and

Russo was fundamental in establishing this idea of Verga's greatness.[13] At first Russo claimed that the author, through his constant use of regression and direct speech, always achieves an immediacy with his characters: he enters into their existence and creates an empathy with their world view, both in his short stories and *The House by the Medlar Tree*.[14] However, when Russo begins to examine the style of the texts, only the novel retains its claim to such an affirmation. All the short stories, after close analysis, reveal, to the contrary, a radical distancing, and Verga is even described by Russo as an "*artista di ferocia*".[15] Russo's intention was to trace an historical evolution in Verga: *The House by the Medlar Tree* together with the collection of short stories, *Vita dei campi* (*Life in the Fields*), represented the height of his work, after which he was seen as reverting to a more distant and decadent style. In fact, although he does not observe this explicitly, Russo was essentially distinguishing between the form of the novel and the short story.[16] It will not then come as a surprise to us, after what we have seen in the last

---

poor family, to raise themselves above their social station as very unimportant sailors in the Sicilian town of Aci Trezza. Verga reproduced the point of view of peasants in not only his style but also his focus. The classic example is that, in the novel, the Battle of Licodia has no more importance than the appearance of rats in the garden of one of the "busybodies".

13 There are three different versions of Russo's *Giovanni Verga*: 1919, 1934, 1941; all references here are to Luigi Russo, *Giovanni Verga* (Bari: Laterza, 1976), unless otherwise stated.

14 Leo Spitzer also gives proof of this in "L'Originalità della Narrazione nei *Malavoglia*", *Belfagor*, 11 (1956), 37-53.

15 Russo (1976), p. 206. In his 1919 edition, it is only in the collection *Vita dei campi* (*Life in the Fields*) that Russo identifies as having this "miracle" of entering in the characters' logic. In the course of this analysis he eliminated the Milanese stories (*Per le vie*) and those belonging to *Little Novels of Sicily*, which reveal an author "more distant from his characters" (p. 180, translation ours). In 1941, Russo added eighty pages of truly stylistic analyses on the problem of this "regression". These analyses, which are much more precise than in the earlier edition, agree on everything except one point: the few stories he had cited as the very example of immediacy no longer withstand such an examination — they are seen now as revealing an irreducible distance from the characters. We find the same dynamics at work in criticism on Luigi Pirandello. Renato Barilli argues that Pirandello's perspective is one of compassion. But, when analysing them, he finally establishes a hierarchy among his various short stories, from satires that cultivate distance to the few texts that, in the course of his analyses, are still considered to have a true attitude of compassion and of immediacy. Several of these texts are not "classic" short stories to my mind, but already what I would classify as "modern" stories. See Renato Barilli, *La Barriera del Naturalismo* (Milan: Mursia, 1964).

16 In his speech in praise of Verga on 2 September 1920, Pirandello also finally recognised that only in *The House by the Medlar Tree* does Verga achieve the goal of immediacy which he had set for himself in *Gramigna's Mistress*. Luigi Pirandello, *Opere di Luigi Pirandello* (Milan: Mondadori, 1956-60), available at http://lafrusta.homestead.com/riv_pirandello.html (accessed 22/10/13).

chapter, that Russo finally emphasised the very intimate interrelationship that Verga's short stories establish between animals and men (particularly in *Jeli il Pastore* [*The Shepherd*]). These "primitive" men, once again, are shown as closer to animals than to the rest of society.[17] While his novel offers nuanced characterisation, Verga's "intimate" portrait of peasants in his short stories largely rests on stereotypes.

After Russo, a series of important Marxist critics further helped to create the colossal stature of "*il caso* Verga" in Italy. Unlike most critics, they saw Verga as a wonderful example of critical-cognitive realism, and they were the ones to bring to light the distancing of his characters in his short stories.[18] Their starting point was diametrically opposed to Russo: they saw this distancing in *all* of Verga's texts, both novels and short stories. But Donato Margarito is forced to recognise that in *The House by the Medlar Tree* the distance does not exist: the heroes are shown to be making disastrous choices, while at the same time holding sympathetic values.[19] Their point of view can be challenged, and the novel does indeed show the failure of their endeavours — and that this failure is a result of contradictions in their value system — but it is a discussion that allows them to have a full "voice" of their own. Their values cannot be refuted in totality, as is the case with

---

17 This, moreover, did not bother Russo who acknowledged the primitivism in Verga, which he saw as a good antidote to the modern world. However, this is only true in the short stories. Russo plays with the two scenarios: on the one hand, he praises the absence of distance in Verga, providing examples, in fact, only from *The House by the Medlar Tree*. On the other hand, taking his examples from the short stories, he salutes the return to the primitive. A cursory reading of his book could ignore that this "primitivism" is, in fact, accompanied by a distance.

18 See Romano Luperini, *Verga e le strutture narrative del realismo: saggio su "Rosso Malpelo"* (Padova: Liviana, 1976); and Donato Margarito, "Verga nella critica marxista: dal 'caso' critico al metodo critico-negativo", in *Verga: l'ideologia, le strutture narrative, il "caso" critico*, ed. by Carlo Augieri and R. Luperini (Lecce: Millela, 1982), pp. 235-89. Baldi (1980) gives a superb example in *Rosso Malpelo*, where he shows the clash between "reality" and how it is actually represented. Rosso is a poor miner, crushed by his work and hated because he is red-haired and "therefore bad". The author denounces the social and economic order of this inhuman society by having the narrator and characters justify it, and then distancing us from their views.

19 "The value system of the Malavoglia, from wisdom to love, is worthy to be considered at a certain narrative level, and acquires a tangible materiality, something noted by both peasant and intellectual commentators, sometimes very sympathetically"; Margarito (1982), p. 273, translation ours. See also Vittorio Lugli, "Lo stile indiretto libero in Flaubert e in Verga" in *Dante e Balzac con altri italiani e francesi* (Naples: Edizioni Scientifiche Italiane, 1952), p. 221-238. For a more complete presentation of this discussion, see Florence Goyet, *La Nouvelle au tournant du siècle en France, Italie, Japon, Russie, pays anglo-saxons. Maupassant, Verga, Mori Ōgai, Akutagawa Ryūnosuke, Tchekhov et James* (doctoral thesis, Université Paris 4-Sorbonne, 1990), pp. 438-45.

the characters of his short stories — for example, the miners and mine-owners in *Rosso Malpelo*, who proclaim that the world of the mine is good. The polyphony of the novel is untenable in the short story.[20]

In passing, we can recognise here one of the criteria necessary for immediacy through direct speech. As Russo and Leo Spitzer have well demonstrated, for immediacy to be possible there has to be a total absence of external intervention. And "total" must be taken literally: this is far from the impersonality of, say, Gustave Flaubert, whose most "objective" passages are shaped by the author's value judgements. In fact, from the moment we allow the possibility of interpreting the character's words other than by the meaning and status he himself gives them, then we fall into irony.[21] However Russo, like Baldi, shows that this is a necessary but not sufficient condition. *Rosso Malpelo* employs the same technique as *The House by the Medlar Tree*; for all that, no one doubts that the worldview presented in it must be rejected. Direct speech is neither an automatic guarantee of immediacy, nor an infallible means of assuring distance, as Margarito would have it. The rhetorical technique in itself is neutral, and its use within a given strategy is what gives it meaning.

Dialect and distancing

The short story uses direct speech in order to energise the poles that it almost always establishes. Maupassant's *Le Réveillon* (*An Odd Feast*) illustrates Voloshinov's point that the objective characterisation of the protagonist prepares our reception of direct speech. The least one can say is that direct speech in this story is not produced in a void: the protagonists are strongly characterised before we hear their voices.[22] The whole narrative centres on

---

20 It is striking to see, in all the discussion of *The House by the Medlar Tree*, to what extent the greatest critics are in opposition over actual linguistic analysis. This begins with Spitzer (1956), who critiques the grammatical analysis of Giacomo Devoto in *Itinerario stilistico* (Florence: Le Monnier, 1975). Then Baldi (1980) refutes Spitzer, and Luperini (1976) is of yet another opinion. It seems to me that the error is in wanting at all cost to *oppose* diametrically what reverts to such and such a character or group of characters. In this novel, the different voices and values match, merge, and encroach on each other. This marks the difference between it and the short stories in which, to the contrary, things are very clear.

21 Because they are skewed by "clashes of style" as described by Wayne C. Booth, *A Rhetoric of Irony* (Chicago: University of Chicago Press, 1974), pp. 67-72.

22 Guy de Maupassant, *The Complete Short Stories of Guy de Maupassant*, trans. by Artine Artinian (Garden City, NY: Hanover House, 1955), pp. 1265-68 (hereafter Artinian). The French text can be found in Guy de Maupassant, *Contes et nouvelles*, ed. by Louis

the fact that the peasants depicted in the story come from the opposite end of society from the narrator — a country squire from Normandy — and his cousin with whom he goes hunting.

An Odd Feast is set on a "horribly" freezing Christmas eve, when the hunters come upon a mass and then go visiting the family of a recently deceased shepherd. The peasants "shiver devotedly" as they perform their "naive and silly" rituals. The sight of the people at midnight mass strikes the hunters as unbearably pointless. In the end they prefer to leave the shelter of the church and walk around in the cold night until they decide to visit the grandson of the dead man. While the shepherd's family will be seen huddling around a "midnight feast" of blood sausage, the hunters reminisce at length on the delights of past Christmas dinners in a friendly expansive mood which suddenly makes them feel very close to each other; they are delighted with the cold weather — even though it transforms the peasants' house into a "Siberian hut" — because it ensures that there will be ducks on the pond the next day.

The peasants' words are presented *within this framework*; their speech is only one of the characteristic traits that emerge for the reader out of the entire picture. It both energises and seals the opposition between the "sophisticated" hunters and the "simple" peasants, and establishes the essential fact that the peasants belong to a universe with what are perceived to be strange and inferior values. The first exchange indicates a difference in the class of education between the peasants and the hunters as the peasants sit around a table made of a grain bin: "'Well, Anthime, so your grandfather is dead?' 'Oh Ay sir, he be passed on'". In response to the narrator's request to see the body, Anthime answers: "What good would it do ee?". Then, when the gentlemen insist, the wife explains: "I told ee I put im in the bin till morning coz there b'aint no other place".[23] Reproducing this stilted dialect is a sure way for Maupassant to reinforce the surprise effect of the revelation that the corpse of the old man is in the very grain bin on which they have been eating. But it is more than that. It is a way of associating intimately the behaviour of these characters with their specificity as peasants. The unaffected way in which the woman makes the statement — interrupting her husband, and not seeing any harm in her action — is as important as the dialect itself. Admittedly, the peasants are bothered that they have been forced to admit what they have done, but in fact they see their action as quite natural:

Forestier, 2 vols (Paris: Gallimard, collection La Pléiade, 1974), II, pp. 336-41 (hereafter Pléiade).

23 Artinian, p. 1267 (Pléiade, I, p. 341).

...it be like this, sir. There be only one bed and we be only three, we slept together... Since he be poorly, we be sleeping on ground. The floor be awful hard and cold now so when ee passed on, we told us 'since he be dead, he don't feel nothing, so ain't no use leavin' him in bed. Ee be comfortable in bin and we be gwain sleep in bed tonight, coz it be awful cold'. I b'ain't gwain sleep with a dead man now, be I?[24]

The narrator's first reaction is to laugh, a laugh very common in such stories, which again plays on the difference between the "civilized" city dwellers and the uneducated peasants. His reaction echoes, perhaps, that of contemporary readers, and the well-to-do readers of *Gil Blas*, the journal in which the story was first published. We are not shocked: there is an assumption that we will accept quite readily the peasants' reasons, but we laugh at them because they are so far removed from our world and our behaviours.

It is hard to maintain, as critics generally do in such cases, that Maupassant is criticising the values of his own circle (and that of his readers); that the implication of these stories is subversive. In *An Odd Feast*, as usual, the peasants are marked by the seal of animalistic brutishness.[25] We certainly find the wealthy cousin's fury to be ridiculous, and see him as a prisoner of his own values, incapable of recognising that there is no other solution for the peasants. However, this judgement is accompanied by a burst of laughter, because it has been made clear from the beginning of the text, through Maupassant's vivid descriptions, that the two worlds have nothing in common.[26] As a result, these characters are confined to their

---

24 Ibid. The text was translated at the beginning of the century in plain English, losing the effect of dialect in the French original: "You see, my good gentlemen, it's just this way. We have but one bed, and being only three we slept together; but since he's been so sick we slept on the floor. The floor is awful hard and cold these days, my good gentlemen, so when he died this afternoon we said to ourselves: 'As long as he is dead he doesn't feel anything and what's the use of leaving him in bed? He'll be just as comfortable in the bin'. We can't sleep with a dead man, my good gentlemen! — now can we?". Guy de Maupassant, *The Complete Short Stories of Guy de Maupassant: Ten Volumes in One*, trans. by Howard Dunne (New York: P. F. Collier, 1903), p. 972. This 1903 edition by Dunne is generally thought of as very questionable; see Richard Fusco, *Maupassant and the American Short Story: The Influence of Form at the Turn of the Century* (University Park, PA: Pennsylvania State University Press, 1994), p. 119.

25 "...a gloomy and brutish expression on their faces [...] [they would] munch in silence"; "Between the two was a single plate of the pudding"; "a suffocating odor of roasted blood pudding pervaded every corner of the room". Artinian, p. 1267.

26 Consider the various and always pejorative mentions of blood sausage, a common peasant food, for example, when they lift the lid to reveal the corpse ("And, removing the dish of blood sausage, she lifted the table top"). The blood sausage is a symbol of their existence as peasants to the socialites: their feast stinks.

existence as peasants by their dialect. We are not facing the spectacle of people akin to us, whom misery has driven to strange behaviour. They are peasants, heavily defined as such, surrounded by circumstances that have made them radically different from "us". Their misery, their piety, their smoke-filled room, tarnished with dirt and their feast of blood sausage, make them and their world finally different *in essence* from the readers of *Gil Blas*.

Built on the same principles, Chekhov's short story *Muzhiki* (*Peasants*) roused very violent opposition.[27] In a Russia where the slogan *"Khozhdenie k narodu"* ("Going to the people"), launched in the 1860s by the Russian Populists (the *Narodniki*), was still quite popular, Chekhov was thought to be defending urbanites against peasants.[28] This was not, however, at all what he intended, and it is interesting to consider how an author of Chekhov's ability could have been so misunderstood.[29] The misunderstanding seems to have resulted from the very characteristics of the short story format. The still important presence of the Narodniks' idea of "back to the land" acted as a backdrop that, for once, enabled readers to be sensitive to the coldness with which the short story treats its subjects.

Peasants tells the story of Nikolay, a *mujik* who at a young age went to Moscow where he became a valet in one of the most elegant hotels in the city. Old, sick, and penniless, he returns to his village where he hopes to find peace and comfort. With this as his starting-point, Chekhov draws a pitiless picture of the life of the peasants. The use of dialect is central: as in Maupassant, it summarises and condenses a vision of the world and firmly anchors the characters' behaviours in their social class. The beginning of the short story is full of paroxystic descriptions of misery and dirt. The old *mujik*, softened by his years in the luxurious hotel, is shocked by the poverty of his old house: there are flies, a broken stove, and walls decorated with

---

27 Anton Chekhov, *The Portable Chekhov*, ed. by Avrahm Yarmolinsky (Harmondsworth: Penguin, 1977), pp. 312-53 (hereafter Yarmolinsky). The Russian text can be found in Anton Pavlovich Chekhov, *Polnoe sobranie sochinenii i pisem*, 30 vols (Moscow: Nauka, 1974-1983), IX, pp. 281-312 (hereafter Nauka).

28 In the 1860s, for an important group of intellectuals, the "people" represented the true Holy Russia. Chekhov and his generation (those of the 1880s) had a conscious reaction against this mythical vision of the profound Russia.

29 In order to show that the city was not a panacea for him, Chekhov published, in the same collection as *Peasants*, *Tri goda* (*Three Years*), a portrayal of urban misery. He also planned a sequel to the story, in which the heroines when they arrive in Moscow, would experience the misery in the capital; but this sequel remained only an outline and was never published (see outline in Nauka, IX, p. 344; there is no English translation that I know of).

bottle labels rather than pictures. At the end of the first page, Nikolay's daughter calls to the cat. A little peasant girl of eight — perched on the stove and totally indifferent to their arrival — alerts her in terms that are roughly equivalent to:

'It can't hear,' said the little girl; 'it's gone deaf.'
'Why?'
'Oh, it was hit.'
Nikolay and Olga realized at first glance what life was like here.[30]

The conclusion is obvious: it is a different world, an atrocious and hopeless place of misery, in which nothing can disturb a young girl's apathy, neither her cousin's arrival, nor a maimed cat. Similarly, when the urbanites ask their sister-in-law whether she is suffering from her soldier husband's absence, she answers by a single exclamation of annoyance: "Deuce take him!".[31] The language locks the character; it *is* the character. For once, the Russian readers were sensitive to this — like Dubliners in the height of Gaelic Renaissance euphoria may have been — because the idea of superiority of peasant life and values was still vivid in Russia.

Foreign terms

The use of foreign terms in short stories, although different from dialect, plays a similar role. By evoking regional or social distortions, or by including a word in Italian in a short story set in Italy, the scene being portrayed is given a voice. Henry James often uses this device, especially in his early short stories about Europe. One passage in particular from *Théodolinde* allows us to see the implications of foreign quotations.[32] The

---

30 Yarmolinsky, p. 311. It is very difficult to translate into English the particular peasant tone, because it does not consist, as in Maupassant, of incorrect phrases and phonetic distortions. It is completely characteristic, but comes about essentially through the use of parataxis and a singsong rhythm, a sort of chant which goes naturally with proverbs: "*Ona u nas ne slishit, —skazala devochka. — Oglokhla. / Otchego? Tak. Pobili*" (Nauka, IX, p. 281).

31 Yarmolinsky, p. 317. The Russian is "*A nu ego!*". The surprise which her answer provokes (she does not miss her husband, she is quite happy that he is away) is intimately associated with the actual expression, and solidifies the idea that "these people neither speak nor think like we do".

32 Edel, IV, pp. 141-207. *Théodolinde* had several US and UK variants, and was also published under the title *Rose-Agathe*. These textual variants can be found in Henry James, *The Tales of Henry James: Volume 3, 1875-1879*, ed. by Maqbool Aziz (Oxford: Clarendon Press, 1984), pp. 396-97.

story is about an American who has been living for some time in Paris. He is sitting at his window waiting for a fellow expat to arrive:

> A Parisian thoroughfare is always an entertaining spectacle, and I had still much of a stranger's alertness of attention […] There was poetry in the warm, succulent exhalations of the opposite restaurant, where, among the lighted lamps, I could see [...] the waiters in their snowy aprons standing in the various attitudes of immanent *empressement*, the agreeable *dame de comptoir* sitting idle [...] there was of course something very agreeable in the faint upward gusts of the establishment in my *rez-de-chaussée* [...] like a Madonna who should have been *coiffée* in the Rue de la Paix.[33]

Doubtless austere Boston readers were not familiar with the institution of the Parisian *dame de comptoir*, enthroned at her cash register in the majesty of officiating over the supreme pleasures of absinthe and roast chicken. However, women went to hairdressers in America in James's day, and first floors existed in Boston — James even used two different words to indicate them, according to his public, for an American reader *first floor* and for the English reader *ground floor*.[34]

The point, of course, is that the French words make it Parisian. They gave the American or English reader the titillation of memory or imagination that made the scene more than an abstract evocation. "*Empressement*" is purely for the pleasure of recalling Paris, and disorientating his reader.[35] It is important once again to note that all of this presupposes not only a linguistic competence in the reader, but also a prior acquaintance with the foreign culture. Someone who does not know the meaning of *dame de comptoir* will not learn it here. The interest is elsewhere: not in making a foreign country familiar, but in recalling it in its concrete form. These terms create "foreign pockets" within the text, exotic morsels. They add greatly to local colour but nothing to knowledge.

The foreign quotes in Mori Ōgai's *Hanako* jump out at us, since they appear at a ninety-degree angle in the Japanese text (see fig. 1).[36]

---

33 Edel, IV, pp. 119-20.
34 For more on James's changes in vocabulary to suit an English audience, see Michael Anesko, *Friction with the Market: Henry James and the Profession of Authorship* (New York: Oxford University Press, 1986), pp. 59-60. These amendments were a necessary condition for publication in London.
35 In 1885, James replaced the word "*empressement*" with "eagerness". However, he did not abandon his practice of using French words: he also replaced the English "modest" with "*pudique*". Similarly, he kept "*coiffée*" while changing the ending "by M. Anatole". In all, more than a dozen French words remained.
36 Mori Ōgai, *Mori Ōgai zenshū*, 38 vols (Tōkyō: Iwanami Shoten, 1971-1975), VII, pp. 189-97.

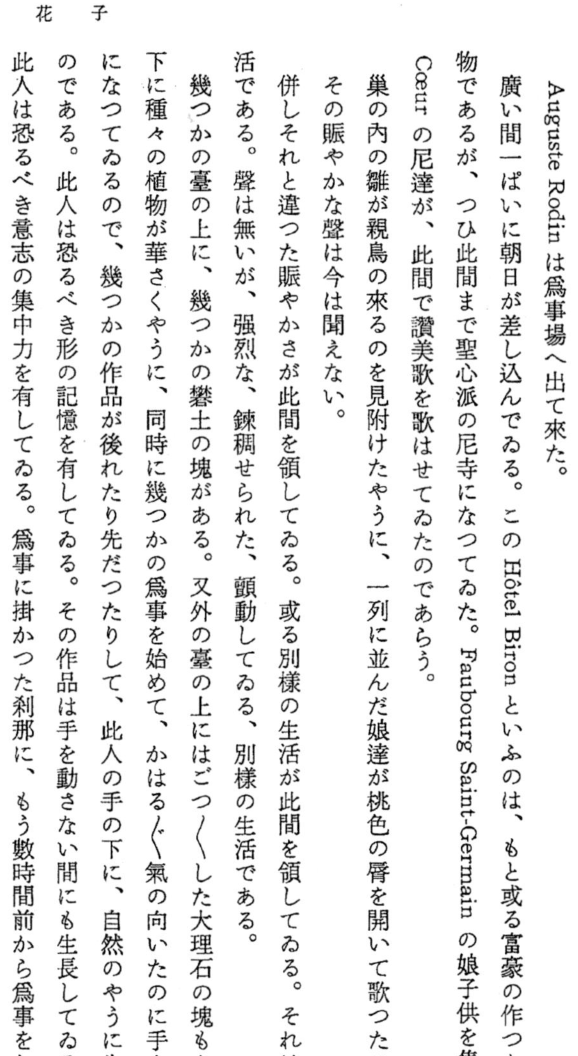

花子

Auguste Rodin は爲事場へ出て來た。

廣い間一ぱいに朝日が差し込んでゐる。この Hôtel Biron といふのは、もと或る富豪の作つた、贅澤な建

物であるが、つひ此間まで聖心派の尼寺になつてゐた。Faubourg Saint-Germain の娘子供を集めて Sacré-

Cœur の尼達が、此間で讃美歌を歌はせてゐたのであらう。

巣の内の雛が親鳥の來るのを見附けたやうに、一列に並んだ娘達が桃色の脣を開いて歌つたことであらう。

その賑やかな聲は今は聞えない。

併しそれと違つた賑やかさが此間を領してゐる。或る別樣の生活が此間を領してゐる。それは聲の無い生

活である。聲は無いが、強烈な、錬綢せられた、顫動してゐる、別樣の生活である。

幾つかの臺の上に、幾つかの礬土の塊がある。又外の臺の上にはごつ〳〵した大理石の塊もある。日光の

下に種々の植物が華さくやうに、同時に幾つかの爲事を始めて、かはる〴〵氣の向いたのに手を着ける習慣

になつてゐるので、幾つかの作品が後れたり先だつたりして、此人の手の下に、自然のやうに生長して行く

のである。此人は恐るべき形の記憶を有してゐる。その作品は手を動さない間にも生長してゐるのである。

此人は恐るべき意志の集中力を有してゐる。爲事に掛かつた刹那に、もう數時間前から爲事をし續けてゐる

Fig. 1. Mori Ōgai, *Hanako*, in *Ōgai zenshū*, vol. 7 (Tōkyō: Iwanami Shoten, 1973), p. 189. Reproduced by kind permission of Iwanami Shoten Publishers, Tōkyō (all rights reserved).

Printing foreign words in Roman script in Japan is the result of a conscious choice, as there are two other ways of transcribing them.[37] When Ōgai begins his text with "Auguste Rodin" in Roman script, he is indicating more than anything else, more even than the meaning of the word, its foreign quality. It is a sample of foreign reality, brought back for display. He includes, of course, place names such as "Faubourg Saint-Germain", any translation of which would be incomprehensible, but he also includes words which one would expect to find in Japanese characters: Prince of "Kambodscha" (of Cambodge), and even "Mademoiselle Hanako". He even goes so far as to repeat the same sentence twice, first in French (in small caps) and then in translation: "Hence the child goes from *physique* to *metaphysique*, from Physics to Metaphysics". Placing these foreign words in their exotic form calls up a whole universe, where one is familiar with "Beaudelaire" (sic), and with the *Physics* and *Metaphysics* of Aristotle. In other words, Ōgai is evoking the fascinating, and so distant world of Rodin's Paris; indeed, there was a great fascination for Rodin at that time in Japan.[38]

******

Short-story authors are great stylists. Each word maintains hidden relationships with the others, achieving the effectiveness of the whole. But this effectiveness tends to be formidable. The classic short story is a trap that imprisons its characters, surrounding them by converging techniques of distancing. Giving characters their own voice within this framework, far from helping the author to efface himself and leave them room to defend their truth, is instead another means of making them *typical*. Their definition becomes all the clearer and more brilliant to the reader in that all the traits converge, but the vivid image they form is terribly confined.

This is a feature that underwent dramatic change in the twentieth century, when the minorities that had been the object of short stories began to author them. When female Chicano writers include quotes in their native Spanish, the effect on the reader is radically different from the use of foreign terms that we have seen above:[39] Postcolonial critics have stressed how minorities

---

37 English words could either be totally assimilated, their content translated by means of sino-Japanese ideograms, or the sounds could be transcribed (without translation) by means of syllabaries. Roman type was very rare and incomprehensible except to intellectuals.

38 Ōgai published his story just before the journal *Shirakaba* released a special issue dedicated entirely to the sculptor.

39 See Consuelo Montes-Granado, "Code-Switching as a Strategy of Brevity in Sandra

have been able to write their own authentic "voice".[40] When minorities become not only the subjects but also the authors of the narrative, we find the short story playing the role described by Mary Louise Pratt: that of allowing for the introduction of new subjects, new social groups.[41] But the classic short stories we have been examining were written for the most part by relatively privileged white men, operating within a strict framework of distancing; their use of direct speech does nothing more than make the distance between the reader and minority characters even greater.

Cisneros' *Woman Hollering Creek and Other Stories*", in *Short Story Theories: A Twenty-First-Century Perspective*, ed. by Viorica Patea (Amsterdam: Rodopi, 2012), pp. 125-36. We are, of course, reminded that this effect is not automatic by authors like Homi K. Bhabha, *The Location of Culture* (London: Routledge, 2004); and Albert Wendt in his Introduction to *Nuanua: Pacific Writing in English Since 1980*, ed. by Albert Wendt (Honolulu: University of Hawaii Press, 1995), pp. ii-iii.

40 See, for example, *Ethnicity and the American Short Story*, ed. by Julie Brown (London: Garland, 1997). See especially Brown's Editor's Note (pp. xvii-xx), Bill Mullen's "Marking Race/Marketing Race: African American Short Fiction and the Politics of Genre, 1933-1946" (pp. 25-46) and Madelyn Jablon's "Womanist Storytelling: The Voice of the Vernacular" (pp. 47-62). Mullen shows that the creation of *Negro Story*, a black literary magazine dedicated to the short story, was part of an attempt to alter the "markings and marketings of race in the short story genre" (pp. 34-40). But, as Rebecca Hernández points out, even in these new circumstances, an author like the Mozambican Luis Bernardo Honwana would generally prefer writing in Portuguese "in order to preserve their psychological profile and their full expressive capacity". Rebecca Hernández, "Short Narrations in a Letter Frame: Cases of Genre Hybridity in Postcolonial Literature in Portuguese", in *Short Story Theories: A Twenty-First-Century Perspective*, ed. by Viorica Patea (Amsterdam: Rodopi, 2012), pp. 155-72 (p. 159).

41 Mary Louise Pratt, "The Short Story: The Long and the Short of It", *Poetics*, 10 (1981), 175-94; also in *The New Short Story Theories*, ed. by Charles E. May (Athens, OH: Ohio University Press, 1994), pp. 91-113 (p. 108). On the role of creative writing workshops in this new outlook of the short story, see Andrew Levy, *The Culture and Commerce of the American Short Story* (Cambridge: Cambridge University Press, 1993), pp. 4-7. See also James Nagel, who insists on the story published in "little magazines" (of this workshops network) as being the ideal tool for minorities to appropriate the telling of *their* dramas; the next step being the publishing of cycles of these stories. James Nagel, *The Contemporary American Short-Story Cycle: The Ethnic Resonance of Genre* (Baton Rouge, LA: Louisiana State University Press, 2004), pp. 255-57.

10. The Narrator, the Reflector and the Reader

The classic short story makes use of the all participants in the narrative process — author, narrator and reader — to create the characteristic distance between reader and characters. The reader shares with the author the exhilaration of enjoying the spectacle of this distance. In this chapter, the short story will once again show its versatility: it can distance the narrator from the reader, or equally it can create a real proximity to him, only to increase the distance from the other characters. We will first spend some time on the concept of the "reflector", as described by Henry James, to show its necessity, but also its dangers: structural distinctions are not enough, we have to take into account the whole context, the whole strategy of the text. The reflector does not *tell* the story — that is the role of the narrator. He is one of the characters, but one privileged by the writer: he is the one who *sees*, and through whose eyes *we* see. In great novels, the reflector can be a powerful device to help the reader to enter the fictional world and to get nearer to the characters' mental universe. But in classic short stories — even in James's — it is one more variation on the common theme of distancing.

The works of James are, of course, good examples of the use of a reflector. Hardly any of his stories is an *Ich-Erzahlung*: we usually have a third-person narrator, but this narrator is not omniscient, and James limits himself to

DOI: 10.11647/OBP.0039.10

what this character knows, hears, sees and, most importantly, feels. It is as if the writer were placing a filter between us and the spectacle. When this filter is, to use James's words, "the most polished of possible mirrors of the subject", third person narration does not prevent us from participating in the mental universe of the characters.[1] In his critical writings, James developed at length the idea that through a discriminating, intelligent, and sensitive reflector, we would appreciate to the full all the subtleties and beauties of a novel's universe.[2]

Although James's distinction between narrator and reflector is necessary, it is not without danger, especially when — as in the works of the French New Critics — it is viewed as having automatic effects. Gérard Genette defined a complete "*grille*" by combining the possibilities of "mode" (reflector) and "voice" (narrator).[3] When the narrator is one of the characters, narration is said to be "intradiegetic"; when he is exterior to it, "extradiegetic"; when the reflector is one of the characters we have "internal focalization"; "external" when he is not. This combination of narration and focalization provides neat divisions, with each "compartment" representing one particular technical example. The danger, of course, is to assume as Genette and the narratologists did after him, that each of these "compartments" implies a particular effect. That is, that by using both external focalization and heterodiegetic narration, one would achieve an "external" viewpoint of the narration; and that by reverting to internal focalization and intradiegetic narration, one would automatically get an "internal" perspective on the narrative. When we begin to examine specific stories, however, we see to the contrary that each of these compartments is susceptible to a wide variety of uses.

Once our interest lies in the problems of the relationship between reader, author and characters — and we are primarily concerned with how the one regards the other — such mechanical, formal distinctions

---

1 Henry James, *The Art of the Novel: Critical Prefaces* (New York: Scribner, 1962), p. 70.

2 The Preface to *Princess Cassamassima* (ibid, pp. 59-78) in particular, is nearly all dedicated to reflections on the necessity of such "intense perceivers": "Their emotions, their stirred intelligence, their moral consciousness, become thus, by sufficiently charmed perusal, our own very adventure" (p. 70). James never stops repeating that the choice of a fine conscience is essential. He almost always has recourse to a third person, except for a few texts that are among his most bitter publishing failures. See also Anne T. Margolis, *Henry James and the Problem of Audience: An International Act* (Ann Arbor, MI: University of Michigan Press, 1985).

3 Gérard Genette, *Narrative Discourse: An Essay in Method*, trans. by Jane E. Lewin (Ithaca, NY: Cornell University Press, 1980), pp. 170-75.

become secondary. We do need to be able to distinguish between the reflector and the narrator, precisely because the short story will use either one to continue to bring the reader and author together in admiration of the distant spectacle. Without it, the profound architecture of some of the most subtle and best stories cannot be understood. But we cannot take for granted its particular effect in the texts.

Wayne C. Booth has provided a useful tool for analysis in his distinction between "reliable" and "unreliable" narrators.[4] Booth's theory helps us to see that, when it comes to the classic short story, unreliable narrators/reflectors represent characters; reliable narrators/reflectors *never* represent characters — but rather represent the reader.[5] The reliable narrator is the person whose word we do not doubt *a priori*; we do not subject his statements, arguments or values to a systematic proof. This does not signify that he is omniscient; simply, that he is in a certain way "transparent". We do not exert before him our capacity for detecting irony. On the other hand, we distance ourselves from the unreliable narrator's discourse. At the very least, we take what he says with a grain of salt; and at the extreme, we systematically interpret the opposite of what he says. The factors that make him unreliable are the same as those that distance the other characters. The superiority of this distinction over that between "voice" and "mode" is that we are no longer describing external traits (whether the narrator is one of the characters or not); we are invited to balance the relations between the different actors in the narrative process by taking into account, equally, the entire context.

Another critic will bear witness to the necessity and the danger of these external, formal distinctions. Japanese criticism uses the concept of "first person disguised as third person" (*sanninshō o kasō ichininshō*), which corresponds to one of the essential "compartments" of Genette's *grille*: "heterodiegetic narration/internal focalization". Etō Jun uses this concept to formalise the difference between western and Japanese narration.[6] For him, western narration is characterised by the use of the third person and

---

4 Wayne C. Booth, *A Rhetoric of Irony* (Chicago, IL: University of Chicago Press, 1974), pp. 57-67.

5 Helmut Bonheim perceives that there can be not only unreliable *narrators* but also unreliable *speakers* and *thinkers*. Bonheim mentions this in relation to detective stories, but the phenomenon seems to me also important in "serious" fiction. See Helmut Bonheim, *The Narrative Modes: Techniques of the Short Story* (Cambridge: D. S. Brewer, 1986), p. 71.

6 Etō Jun, "Nichiōbunka no taishōsei to hitaishōsei", *Bungakkai*, 43:1 (1989), 240-52.

of the past tense, whereas Japanese narration is characterised by the use of the "timeless" and of the first person, either "disguised" or not.

Etō's argument ignores the fact that western narratives also make use of all the resources of voice and mode. But interestingly enough, he immediately connects this fact of syntax with other rhetorical techniques. His aim is to show that Japanese is the language of proximity to a character, and he bases his proof on the distortions that an English translation inflicted on a novel by Tanizaki Junichirō. Etō's contextual analysis is subtle enough to enable him to show that this technique is only one element of a complete tableau: having recourse to the timeless and to an internal focalization is accompanied, for example, by the use of a specifically affective vocabulary (*jōigo*), which brings the reader into the character's subjectivity.[7]

Unreliable narrators and reflectors

Unreliable narrators and reflectors in short stories are members of the world being described. They are characters among other characters, distanced from the reader by the same methods we have seen in previous chapters. A classic example is Herman Melville's *Bartleby, The Scrivener* where the interest rests on the growing suspicion about the reliability of the narrator, the Wall Street lawyer, and on our awareness of a double spectacle: the scene as narrated *and* the distortion which we suspect has been imposed on the scene.[8] This doubt about what is said or perceived by a narrator or reflector who is one of the characters is a constant feature of the classic short story.[9]

---

7   However, Etō still considers this process to be mechanical, thinking that recourse to one voice and one mode are automatic guarantees of proximity, whereas obviously the same affective terms can be included in a strategy of irony in Japanese as well as in European languages. Note too, with the same reservations on my part, Aleksandr V. Ognev, who talks about the same "compartment" of Genette's grille in similar terms, and sees in it a general characteristic of the contemporary short story: "*ot avtora, no s tochki zreniya geroya*" ("in the author's voice, but with the point of view of the character"). Aleksandr V. Ognev, *O Poetike sovremennogo russkogo rasskaza* (Saratov: Izd-vo Saratovskogo Universiteta, 1973), p. 214.

8   R. Bruce Bickley clearly shows that Melville shares our point of view and not his narrator's in his short stories (and not only in *Bartleby*). R. Bruce Bickley, Jr., *The Method of Melville's Short Fiction* (Durham, NC: Duke University Press, 1975).

9   John M. Ellis, for example, points out that in all the short stories he has analysed, the text only gains its full value if the reader recognises the unreliable character of the reflector. The meaning of a text such as Heinrich von Kleist's *Erdbeben in Chili* (*Earthquakes in Chile*) is created in a kind of stereoscope in which we see at the same time the scene presented by the reflector and distortion of it. However, undoubtedly because his

As we are very near here to what we have seen at length in the previous chapter, I shall give only one example to make clear the neutrality of devices: Arthur Schnitzler's *Lieutenant Gustl*.[10] This short story, based entirely on an interior monologue, was written in 1900, a decade or so after Edouard Dujardin's pioneering use of the device in *Les Lauriers sont coupés*, and long before James Joyce's *Ulysses*. In this instance we are *inside* the mind of the character: the narrator's voice is the only one we hear. We should, therefore, be as close as possible to the character, to his "voice", to his inner truth. In reality, we are no closer than when dialect is used. Gustl is as effectively discredited "from within" as he might be in an external narrative.

This distancing begins from the outset with the young officer's reflections on music. He is bored at a concert; he mistakes a mass for an oratorio, and admits to failing to recognise any difference between the choir and cabaret singers. Note that the story was published in the *Neue Freie Press*, one of the favourite newspapers of the Viennese upper middle class, for whom music — originally a means of obtaining social status in the eyes of the aristocracy — had become a widespread passion.[11] By presenting the hero, before any other description, as fundamentally incapable of appreciating music, Schnitzler has already effectively "labelled" him as separate from the readers more clearly than any explicit judgement could have done.

But Schnitzler does not stop there. Not only does Gustl have bad taste, not only is he a conceited junior officer who imagines that all women are attracted to him, but he is in total contradiction to his own values. His bragging about duels at the beginning of the story is totally out of keeping with his confusion later that night, and above all his great speeches on honour are ultimately contradicted by his actions. Schnitzler's ridiculing of the lieutenant is quasi-explicit in the precise contradiction in terms. Right

---

limited corpus does not allow for generalisation, he does not extract all the consequences of his analyses. John M. Ellis, *Narration in the German Novelle: Theory and Interpretation* (Cambridge: Cambridge University Press, 1974).

10 Arthur Schnitzler, *Plays and Stories*, ed. by Egon Schwarz (New York: Continuum, 1982), pp. 249-79 (hereafter Schwarz). The original German version can be found in Arthur Schnitzler, *Das erzählerische Werk* (Frankfurt: Fischer Taschenbuch, 1981), pp. 207-36 (hereafter Fischer).

11 For more on music as a passion shared by all classes of society in Vienna, see Carl E. Schorske, *Fin-de-siècle Vienna: Politics and Culture* (New York: Knopf, 1980). For more on the story and its use of interior monologue, see Heidi E. Dietz Faletti, "Interior Monologue and the Unheroic Psyche in Schnitzler's *Lieutenant Gustl* and *Fräulein Else*", in *The Image of the Hero in Literature, Media and Society*, ed. by Will Wright and Steve Kaplan (Pueblo, CO: Society for the Interdisciplinary Study of Social Imagery, 2004), pp. 522-57.

after he is insulted by a baker, Gustl states the need to end his life: "And even if he [the baker] had a stroke tonight, I'd know it [...] I've got to do it — There's nothing to it. —".[12] When he learns that the baker in fact died of a stroke, this completely restores his peace of mind, and he can pretend that his honour has not been damaged.

The ending underlines the contradiction even further: one would have thought that the night's anguish would have transformed the lieutenant, and prompted him to question his somewhat automatic adherence to the code of military behaviour. Yet Gustl experiences no revelation. The story ends with what is going through his mind at the thought of fighting a duel with another man: "Just wait, my boy, I'm in wonderful form... I'll crush you into mincemeat!".[13] The culinary allusion here reminds us of the baker from earlier in the story, creating the sense of an endless cycle. The "stroke of joy" that overwhelms him is the joy of a brutal mercenary. As was often the case, the objects of this ridicule were quite aware of the distancing at work — the army was outraged by the derision implied in the story and went so far as to demote Schnitzler for writing it.[14] In *Lieutenant Gustl*, we remain completely exterior to the character, even though, technically speaking, we have remained within him: the technical point of view has no automatic bearing on the perspective.[15]

Before proceeding to the more complex case of the reliable narrator/ reflector, we must note once again that the fantastic short story uses the techniques of the classic short story in a much more complex fashion. In supernatural tales, unreliable narrators/reflectors are an exception; but this exception allows for powerful effects. For example, by choosing for

---

12 Schwarz, p. 261.

13 Ibid, p. 279. I have modified the translation here ("I'll knock you to smithereens!") to be closer to the original: *"Dich hau' ich zu Krenfleisch"* — where *Krenfleisch* is a beef-meat slice to be eaten with horseradish. See Fischer, p. 236.

14 Details of the negative reception of *Lieutenant Gustl* by the army can be found in Evelyne Polt-Heinzl, *Arthur Schnitzler: Leutnant Gustl* (Stuttgart: Reclam, 2000), pp. 42-61.

15 Very much akin to this, to my mind, is Simone de Beauvoir's use of the diary as a framing device in *La Femme rompue*. Ray Davison emphasises the surprising distance of this intimate format, and quotes the many passages in which the heroine, Monique Lacombe, reveals her petty bourgeois interests and fears. However, Davison is interested in something else: the means that this gives Beauvoir to recognise the pain of Sartre's behaviour towards her: "In other words, and paradoxically, because Beauvoir is so distanced in her conscious mind from Monique Lacombe [...] she does manage to talk about herself [Beauvoir] more interestingly than when she uses the direct autobiographical mode". Ray Davison, "Simone de Beauvoir: 'La Femme rompue'", in *Short French Fiction: Essays on the Short Story in France in the Twentieth Century*, ed. by J. E. Flower (Exeter: University of Exeter Press, 1998), pp. 71-88 (p. 72).

once not to have a reliable reflector, James strengthens the ambiguity in *The Turn of the Screw*. There is still lively controversy about whether the young English teacher in the story actually sees the two ghosts, and it has often been stressed that the text's interest lies in this very ambiguity. The governess's point of view is not immediately doubted, and it is never openly contradicted by the author; but a whole series of indices prevent her from reaching the status of reliable reflector. As a result, suspense is reinforced, and the entry into a fantastic world becomes more troubling than usual: the reader is constantly invited to question the reality of what is being conveyed. Thus James creates a stereoscope: the scene and the way it is perceived.[16]

Reliable narrators and reflectors

Reliable narrators/reflectors are never representatives of the world portrayed; and they are the only "characters" not to be distanced. Yet for all that, they are not necessarily representatives of the reader, either; sometimes the narrator is both reliable and foreign. In Voltaire's *Micromegas,* for example, the narrator Micromegas, a "little giant" from the far-away planet Sirius, comes to Earth on a mission of discovery. His impressions of Earth of course bear the stamp of strangeness, as did those of Jonathan Swift's Gulliver: customs of the Earth creatures — or the Houyhnnhnms — are quite different from those at home in Sirius. By describing eighteenth-century France and England through "foreign" eyes, familiar customs suddenly look very strange, and their faults become more apparent. This device was quite popular in the eighteenth century, but was used much less frequently at the end of the nineteenth. However there are still some examples of its use in classic short stories, including Leo Tolstoy's *Kholstomer.* The author provides a satire of Russian society through the eyes of a horse — a narrator as far removed from our own ideas as Gulliver or Micromegas. From the moment we are presented with such a reflector, all that is obvious collapses: the very idea of owning an animal, for instance, becomes monstrous; and with it the social structure of Alexander II's Russia.

---

16 The same device is found in Maupassant, whose fantastic stories are perhaps the stronger of his works. In the second, *Horla,* the narrator is so clear-minded that he forestalls each of our comments and suspicions. As a reflector, he is not reliable, but he is reliable as a narrator (in that he analyses what he recounts), and the text gains its power from what is almost schizophrenia; through this we enter a different world, where our logic is no longer valid.

This device is not only powerful as a tool for satire. James's most famous short story, *Daisy Miller,* owes much of its strength to his choice of a reflector from "the Sirius point of view". Frederick Winterbourne is a member of a very good American family but he has been brought up in Switzerland. His outlook is stamped with a freshness of perception: he does not know any other young American girls, so he does not compare Daisy to them and come to the hasty conclusion that her free and simple manners are bad. In this way, James can present Daisy as foreign and incomprehensible, but without "cataloguing" her. James's readers followed Winterbourne's opinion because he shared their fundamental values. Morality is essential for him: he is not a Frenchman for whom a young woman's flirtatious behaviour would be an attraction. As a result of Winterbourne's fresh perception, readers understood that Daisy could not be described according to their pre-conceived categories.[17]

This "Sirius point of view" exploits the potentialities of the short story genre to the fullest; it provides enormous vivacity of perception and a radical exteriority in relation to the subject. For once the readers' prejudices are called into question. But this device does not signify immediacy any more than in Voltaire, Swift or Tolstoy: Micromegas is interested in men and their problems, but never gives up his standpoint as an outsider. If the readers followed Winterbourne in his judgement — or rather his absence of judgement — of Daisy, it is precisely because he is not part of her universe. And even at the end of the story, the readers do not share in the values of the young woman — they have simply ceased to see her in the same light as they did at the beginning. The short story is able to renew our perception of an object, but, for all that, it does not take us into its logic. It is not the Houyhnnhnms' values that the reader is invited to share, but those of Gulliver. *Micromegas* and *Gulliver's Travels* show us very clearly the fundamental law: when there is immediacy in a short story, it is always with an intermediary. The reliable narrator/reflector is the mediator between the reader and a bizarre world. He is the Parisian of the Normandy stories who introduces us to the special world of the peasants; he is the Japanese student in Mori Ōgai's *Hanako* who interprets the world of Auguste Rodin.[18]

---

17 On this "American girl", see Virginia C. Fowler, *Henry James's American Girl: The Embroidery on the Canvas* (Madison, WI: University of Wisconsin Press, 1984).

18 He is also, except in the cases mentioned above, the narrator in fantastic stories. In order for us to want to follow the character into this other world and to accept the account of events which will make us lose our most obvious points of reference, the short story will

Side by side with these Sirians who enable us to see the object in a different light and judge our world *a novo*, we find any number of reliable narrators/reflectors who are the representatives of the reader. The typical example here would be Franz Kafka's *Strafkolonie* (*In the Penal Colony*). The narrator-reflector is a European who has come to visit a remote colony where torture is a fundamental means of government. He represents a world where torture could never be legitimated or praised (even if it could be practiced); his presence, therefore, is a very economical way of showing the radical foreignness of the values of the officer commanding the colony. By the insistent mention of the "normal" values and reasoning of the narrator's world, Kafka refuses to justify the brutal laws that govern this world. This does not eliminate a certain fascination, but it is produced through horror, terror, and distance.

Similarly, the central device of Chekhov's *Muzhiki* (*Peasants*), the story we saw in the previous chapter, may well be the author's choice of reflector.[19] Nikolay was born a peasant, but he left his village as an infant and spent all his life in Moscow, where his work in the best hotel in town put him in constant contact with all that is most refined. Returning to his village, he has the reactions of a city-dweller: he looks at the hut from an external perspective, and through his mediation Chekhov constructs a truly terrifying vision of rural poverty. The denunciation of the misery and dirt of the peasants' life by one of their own is much more powerful than if it had come from a country gentleman. What is even more remarkable is that Chekhov abandons Nikolay as reflector part way through the story. At this point, Nikolay joins the other characters and will, like them, be distanced. But the effect has already been accomplished: that first impression of horror in the face of such tremendous misery will never be questioned. Right up until the end of the story, Nikolay's impressions of the village will be considered valid, and will serve to distance the scene, even though, as a character, his behaviour and his values will be challenged.[20]

---

usually resort to a narrator or a reflector in whom we have confidence. But it is always in order to stress the strangeness of the world described.

19 Anton Chekhov, *The Portable Chekhov*, ed. by Avrahm Yarmolinsky (Harmondsworth: Penguin, 1977), pp. 312-53 (hereafter Yarmolinsky). The Russian text can be found in Anton Pavlovich Chekhov, *Polnoe sobranie sochinenii i pisem*, 30 vols (Moscow: Nauka, 1974-1983), IX, pp. 281-312 (hereafter Nauka).

20 Nikolay's wife, too, is used as a reflector at the beginning of the story. Very quickly her style, and her religiosity put her at a distance from the reader; but she will have already fulfilled her role as reflector, which is to jolt us into utter horror.

The definition of the narrator as the "representative of the reader" allows for a variety of criteria. When James writes about Europe, he is an American talking to Americans — or to us for whom Europe at the beginning of the century is just as distant. When Verga describes the misery of the peasants in the *Rivista Italiana di Scienze, Lettere ed Arti*, he is an intellectual speaking to intellectuals who also share his interest in social problems. But that the narrator/reflector is the representative of the reader in no way implies that he belongs to this world by birth: it will be necessary and sufficient for him to share his values, his ways of judging and of expressing himself.

In Maupassant's *Mon oncle Jules* (*My Uncle Jules*), the narrator is walking with his friend, Davranche, when he sees him give twenty francs — a lot of money — to a beggar.[21] Noting his surprise, Davranche explains how, as a young man, he found his "Uncle From America" humbly at work on one of the imitation steamboats that crossed from Jersey to the mainland. Uncle Jules — the great hope of the family, expected to become a millionaire — had in fact failed to make his fortune in America and had not dared to return to Le Havre where his relatives lived. In order to survive, he became an oyster-shucker on one of these cheap steamers. Now a rich man himself, Davranche gives a lot of money to someone who reminds him of his uncle. What is interesting is that Davranche takes the opportunity provided by this account to paint a lurid picture of the material hardships of his own family, hardships that are basically seen as pitiful and ridiculous:

> I remember the pompous air of my poor parents in these Sunday walks, their stern expression, their stiff walk. [...] Jersey is the ideal trip for poor people. It is not far; one crosses a strip of sea in a steamer and lands on foreign soil, as this little island belongs to England. Thus, a Frenchman, with a two-hours' sail, can observe a neighboring people at home and study the customs [...] [My father] spread around him that odor of benzine which always made me recognize Sunday. [...] My father was probably pleased with this delicate manner of eating oysters on a moving ship. He considered it good form, refined [...][22]

From this description it is clear that a first person account is no guarantee of immediacy, as so often has been said, even when there is a reliable narrator/

---

21 Guy de Maupassant, *The Complete Short Stories of Guy de Maupassant*, trans. by Artine Artinian (Garden City, NY: Hanover House, 1955), pp. 1308-12 (hereafter Artinian). The French text can be found in Guy de Maupassant, *Contes et nouvelles*, ed. by Louis Forestier, 2 vols (Paris: Gallimard, collection La Pléiade, 1974), I, pp. 931-38 (hereafter Pléiade).

22 Ibid, pp. 1309-10 (pp. 934-35).

reflector. It is not because the narrator says "I" that there is no distance between us and that which he describes, because often he feels distant from his own surroundings. This is an exemplary case, since the narrator introduces his own family: the fact that it is his father who is involved does not lessen the ridicule in the least. The reason for this is that the narrator has been distinguished from the other characters from the beginning of the text. The story framing the story showed him walking with the narrator who can be assumed, at this time, to be a Maupassant, whose image as a worldly storyteller and elegant gentleman is firmly fixed in the mind of the readers. This son of a provincial clerical worker has become a true Parisian, with intimate connections in society: he has very little in common with the workers of Le Havre. Like Nikolay in *Peasants*, he has changed his universe: his tale can therefore distance this world without embarrassment.[23] This gesture seals his membership in Maupassant's world, in a community whose judgements the reader is supposed to share, and which the entire text reinforces.

There are from then on two possible outcomes. The reader can reject the text as presented. This is what happened with Chekhov's *Peasants* in the face of "populist" readers, or with *Lieutenant Gustl* when it was read by Schnitzler's fellow military officers. The readers saw the fierce distancing operating against the peasants and officers, and they rejected it in the name of their own values. We see this amongst more recent critics in the light of postcolonial and feminist theory; for example, in the reaction of Chinua Achebe to Conrad's *Heart of Darkness* or Virginia Llewellyn Smith to the distancing of female characters in Chekhov.[24] Too strong an ideological distance forbids acceptance of a short story. The text will be considered false, partisan, ill-informed: it is scarcely possible to read a story whose value system is too foreign, even though a strongly ideological novel like Tolstoy's *Voskresenie (Resurrection)* can be read without accepting his system of philosophy.

But usually the reader goes along with the distancing that occurs. There is enough objective difference — whether it be social or temporal — between

---

23 To use Andrew Levy's words: this is a case, not of having "no link with those socially disenfranchised groups", but of having "left them back home". Andrew Levy, *The Culture and Commerce of the American Short Story* (Cambridge: Cambridge University Press, 1993), p. 109.

24 Chinua Achebe, *Hopes and Impediments: Selected Essays* (New York: Doubleday 1989), pp. 1-20; and Virginia Llewellyn Smith, *Anton Chekhov and the Lady with the Dog* (Oxford: Oxford University Press, 1973).

the readers and the character to justify the distancing in the reader's eyes. At this point, the text has created precisely two groups: in one we find the characters and the unreliable narrator/reflector; in the other will be found the author, the reliable reflector/narrator, and with them the reader. By definition, the reliable narrator expresses values that will tend to be accepted; when he judges a character, we join in the judgement. It is Davranche laughing at his pitiful father, it is Kafka's traveller, and it is Nikolay denouncing the terrible state of Russia in *Peasants*. If the reader does not join with the author and the narrator/reflector in distancing the characters, he or she cannot enjoy the story. We can only read in the way the text invites us. In a sentence such as: "[My father] considered it good form, refined" from *My Uncle Jules*, we are invited to laugh at the father, and to question his taste.[25] Similarly, in *Peasants*, when the narrator says "[...] going into the log cabin, he was positively frightened: it was so dark and crowded and squalid [...] black with soot and flies. [...] The poverty, the poverty!", we are invited to share in the reflector's disgust.[26] The reader will adopt the reliable narrator/reflector's "perspective point" in the technical sense that is used in painting: that is, the point from which one gains the "correct perspective" on the picture. This positioning is imperative to the reader's enjoyment of the short story.

25 Artinian, p. 1310 (Pléiade, p. 935).
26 Yarmolinsky, p. 312 (Nauka, p. 281).

11. Distance and Emotion

In Mikhail Bakhtin's terms, a text is monologic and diametrically opposed to the polyphonic novel when it lets us hear one truth only, privileging one voice over all others.[1] In the classic short story this voice is that of the reader through his representatives — the narrator and reflector. The polyphonic text can claim an ethical superiority, but this does not mean that monologic texts are without power, charm or value.[2] The classic short story is perfectly adapted to satire — the ethical value of which is evident. It can help readers to see vividly all the shortcomings of a character or a situation (social or moral) by putting it at a distance. It can even — although it does not avail itself of the possibility very often in the period we are considering — put the readers themselves at a distance. But the short story does all this without ever renouncing its monologism.

The short story with a dilemma

In order to create polyphony, as defined by Bakhtin, the different voices involved must be "a plurality of consciousnesses, with equal rights"

---

1 See Mikhail Bakhtin, *Problems of Dostoevsky's Poetics*, ed. and trans. by Caryl Emerson (Minneapolis, MN: University of Minnesota Press, 1984), pp. 5-6.

2 For more on the potential superiority of polyphonic over monologic texts (in relation to epic, see Florence Goyet, *Penser sans concepts. Fonction de l'épopée guerrière* (Paris: Champion, 2006).

DOI: 10.11647/OBP.0039.11

— each of them must have their own validity.[3] Not one of the characters in Fyodor Dostoevsky's *The Brothers Karamazov* or *The Idiot* is discredited; faced with contradictory truths, the reader recognises the impossibility of choosing between them. There are very few classic short stories that expose us to several "voices". Even in the exceptional examples where we find two voices in a short story, both characters are equally discredited. Instead of polyphony, the result is the narrative image of aporia.

A good example of a short story with two voices is Anton Chekhov's *Vragi* (*Enemies*).[4] Kirilov, a doctor whose son has recently died of a drawn-out illness, is called upon by a local landowner, Abogin, who asks him to attend to his sick wife. At first the doctor refuses — he is exhausted from his son's illness and death — but in the end agrees. When they get to the landowner's house, they discover that his wife was feigning illness so that she could run off with her lover while her husband was fetching the doctor. Desperate, Abogin unloads his conjugal problems on the doctor who resents him for having brought him there. A terrible scene in which they insult each other is followed by some abstract remarks from Chekhov about how misfortune separates the unfortunate instead of bringing them together.

There is an important difference here from the stories we have seen so far: the two characters face off without either one getting the better of the other, without truth being on one side. Chekhov is careful to prevent us from being able to make a choice. We are no longer in the more common situation, as in Guy de Maupassant's *My Uncle Jules*, which we saw in the last chapter, where the character is discredited in favour of the narrator's values. At first glance, we even have the feeling that, for once, Chekhov gives each of these characters a certain credibility. The story begins by portraying the doctor without any attempt at distance. Through a powerful description of his distress at his son's death, he is sympathetic to the reader. Chekhov takes great pains to detail — concretely and very vividly — his terrible exhaustion. His shock has left him no longer in possession of his faculties: he cannot find the door of his study, for example, and he lifts his right foot

---

3 Bakhtin (1984), p. 5.

4 Anton Chekhov, *The Schoolmaster and Other Stories*, trans. by Constance Garnett (New York: Macmillan, 1921), pp. 15-34 (hereafter Garnett). The original Russian can be found in Anton Pavlovich Chekhov, *Polnoe sobranie sochinenii i pisem*, 30 vols (Moscow: Nauka, 1974-1983, VI, pp. 30-43 (hereafter Nauka). Page references will be given first to the translation, then to the original in brackets.

too high to cross the threshold.[5] The reader is "with" the character because of his vulnerability, and ready to react to the total incongruity of Abogin's demands on him. At the beginning of the story, Abogin is one of those classic characters of Chekhov, the "prisoner of his own preoccupations",[6] who treats a child's death on the same level as a mild discomfort.[7] Kirilov, then, obviously interprets his own adventure as a simple antithetic tension: an exhausted doctor, affected in both body and emotions, is taken twenty kilometres from home to be used as an accessory in an adulterous episode.

What is remarkable here is that the entire story prohibits the reader from sharing in Kirilov's interpretation. After bringing the doctor into true proximity with the readers' sympathies, it then distances him and brings Abogin closer. Faced with the unfortunate doctor, Abogin is not, in fact, the tedious person we first see, but a man "in whose face there was a suggestion of something generous, leonine";[8] he is truly suffering over his wife's illness and is afraid she will die. The story then reveals that the young woman's father died from an aneurism, making the landowner's anguish all the more understandable.

But the interest of this unusual closeness to the character becomes clear as soon as we see the portraits that Chekhov draws one after the other. The essential trait is then revealed: Chekhov, by reversing their roles, creates an absolute *symmetry* between his protagonists. Abogin — the annoyance — is described in a purely meliorative way, whereas the doctor — for whom we were ready to feel sympathy — is distanced:

> The doctor was tall and stooped, was untidily dressed and not good-looking. There was an unpleasantly harsh, morose, and unfriendly look about his lips, thick as a Negro's, his aquiline nose, and listless, apathetic eyes. [...] Looking at his frigid figure one could hardly believe that this man had a wife, that he was capable of weeping over his child. *Abogin presented a very*

---

5   Ibid, p. 18 (pp. 32-33). The absence of distance in this opening is summed up in the strange passage on the "subtle beauty [...] of human sorrow [...] which... only music can convey" (p. 19 [p. 33]): to define the beauty of this grief is to invite the reader to share in this truly musical emotion.

6   See Kataev's analyses of this incapacity of Chekhov's heroes to emerge from their preoccupations, which is one of his great methods of discrediting. V. B. Kataev, *Proza Chekhova: Problemy Interpretatsii* (Moscow: Izd-vo Moskovskogo universiteta, 1979), p. 62. For a partial translation, see Vladimir Kataev, *If Only We Could Know: An Interpretation of Chekhov*, trans. by Harvey Pitcher (Chicago, IL: Ivan R. Dee, 2002).

7   When hearing of the death of the child, Abogin is upbeat: "A wonderfully unhappy day... wonderfully! What a coincidence... It's as though it were on purpose." Garnett, p. 17 (Nauka, p. 32).

8   Ibid, p. 25 (p. 38).

no full shop

different appearance. He was a thick-set, sturdy-looking, fair man with a big head and large, soft features; he was elegantly dressed in the very latest fashion. In his carriage, his closely buttoned coat, his long hair, and his face there was a suggestion of something generous, leonine;[9]

The phrase in emphasis clarifies the antithesis present in every feature. The portrait of the doctor is astonishingly clumsy, and the narrator goes so far as to make an improbable judgement: "one could hardly believe that this man had a wife, that he was capable of weeping over his child". The portrait of Abogin, on the other hand, is enough to moderate his violent arrival in the grieving household. The two presentations, then, are balanced so that neither one is favoured.

Nevertheless, it cannot be called polyphony. The central direction of the text is to position these two characters *back to back.* We could say that Abogin is only rehabilitated to the precise degree to which Kirilov is discredited: he is Kirilov's pendulum, negative and positive to exactly the same degree. Once again the proximity permitted by the short story is *transitive.* The two enemies have been built in perfect symmetry in order to make it possible for Chekhov to state the dilemma.[10] To achieve this it was necessary that the two men not despise each other at the outset — their hatred had to come from the situation itself. If Abogin had been a comic cuckold, there would have immediately existed the classic tension between the "heroic, dutiful doctor" and the "amorous, ridiculous landowner", both well-known types in Russian literature. Instead the diptych allowed Chekhov to clarify the abstract problem he is dealing with, a problem whose terms he explicitly articulates at the very end of the text: instead of bringing the characters together as we expect, their misfortune makes them loathe each other.

Even the unusual nuances of the characters do not prevent Chekhov from judging them definitively and conclusively. Half way through the story, Abogin will again be discredited. The moment he discovers his young wife's deception, he burdens Kirilov with his complaints about the fugitive as well as a very complete picture of his family life. Chekhov ironically disowns him, as is clear in a short passage about the remedy which should be applied to this so-called incurable grief: "If he had talked in this way for an hour or two, and opened his heart, he would undoubtedly have felt

---

9   Ibid (emphasis mine).

10 We can only comprehend the meaning of the title *Enemies* when we recognise that it refers to the fundamental confrontation at the heart of the text, and not to the history of either one of the characters.

better".[11] That is: if he had received a sympathetic reception from the doctor, his burst of confidence would have allowed him to assuage his grief and prevented him from doing "anything needless and absurd". Chekhov here takes his distance from the grief of Abogin.[12] For his part the doctor will be explicitly discredited at the end, in two almost identical formulae: he will retain "unjust and inhumanly cruel" thoughts from this confrontation, a conviction "unjust and unworthy of the human heart".[13]

In this indictment of the two men, neither one is given preference, yet, for all that, neither logic is shown as valid. Superior to them both, the narrator dispenses abstract explanations, and unyieldingly contrasts the two behaviours, carefully and symmetrically discrediting first one and then the other. What is gained from this is a proof: a precise and utterly inescapable vision of the narrowness of these two worlds. Chekhov is using, in a particular way, the essential techniques of the genre, such as I have been describing from the beginning of this book. What makes this very different from the other short stories is his thematic exploitation of tension. Instead of simply being used to structure a story and give it sufficient autonomy, the tension serves to bring the two worlds face to face, revealing their radical narrowness. In every other respect, these "stories with a dilemma" are very standard. They operate on paroxysms.[14] They are based on the reader's preconceptions: the figure of the doctor caught between his duty and his personal grief and the landowner trapped in his ideas of "modern" love are typical. The confrontation serves to invert each of the presupposed concepts (doctor who is scarcely human, amorous

---

11 Garnett, p. 30 (Nauka, p. 41).

12 Following the pattern with which we are now so familiar in the classic short story, all the techniques converge to prevent our comprehension of Abogin's behaviour: once he has got hold of Kirilov in his car, he does not give a single word in response to the doctor's request to return home for a moment to get someone to stay with his wife, who is all alone in the house with the dead child. Both men sit without any communication, and their perception of nature is purely mimetic of their own feelings, whereas we know that for Chekhov the capacity to see the beauty of nature for itself is the touchstone of a character's soul. On the importance of "details" in Chekhov, see Aleksandr P. Chudakov, *Poetika Chekhova* (Moscow: Nauka, 1971).

13 Garnett, p. 33 (Nauka, p. 42).

14 Examples of paroxysms in the story include not only the death of the child but also the fact that Kirilov and his wife are too old to have another ("Andrey was not merely the only child, but also the last child", p. 19); Abogin's arrival *just* when the boy has died; the trivial reason for the drama (adultery); the extreme style of the character portraits; the fact that Abogin loves his wife like a slave; and Abogin's risible readiness to apply all modern ideas.

landowner who has nobleness). When the short story does present two voices, it sets them back to back, like fraternal enemies.

In this respect, the short story works counter to the great novel. For proof we need only examine James's different use of the international theme in his short stories and novels. James, a voluntary exile in England, loved the country enough to apply for citizenship: unquestionably he was predestined not to be able to choose between the often antithetic Old and New World. What is striking is that, in his short stories, this dilemma goes through a distancing of the two cultures, through a dramatisation of the conflict between them. We have a particularly clear example of this in the difference between the novel *The Golden Bowl* and its sketch, the short story *Miss Gunton of Poughkeepsie*. Both are centred around the marriage of a young American woman and an Italian prince. In the short story, the prince is desperate to marry Lily Gunton — a fresh incarnation of Daisy Miller — and she burns with the same ardour. The obstacle that arises between them is none other than the symmetrical intransigence of Lily and the prince's family over one of their many different social customs: the prince asks that Lily be the first to write to his mother, and the young woman absolutely refuses.

As in all short stories that deal with an international theme, the tension in *Miss Gunton* is created between the two opposite worlds. It is further emphasised by the use of a young English woman as reflector, Lady Champer, through whose eyes we see Lily. From her first words — "It's astonishing what you take for granted!" — Lady Champer poses the problem of different, irreconcilable concepts; for an English lady as for an Italian prince, what Lily considers "natural" is constantly a source of amazement. As Lady Champer explains to the prince, it is the responsibility of the family in the American's universe to welcome a young fiancée, especially if she is an orphan. But, nevertheless, Lady Champer goes on to explain to Lily that, for an Italian princess, there is no question of sacrificing the homage due to her rank, especially if the fiancée is a foreigner. Lily ends up marrying an American, to the prince's great despair. It is not really surprising that James was able to publish the text at the same time in both countries: in the London *Cornhill*, and in *Truth* in America. He is not in fact dealing with either Americans or Italian princes, but with the gulf that separates them both. The strangeness of each custom is delineated and underlined, because the presence of the other universe puts it in perspective.

We never find in James's great novels this unyielding opposition between the Old and the New World; instead there is a progressive discovery, a true interpenetration. In *The Golden Bowl*, the two worlds interact in a much more subtle, dialectic fashion than in the short story. The friend of the two young people is no longer an English noblewoman, but an American.[15] The interior world of the young woman and her value system are not a source of surprise for her as in the short story. She no longer serves to reveal the potential foreign quality of the character of the young American; rather she allows us to penetrate more deeply the subtlety of her feelings and attitudes.

Clash, confrontation, unyielding opposition: the pictures of Europe and America in the short stories are based on radical incomprehension. James's *The Modern Warning* perhaps provides the most exemplary expression of this dilemma between the two worlds: in it the heroine dies from having tried to be faithful to both universes at the same time. The young American, Agatha, marries a high-ranking English conservative, Sir Rufus — ignoring the warnings of her brother, a Yankee patriot lawyer. For many years she is untroubled by her "international" position, living as a married woman amid her house and her garden, her children and her social circle. But after a journey to America, her English husband decides to write a book explaining the mistakes and perversities of the young democracy. Agatha tries to persuade him that he has misjudged her country, just as she had tried to convince her brother of his unfairness towards Sir Rufus. Unable to reconcile the two countries' world visions, she finally commits suicide.

This death is more than a melodramatic end to a story that had dangerous leanings in this direction already. It is the *only* possible conclusion if we are to take into account both sides of the problem as presented by James throughout his tale. Obviously, like many an aporia, it is perfectly possible to go beyond this fundamental tension, but only within a dialectic framework. Having built its characters as exemplary representatives of their category, defined by their bizarre or ridiculous foibles, the short story does not have sufficient flexibility to change them in any meaningful way.

We should note in passing that, in the best of cases, the short stories with dilemmas can lead the reader to question his or her own values. When an English person reads *Miss Gunton of Poughkeepsie, An International*

---

15 James often used confidants like this, who play the role of a reflector: they show the hero outside of his own self-awareness, and they also make it possible to understand the richness of the feelings and thoughts he articulates.

Episode, or *The Modern Warning,* the symmetrical and reciprocal distancing of the two universes brings about a "boomerang effect", in which even the reader's values are also discredited. At the beginning of *An International Episode,* an Englishman laughs at the bizarre qualities of the New World, but ultimately he will be dislodged from the comfortable position he usually occupies in the short story. If the reader is ready to accept the distancing in the first panel of the diptych then she will hardly be able to deny it in the second, even when it concerns her directly.

As we have seen, the short story concentrates on a "case", an abstract little problem, a dilemma for which no character has a satisfactory solution.[16] The reader is generally invited to remain above the fray and can therefore maintain a position of superiority in relation to the spectacle. But here, as in some of Chekhov's short stories, the reader is encouraged to use her superior position to distance herself from her own ideas and prejudices and gain a new perspective on her own preconceptions. The "short story with a dilemma" belongs at the outer limits of the universe of classic "exotic" short stories, while still functioning in essentially the same way.

Readers' emotional response to the classic short story

In his work on Nikolai Gogol's influential *Shinel'* (*The Overcoat*), Boris Eikhenbaum has made clear the profound dual aspect of the short story genre.[17] The story's central character, Akaki Akakevich, is defined mostly by his persona as a "pitiful" hero, someone who simultaneously stirs both our sympathy and our ridicule. Eikhenbaum laid bare the signs of what I have called distancing in this idea of ridicule. In particular, he showed that the famous passage with the refrain "why are you mistreating me?" is not a plea for Gogol in favour of his pathetic hero.[18] Rather, the passage creates a contrast with the neutral, impersonal tone of the narration. Eikhenbaum's analysis takes into account the puns and wordplays on the name of Akaki, the heroic-comic tone, and the use of absurd-sounding "grandiose and

---

16 "We're simply the case…" as the character of Stuart Straith says in *Broken Wings*. Henry James, *The Complete Tales of Henry James,* ed. by Leon Edel, 12 vols (New York: Rupert Hart Davis, 1960), XI, p. 232.

17 Boris Eikhenbaum, "How Gogol's 'Overcoat' is Made", in *Gogol's "Overcoat": An Anthology of Critical Essays,* ed. by Elizabeth Trahan (Ann Arbor, MI: Ardis, 1982), pp. 21-36.

18 Ibid, p. 28.

fantastic" words like "hemorrhoidal".[19] This total strategy establishes what Eikhenbaum calls a "grotesque" relationship with the subject in which "the mimicry of laughter alternates with the mimicry of sorrow".[20]

One of the most common manifestations of this tension characteristic of the classic short story is the coexistence of ridicule and sympathetic emotion, although some stories unite "sordid realism" and emotion (without ridiculing the characters) or intellectual understanding without compassion — in all three cases, however, the framework is provided by the essential monologism of the genre. Akutagawa Ryūnosuke, in particular, has manipulated with extraordinary dexterity this mix of cruelty and pity for his characters. At the heart of a short story such as *Imogayu* (*Yam Gruel*), there is both distancing and the recognition of the hapless hero Goi's humanity — which will lead to our pity for him.[21]

What is interesting is the extreme to which distancing is carried in a story that also portrays the hero as one of our "brothers". Not only does Akutagawa prevent the reader's attachment to the character at the beginning of *Yam Gruel* by interrupting his argument under various different pretexts, but he also provides a portrait of Goi that is deliberately paroxystic and predictable: he is ugly, cowardly, slovenly and is seen as the anti-hero, adorned with an Homeric epithet "the red-nosed Goi".[22] Akutagawa then inflicts on Goi an heroic-comic treatment with the great theme of "the unique goal of existence": Goi lives in the hope of one day eating his fill of yam gruel, and on the day when a practical joke fills him with disgust for this meal, he will literally no longer have an existence.

It is strictly within this framework that there arises another aspect, latent in the very definition of the character: the pathetic being, worthy of our sympathy. Like Akaki Akakevich in *The Overcoat*, Goi complains pitifully that he is being persecuted. This takes the form of an antiphon of drawling echoes: "'Why did you do that'".[23] Such disarray interjects a few seconds of

---

19 Ibid, p. 27. This does not, of course, explain why the text has always been understood as the expression of a sympathetic point of view. Note, however, that Gogol's tone is grossly distorted in translation by the suppression of the frequent play on sounds considered ridiculous by the Russians.

20 Ibid, p. 29.

21 Akutagawa Ryūnosuke, *Japanese Short Stories by Ryūnosuke Akutagawa*, trans. by Takashi Kojima (New York: Liveright, 1952), pp. 45-71. For the original Japanese, see Akutagawa Ryūnosuke, *Akutagawa Ryūnosuke zenshū*, 19 vols (Tōkyō: Iwanami Shoten, 1954-1955), I, pp. 85-105.

22 Ibid, p. 48 (p. 87).

23 Ibid.

trouble in the mind of his persecutors, and Akutagawa develops this theme by introducing the character of a young provincial officer, who does not belong to the closed little world of this feudal court. Through his eyes, Goi suddenly changes status, for him and for us:

> Of course, at first he, too, joined the others in ridiculing the red-nosed Goi without reason. But one day he happened to hear Goi's question, 'Why did you do that?' and the words stuck in his mind. From that time on he saw Goi in a different light, because he saw a blubberer, persecuted by a hard life, peeping from the pale and stupid face of the undernourished Goi.[24]

Note the "pale and stupid face" from which this new visage of Goi is "peeping". In other words, the story works on the same material in two contradictory ways, in order to release the opposing potentialities. We are not led to question our judgement of Goi as an individual: we are offered a proof of an abstract truth. Basically Akutagawa is saying that every man is your brother, no matter how ridiculously wretched he may be.

This development in our perception of Goi's character is by no means the climax and end of the story. It goes on to tell us about a nasty trick played on Goi: a superior officer takes him far away from his home and serves him so many pitchers of yam gruel that he becomes sick. The revelation of Goi's "humanity" in the eyes of the young provincial functions as the background against which emerges our reading of this grotesque episode. His ridicule is constantly driven home at the same time as we witness his rehabilitation. The young officer's reaction enlightens our vision of the hero without destroying the effect of distancing: the constant insistence on Goi's cowardice, for example, does not allow us to ignore how ridiculous he is.[25]

"Sordid realism" is another mode of the short story, in which the innumerable "little men" (to use Gogol's words) of the time are also subjected to a double treatment by the author. In these stories, scenes will be loaded with unbearable misery, making us feel an immense pity for the character, while at the same time firmly distancing him. Examples from our body of authors include: Maupassant's *The Vagabond*, Akutagawa's *The Tangerines*, Verga's *Nedda* and *Rosso Malpelo*, and Chekhov's *Sleepy*, *Vanka* and *Anyuta*. The latter of these stories provides an exemplary summary of

---

24 Ibid, pp. 48-49 (pp. 87-88).

25 Crossing the moor on the way to the officer's house, Goi trembles like a leaf. One day, he finally dares to defend an unfortunate dog because he is only dealing with children: "But on this occasion, since they were children, he could muster up some courage". Ibid, p. 50 (p. 89).

the problematic I am trying to untangle here.[26] First we should note *Anyuta*'s extraordinary effectiveness: from Tolstoy to Lenin and the Moderns, this is one of the stories most loved by the Russians. It is also a complete anthology of the techniques of sordid realism, based on paroxysm. Anyuta is a poor girl who lives with a destitute medical student in a seedy hotel where they occupy the cheapest room. They have no fire, "no tobacco and no tea", and the young woman, who is extremely thin and pale, takes up sewing in order to support them both. The description of the state of their room speaks for itself:

> Crumpled bedclothes, pillows thrown about, books, clothes, a big filthy slop-pail filled with soapsuds in which cigarette ends were swimming, and the litter on the floor — all seemed as though purposely jumbled together in one confusion.[27]

This extreme misery is the backdrop for the development of the essential tension: the paroxysm of indifference on the part of the student, Klochkov, is contrasted with Anyuta's extreme devotion. There is an example that captures this tension perfectly: in order to review his anatomy lesson, the future doctor draws ribs in crayon on Anyuta's nude body, so that she looks "as though she had been tattooed".[28] Anyuta shivers with cold and is afraid that "the student, noticing it, would stop drawing and sounding her, and then, perhaps, might fail in his exam".[29] Klochkov scolds her when she complains timidly of cold hands, and leaves her to shiver even after he has finished: "You sit like that and don't rub off the crayon, and meanwhile I'll learn up a little more".[30]

I will not elaborate here on the central development: Chekhov shows Anyuta's silent memory of all the students she had known, all of whom had gone on to achieve great success in life:

> Now they had all finished their studies, had gone out into the world, and, of course, like respectable people, had long ago forgotten her. One of them was

---

26 Anton Chekhov, *Anton Chekhov's Short Stories*, ed. by Ralph E. Matlaw (New York: Norton, 1979), pp. 20-23 (hereafter Matlaw). For the Russian text, see Nauka, IV, pp. 340-44.

27 Ibid, p. 20 (p. 340).

28 I had the opportunity to see this story "performed" by Soviet actors in Paris in 1988. The audience of course laughed at the assimilation, in the same breath, of Anyuta and a skeleton ("One must study them in the skeleton and the living body... I say, Anyuta, let me pick them out", p. 21). The actors were following the "drift" of the text by emphasising the effects: after Klochkov had drawn her ribs, Anyuta really did look like a skeleton.

29 Matlaw, p. 21 (Nauka, p. 341).

30 Ibid.

living in Paris, two were doctors, the fourth was an artist, and the fifth was said to be already a professor.[31]

We simply note that this is the great Chekhovian theme of "deceptive representations" of reality. Anyuta, an unreliable reflector, unleashes a chain of logic that is in no way acceptable to the reader: because they are now "respectable people", they have forgotten her. What follows will also develop the deceptive representations of Klochkov, who wants to get rid of Anyuta when a painter friend makes him ashamed of his "unaesthetic" life. Blinded by his wish to be "respectable", he wants to remove Anyuta from his life, and does not understand that it is she, alone, who gives his life substance.

In Russian society at the end of the nineteenth century — bathed in good sentiments and an atmosphere of Christian piety that dictated values if not behaviours — such a story was a powerful denunciation. It revealed with terrible force the hypocrisy of the time and showed readers that it was wrong to allow such situations to happen around them. But it is important to understand that the very source of this effectiveness, of this powerful emotion that has captivated generations of readers, is created *in and by* the radical distancing. Anyuta is worthy of all our pity, but her world vision is not in the least valid. We are moved because we see the degree to which she errs, the degree to which she is excluded from society as a whole and incapable of even participating in its ways of thinking. The author places us totally outside the world of the young protagonists, in a place where he can show us the architecture of this strange spectacle, and the inescapable destiny awaiting its characters.

Presenting us with characters whose behaviour we shall understand, but from afar, is another of the usual ways of creating emotion in the classic short story.[32] A good example of this is found in a simple and also famous story: Maupassant's *Le Vieux* (*The Old Man*), also known as *Les Douillons* (*Apple Turnovers*).[33] The Chicots are a peasant couple in Normandy. The old

---

31 Ibid.

32 Although he does not see distance as a characteristic trait of the short story, I find parallel analyses in Martin Scofield, *The Cambridge Introduction to the American Short Story* (Cambridge: Cambridge University Press, 2006). See especially his analysis of Ambrose Bierce's *Chickamauga*, pp. 70-71.

33 Guy de Maupassant, *Complete Short Stories of Guy de Maupassant*, trans. by Artine Artinian (Garden City, NY: Hanover House, 1955), pp. 544-48. For the original French text, see Guy de Maupassant, *Contes et nouvelles*, ed. by Louis Forestier, 2 vols (Paris: Gallimard, collection La Pléiade, 1974), I, pp. 1130-37.

father is dying, and the couple is annoyed because he is taking his time to do so. Since they are sure his death is imminent, they decide to invite the neighbours immediately to his funeral, so as not to delay the farming work, and the wife makes apple turnovers to offer to the guests. But, as we know, the father will not be dead when the guests arrive, and the peasants will have to give another burial reception.

What is interesting about this short story is the extreme clarity of what is at stake; the logic of the characters is convincingly followed through to the end. And yet the comprehension of the reader is essentially limited, and allows for the defining of our emotion. The author makes it clear that the Chicots are not departing in any way from the rural customs in counting on the father's death. They know that the mayor will authorise them to hold the funeral immediately after he dies, despite the law, as he did for "old man Renard, who died just at sowing time":[34] in this community, farming comes first. The reader feels convinced of this: we are ready to recognise the necessity of not endangering the harvest in order to follow what is no more than a simple custom. In a world that is so poor, it seems normal to ignore the sentimentality of a death, since the deceased will not know any difference. But acknowledging this necessity can only be done by establishing a radical difference between our universe and theirs. The portraits, first of the wife and then of the husband, are predictably marked with bestial imagery:

> Her bony figure, wide and flat [...]. A once white bonnet, now yellow, covered part of her hair, pulled tight over her head. Her dark face, thin, ugly, toothless, showed that wild animal-like expression peasant faces often have. [...] probably no more than forty, but he looked sixty, wrinkled, gnarled [...]. His outsized arms hung down along his body.[35]

This description does not prepare us to share in the logic of these characters on an equal footing and accept the validity of their reactions, their judgements and their behaviour. Signs of their strangeness continue to accumulate: the legions of rats which scurried about "day and night" in their attic; the "earthen floor, rough and damp" which seemed slippery with grease; their rooms separated by a "ragged piece of local calico".

And of course Maupassant's use of direct speech leaves no room for empathy. The author describes the dying old man as a disembodied sound: "A regular, rough sound — hard breathing, gasping, whistling,

---

34 Ibid, p. 547 (p. 1134).
35 Ibid, pp. 544-45 (pp. 1130-31).

with a gargling like a broken water pump — came from the shadowy bed on which an old man was dying, the peasant woman's father".[36] The peasant woman repeats the narrator's brutal image when she talks to her husband: "He's been gurgling like that since noon [...]. [It's] still gurgling [...] Doesn't [it] sound like a pump that's got no water?".[37] There is a rapid transition from indications of a person ("He's been gurgling") to those of inanimate objects: "a pump"; "it's" and "it" referring to the man. Mistakes and mispronunciations are another way of creating a contrast between our way of speaking and that of the peasants. So is, of course, the insistence on the material aspects of the father's death. French readers tend to remember the title of this story as *Les Douillons* (a French dialect word for "dumplings"), which embody the peasants' unemotional view of death: the peasant woman is so absorbed in the preparation of her dumplings, and so unwilling to lose any time, that she does not even check on her dying father.

Yet again note that there is as much sympathy for the characters as is possible in a classic short story: the reader is well aware of the peasant woman's anxiety during the aborted funeral, when she "kept going to the cellar for cider. Pitchers came up and were emptied with the utmost speed".[38] Food and cider are the woman's only thought: she is going to have to make another batch of dumplings, she and her husband will have to invite everyone again — it's a catastrophe for their poor household. We understand, but this understanding brings with it the recognition of the essential difference that exists between their world and ours, the gulf separating two kinds of humanity: one which honours the dead, and one which treats death with brutal practicality.[39]

In a different, more political and less literary context, all this would no doubt have been considered classist.[40] Obviously the reader can always

---

36 Ibid, p. 545 (p. 1131).

37 Ibid, pp. 545-46 (p. 1131). I have modified the translation slightly to be closer to the original.

38 Ibid, p. 548 (p. 1136).

39 This is a recurring idea in Maupassant's representation of peasants. See for example this passage from *En famille*: "In the suburbs of Paris, which are full of people from the provinces, one meets with the indifference toward death, even of a father or a mother, which all peasants show; a want of respect, an unconscious callousness which is common in the country, and rare in Paris". Ibid, p. 1032 (p. 206).

40 And indeed when it comes to racism, the short story is recognised as the "most heinous" genre in the representation of black people until the 1950s. See Bill Mullen, "Marking Race/ Marketing Race: African American Short Fiction and the Politics of Genre, 1933-1946", in *Ethnicity and the American Short Story*, ed. by Julie Brown (London: Garland, 1997), pp. 25-46.

decide to recognise a real connection between his own world and that of the peasants. This supposes, however, an external detour, a prior decision. If the reader decides *a priori* that the values of her own world are not superior to those of the peasants, if she assumes that her own are hypocritical, then she will praise the story for its honesty. But even in this case, the reader still remain within the framework described previously: it is not a question of adopting the peasants' values, but of comparing side by side their values and ours, one set challenging the other.[41]

******

The three different strategies we just saw for creating "sympathy" in a short story are profoundly akin to one another. In them, as in so many simpler texts, the short story brilliantly exploits its status as an "exotic" text in relation to its readers. Its own mode of action is precisely by way of establishing a maximum distance between the reader and the spectacle. The "Sirius point of view", of which we talked in the previous chapter, allows a familiar reality to be seen in a different light. By revealing, in *Kholstomer*, contemporary Russian society through the eyes of a horse, Tolstoy was extracting the maximal distance and most powerful emotion of which the genre is capable. All the short stories present, in a strikingly lively fashion, scenes we probably have not been able to see, and characters whom we have approached without realising: prostitutes and pariahs of all kinds, of course, but also the petty clerical workers whose mediocrity hides their misery. We no longer ignore them but rather recognise their spectacular strangeness.

We can now understand why the short story was celebrated by all the revolutionary governments (the prize for the "best short story" has been a characteristic trait of socialist countries, from Tunisia to Eastern Europe): it is the perfect vehicle for denunciation. It should not surprise us that Lenin was so fond of Chekhov's *Anyuta*. Not only did the short story succeed brilliantly in making the atrocity of a situation apparent, it was also able to show that the horror of the characters' behaviour was rooted in the "deceptive representations" which they had of reality, in their incapacity to understand correctly the relationships of power and their own situation.

---

41 In any case I do not think that this is the effect that the story was supposed to produce on the readers of *Le Gaulois*: the peasants are too clearly distanced and the discourse on peasant indifference in the face of death is too characteristic.

The short story is the tool of political awareness, and politicians like Lenin saw it as a wonderful means of enlightening their contemporaries.

But we can, of course, make the same reproach as Hegel made to the philosophers of the French Enlightenment: the very idea of philosophy bringing light to those who do not possess it, in the same way the idea of transforming the life of peasants in Normandy or the Russian petty bourgeoisie, implies a position of superiority. It implies belief in the universality of one's own values, in the necessity of establishing them in these foreign worlds — social or geographic. Postcolonial studies have taught us that the concept of exoticism is only apparently neutral, and that to consider an object or person exotic implies a very definite world orientation: on the one hand the West, and on the other a foreign world, perceived from the superior perspective of a "civilized" country. The emotion may be very strong, and the short story can impart to its readers a profound interest in the misery of the masses, or the fate of petty nobility like Goi. It makes no difference: the essential attitude is a form of condescension: one *looks down* on these characters.

In so far as this, the classic short story is quite naturally the progeny of the end of the nineteenth century, as is exoticism. Vincenette Maigne summarises the traits we have seen deployed in this chapter:

> the term 'exoticism' itself appears moreover in the period of colonial expansion when all the representations of the French [...] comfort the country in its image of the superiority of western civilization, with a benevolent overture to the distant foreign lands, looked on as inferior, barbarous, but interesting (cf. the very formal 'orientalism' of this period which does not consider the indigenous representative to be equal in dignity, but simply a spectacle which is picturesque in its costumes or strange in its customs).[42]

In this framework, the validation of the short story lies precisely in the belief in progress that ruled the last decades of the nineteenth century. When Chekhov treats the subjects of the story Peasants so harshly, when Verga willingly dwells on the sordid realism of his settings, and when Maupassant accumulates portraits of limited, ignorant and superstitious peasants, it is because they are all trying to advance "civilization".

Maupassant's *Le Baptême* (*The Christening*) is emblematic of this approach — an intellectual approach for once rather than the desire to make his reader

---

42 Vincenette Maigne, "Exotisme, évolution en diachronie du mot et de son champ sémantique", in *Exotisme et création. Actes du colloque international* (Lyon: L'Hermes, 1985), pp. 9-16 (p. 12, translation ours).

laugh or procure for him any strong sensation. In this horrifying story, a doctor relates how peasants, in order to show respect for the baptismal customs of their region, have exposed their baby to the rigorous cold of winter (their tradition has it that the baby should wait naked for the priest) then, having all got drunk, have left him to die of cold in the ditch where they had fallen. This story certainly belongs among the innumerable caricatures of peasants, and it displays the characteristic refusal to participate in the logic of the "other". But in this case, the refusal is explicitly justified, and reveals the general direction of the genre: participation in the logic of the peasants would have meant granting validity to a pernicious practice.

It is almost always possible to accuse the short story of "western centrism", and to show that it is based firmly on the reader's values. But at the end of the nineteenth century, there was not an ethnology respectful of the rites and customs of so-called "savages". Instead, there was a focus on the virtues of "reason" and "progress". To publish short stories in the newspapers was to preach the "good word", to try to transform the world (many publications — one of which is still published in Lyon —bore the title of *Progress*). This may be what makes the classic short story so very much a product of its time: its positivist belief in the virtues of education in the simplest possible terms.

12. Conclusion to Part III: Are Dostoevsky's Short Stories Polyphonic?

We have seen in Part III that the classic short story is a resolutely monologic genre, in which only the author-reader group has a fully-fledged "voice" of its own. Every possible rhetorical technique is used to distance the characters from the reader. The primary focus is on the characters' difference, their exotic strangeness, and the result is that the reader judges their voice even before it has been heard. To conclude this section we should, then, return to Mikhail Bakhtin in order to justify the use I have made of the notion of polyphony. Actually, I find that I have gone in a direction not explicitly foreseen by Bakhtin: when he developed the concept, it was for the purpose of contrasting Dostoevsky with all other writers, and the difference between novels and short stories was not one of his concerns.[1] However, it seems to me that we can and should pursue the analysis of Bakhtin in the terms that he himself set. If we are attentive to the development of his arguments in *Problems of Dostoevsky's Poetics* it is clear that he talks of Dostoevsky's short works and novels quite differently. This should lead us to make a

---

1   Mikhail Bakhtin, *Problems of Dostoevsky's Poetics*, ed. and trans. by Caryl Emerson (Minneapolis, MN: University of Minnesota Press, 1984).

DOI: 10.11647/OBP.0039.12

distinction that is as important as it is seldom made, between polyphony and dialogism.

First of all let us note that Bakhtin explicitly states the difference between novels and short stories: "Other autonomous consciousnesses appear only in the longer novels".[2] The movement towards polyphony, characteristic of Dostoevsky, is not fully realised in the short stories: the "other" is not seen as having a full and autonomous status. Since Bakhtin's goal is not to distinguish the different facets of his author, but to indicate his true place in world literature, the fact that he does not make a point of developing this distinction between the genres is not surprising. That he happened to remark on this, however, is because all the analyses he gives of short stories pointed to it. The difference between the novels and the short stories can be said as a difference between polyphony and dialogism.

Polyphony, as put to light by Bakhtin in Dostoevsky's novels, is when the relationships between all the "voices" are based on *equality*.[3] To take a classic example, in *The Brothers Karamazov*, when Alyosha says to Ivan Karamazov: "You are not the one who killed our father", Alyosha's voice has the same status as the voice of the Devil who persuades Ivan that he is guilty. Alyosha makes this assertion to balance that of Satan, and the whole construction by Dostoevsky of the character of Alyosha makes this equilibrium valid.[4] Similarly, in *The Idiot*, it is impossible to despise Rogozhin, because of his rival Myshkin's attitude towards him. As the characters interact with one another, all the "typifying" traits given at the beginning of the book are steadily deconstructed — as are the reader's prejudices, which would lead him to think of Sonya in *Crime and Punishment* as a "prostitute". Everything in these novels makes it impossible for the reader to pass a judgement on the characters. Renouncing this means to renounce social prejudices: to renounce taking a position of superiority toward "other" social categories, genders or races. This is polyphony, "a plurality of consciousnesses, with equal rights", where the character's "word about himself and his world [...] sounds, as it were, alongside the author's word and in a special way combines both with it and with the full and equally valid voices of other characters".[5]

---

2 Ibid, p. 267, note 16. See also p. 220: "But these voices [in *The Double*] have not yet become fully independent real voices, they are not yet three autonomous consciousnesses. This occurs only in Dostoevsky's longer novels".

3 Ibid, pp. 5-6.

4 See ibid, pp. 255-26.

5 Ibid, respectively p. 6 and p. 7.

Now, dialogism in Dostoevsky's short stories is quite distinct from this. Bakhtin similarly puts to light two voices, but here he is not talking about the symmetry or variety of voices of equivalent status. It *is* "dialogism" because the relationship between narrator and character is a direct one, a dialogue. Here too Dostoevsky's heroes are "consciousnesses", fully and constantly aware of everything that can be said of them, of every comment or judgement that could be developed about them. Their major trait could even be said to be this "sideward glance" by which they are always in search of the other characters' assessment of them — both materially and ethically.[6] The characters are in a relationship of dialogue with the narrator, who does not have the last word on them: the narrator cannot give a definite picture of them from an exterior perspective. But this is not polyphony because there is, in fact, a hierarchy between two totally dissimilar partners in the communication process, with one of them — the character — being discredited. Bakhtin continues to speak of two voices, but they are in no way equal.

In the short stories' dialogism, the first voice is that of the hero's self-justification. But — and Bakhtin insists on this — it has no real autonomy, nor any "ontological weight". Neither the "heroes of the underground", nor the hero of *Dvoinik* (*The Double*), nor of *Krotkaya* (*The Meek One*) will be able to persuade the other or themselves that they are right and that the outside world is wrong. And never will some other voice speak about them a truth that would balance the condemnation they are passing on themselves.[7] If we try to adhere strictly to Bakhtin's terms, we are forced to conclude — as he himself usually does — that ultimately it is *the other's truth* which dominates, crushing that of the hero. The "heroes of the underground" can never make their own voice seem valid, even to their own ears. In other words, the monologue wins out over the dialogue and the character admits defeat. Even for Dostoevsky, an author who puts polyphony at the foundation of his fictional universe, the short stories are incapable of giving the hero a separate voice that would be equal to that of the narrator. Although in Dostoevsky's stories too there is "intense anticipation of another's words" through the process of dialogism, this

---

6 Ibid, p. 196.
7 As did Myshkin's voice in *The Idiot*, when he forcefully affirms to Nastassia Filipovna: "'Aren't you ashamed? Surely you are not what you are pretending to be now? it isn't possible!'"; to which she replies "'I really am not like this, he is right'". Quoted in ibid, p. 242.

theoretical "orientation towards another's discourse" is not exploited so as to give him a full narrative and ontological status.[8]

The short story, admittedly, is not alone in this respect. To illustrate my thesis, I propose to imagine an axis. At one end are Dostoevsky's novels, which allow each of his characters a totally valid voice. Here there is a radical absence of judgement, no value wins out definitively and *a priori* over the others; Dostoevsky favours proximity with the character, even if he is debauched, impious or murderous. He allows us to see him *a novo*, in a light freed from all prejudices. At the other extreme of the axis is the classic short story, which refuses to enter to any degree into the logic of its characters; which almost always discredits their vision of the world, and always favours the external viewpoint; which increases distance, even in those rare cases when it is used to extol the merits of a "great man". Between the two extremes are both the other novels of western literature and "short fiction".

These other novels of the western tradition, according to Bakhtin, are not polyphonic. But although they usually define a non-polyphonic hierarchy, with a hero whose voice has fuller status than that of his protagonists, this hero is not himself systematically distanced from the reader as he is in the classic short story.[9] For example, the secondary characters in Maupassant's novel *Une vie* (*A Life*) are treated as caricatures. The heroine's parents, her husband, the priest, the elderly aunt, could all be short story characters (as is in effect the case with the aunt in *Clair de lune* [*In The Moonlight*], and the priest in *Le Saut du berger* [*The Shepherd's Leap*]). But the heroine Jeanne herself is not. The lack of distance from Jeanne is all the more remarkable because the portraits of women and the treatment of love in Maupassant's short stories are so deeply lacking nuance; here, Maupassant achieved for this heroine something he never did for his short stories characters.

Another "intermediary" form between the novel and the classic short story is "short fiction" — from Nathaniel Hawthorne's tales to the "modern", non-narrative story. Short fiction is epiphanic and suggestive. Renouncing the anecdote, it moves beyond the narrowly prescribed outlook on society and characters that make the classic short story monologic, and it is much nearer on the axis to Dostoevsky's novels. As an epilogue to this study, I will briefly look at how the genre moved from one end of the axis to the other.

---

8   Ibid, pp. 205 and 193.
9   At the end of his life, Bakhtin abandoned the idea that Dostoevsky is the only representative of polyphony in a western novel that is totally monological; and he does allow for gradations.

Epilogue: Beyond the Classic Short Story

The title of this book has given a chronological indication: 1870-1925, the period that represents the heyday for the "classic" short story. Before 1870, or rather at the beginning of the nineteenth century, short stories had a very different form, for example those of Nathaniel Hawthorne.[1] After 1920, there emerged a new type of short story that renounced all the characteristic traits we have described. Classic short stories continued to be written — and continued to sell — but beside them the twentieth century saw the rise of something quite different, which corresponds to what Clare Hanson calls "short fiction", and which she has showed to be linked with the advent of Modernism.[2] Structure was no longer based on antithesis or even paroxysms, and the distant look at the subject completely disappeared,

---

1   See Mary Rohrberger, *Hawthorne and the Modern Short Story* (The Hague: Mouton, 1966); and Mary Rohrberger, "Origins, Development, Substance, and Design of the Short Story: How I Got Hooked on the Short Story and Where It Led Me", in *The Art of Brevity: Excursions in Short Fiction Theory and Analysis*, ed. by Per Winther, Jakob Lothe, and Hans H. Skei (Columbia, SC: University of South Carolina Press, 2004), pp. 3-13. On Rohrberger's influence on recent criticism, see for example Susan Lohafer, Introduction, *Short Story Theory at a Crossroads*, ed. by Susan Lohafer and Jo Ellyn Clarey (Baton Rouge, LA: Louisiana State University Press, 1990).

2   Clare Hanson, *Short Stories and Short Fictions, 1880-1980* (New York: St. Martin's Press, 1985), pp. 1-9.

DOI: 10.11647/OBP.0039.13

together with the author's and reader's superior attitudes; monologism was no longer a standard feature.

This transition between the "classic" short story and what I call the new "modern" form started in the very corpus of work we have been investigating. The authors we have analysed, who practiced the classic form with extraordinary success, also published texts that can be taken as heralds of the new form. To finish this book, I shall describe two types of stories — lengthy stories and fantastic tales — that led to the emergence of this new type of short fiction, and explore in more detail the work of authors that sat at the "crossroads" between the classic and modern short story.

Lengthy stories: the long Yvette after the brief Yveline

Among the classic short stories of the time, the "lengthy stories" are quite special. Of course, not all lengthy stories are exceptions to the "classic" rule of monologism, but in certain cases the long short story repudiates the classic format, in that it foregoes both the strong structure of antithesis and the "exotic" perspective.[3] Lengthy stories or novellas can be said to "dilute" the narrative, and the change in length then changes everything. Guy de Maupassant's *Yvette* is a telling example, as we can compare it with a classic short story previously written by Maupassant on the same subject, the briefer *Yveline Samoris*.[4] Both texts tell the story of a girl ("Yveline" who becomes "Yvette" in the long story), the daughter of a "*demimondaine*", one of the high class prostitutes of nineteenth-century Paris who pretended to be aristocrats, and entertained wealthy men who joined in the illusion. The girl is very young and naïve, taking people at face value, living a free, gay life in what she thinks is a real salon. Sérigny, a newcomer to her mother's

---

3   Examples of longer stories that retain a "classic" monologism — and that we have been able to use as examples of the classic format — include Chekhov's *Skuchnaya istoriya* (*A Boring Story*) and *Poprygun'ya* (*The Grasshopper*), as well as Henry James's *Daisy Miller*, *The Figure in the Carpet* and *The Beast in the Jungle*.

4   A translation of the briefer *Yveline Samoris*, titled *Yvette Samoris*, is on Project Gutenberg http://archive.org/stream/completeoriginal03090gut/old/gm00v11.txt   (accessed 16/10/2013). For the original French text, see Guy de Maupassant, *Contes et nouvelles*, ed. by Louis Forestier, 2 vols (Paris: Gallimard, collection La Pléiade, 1974), I, pp. 684-88 (hereafter Pléiade). The longer *Yvette* can be found in Guy de Maupassant, *Complete Short Stories of Guy de Maupassant*, trans. by Artine Artinian (Garden City, NY: Hanover House, 1955), pp. 104-48 (hereafter Artinian). For the original French text, see Pléiade, II, pp. 234-307.

house, is attracted to Yveline/Yvette but cannot decide whether he should seduce her.

In the brief story, *Yveline Samoris*, the antithetical tension established between the two contrasting images of the young woman provides, as usual, a strong structure. Sérigny is trying to decipher a riddle: is Yveline/Yvette totally, absolutely corrupt or totally, absolutely innocent?[5] The ending will prove that she was, in fact, totally innocent; when she realises what is going on in her mother's house she finds herself caught between two equally unbearable (and equally paroxystic) possibilities: living with Sérigny, whom she has come to love, and leading a corrupt life; or sticking to her ideals and renouncing him.

Her answer — a typical answer in classic short stories (see, for example, Agatha's decision in Henry James's *The Modern Warning*, discussed in Chapter Eleven) — is to commit suicide. Distance from the subject takes on the very familiar form of satire of this all too worldly world. The twist-in-the-tail strengthens both the distancing and the powerful effect of the anecdote by forcing the clash between the two antithetical poles of innocence and corruption. The debased society around her refuses to learn from this act of desperation, and her death is officially attributed to an accident caused by a faulty furnace. We have here a particularly vivid display of the traits encountered throughout this study. The characters are not only distanced from the reader, they are straightforward types; not only what we have called "objective types" (social or psychological "roles" which the reader has already met or heard about), but this time clear literary types: the "coquette", the "libertine" and the "ingénue".

In the lengthy short story, *Yvette*, little is left of these typical features. When reworking his tale into a seventy-page novella, Maupassant abandons nearly everything that made it so "classic" a short story. The antithesis and the paroxysms on which it was based disappear. Already by the end of the third chapter, the riddle (corrupt or innocent?) is solved, because we enter into the mind of Yvette and discover that she is neither one nor the other. From then on, the text no longer plays with contradictory ideas — either harlot or virgin — but dwells on a world vision that is complex, ambiguous and still truly unformed. From this point of view, the scene in the riverside

---

5   At the beginning of the longer tale, Sérigny says of Yvette: "She provokes me and excites me like a harlot, and guards herself at the same time as though she were a virgin [...] Sometimes I imagine that she has as many lovers as her mother. Sometimes I think that she knows nothing about life, absolutely nothing". Artinian, p. 107 (Pléiade, II, p. 239).

café, that takes place in the novella but not the short story, is extremely important. The young woman swims beside Sérigny, happy to let him see her body — a completely sensual yet innocent happiness — because she is only conscious of the moment and not of what this sight might arouse in him.[6] The story no longer bears the stamp of the dilemma; the suicide is no longer the natural solution to a narrative situation which is no longer set in terms of irreducible contrasts. Yvette will live amid contradictions.

The consequences of this reworking of the material are not minor. Length has been used to develop hidden potentialities in the subject in a way that contrasts with the usual short story format. In this novella, the heroine is no longer in the least strange or foreign, and she has a full and autonomous "voice". We are finally "with" the character, whose initially strange qualities are superseded by a truly profound perspective of her.

Fantastic tales: the deconstruction of the self

Fantastic tales (especially those dealing with madness), even more than lengthy short stories, could be seen as the "missing link", the step that took the genre from its "classic" to "modern" format. Here, the narrative is not "diluted" (as it is in lengthy stories or novellas) but rather fragmented, in order to portray an unexpected mental universe. Throughout this study, we have seen that fantastic tales used the same material as other classic short stories, but in their own way. Like the classic short story, they present the reader with an unquestionably strange world; but at the same time they exceed the restraints of the framework because they try to let us penetrate a different logic. To be successful, these stories must achieve a sort of quivering of meaning: that oscillation of the readers' belief between the possible and the impossible, between what is rational and what is not. The fantastic narrative entices us to participate for a few moments in a strange world, or, in the case of tales of madness, in an unfamiliar way of thinking. In the latter case, the whole point rests in the display of a "sick" mind as a somewhat viable perspective on the world. Contrary to the realistic classic short stories, which painstakingly build and strengthen the distance between the spectacle and the reader, these tales will try to lessen that distance.[7] In the fantastic story, the reader can no longer be sure of

---

6   Ibid, p. 124 (pp. 267-68).

7   To take a simple example: when the character could appear to us as a coward, the narrator (or the "reflector") quickly shows that their fear is more than understandable

anything, and is unable to occupy the usual comfortable and clear position he was granted in the classic short story.

These fantastic tales retain the structural features of the classic short story, but only in order to rework them along these new lines. For example, they do not hesitate to use the tools that accelerate the reader's entry into the narrative. We see in them antitheses, quasi-abstract entities, and sometimes even character types. Yet these usual short story devices led to a dramatically different outlook when used in fantastic stories: they participate in arousing an emotion in us rather than simply conveying an anecdote. The paroxysms, for example, are used for their thematic presence, and contribute to establishing a world different from ours. Unlike classic shorty stories, in which these devices are so inconspicuous that they mostly go unnoticed, the fantastic story makes the reader oversensitive to them, destabilising his relationship to the text. What has been destroyed is the fundamental ground on which the classic short story was built: that of the reader's certainties.

We saw, throughout the analyses in Part III, that the reader is invited in classic short stories to look upon a profoundly different world. Whether they laugh at the characters, or pity them, or denounce their customs, the readers do so from the position of superiority, for example that of one who knows they could introduce the characters to "progress". However, readers can only do this when their belief in themselves and the "correct" path are strong and unshaking. Stories about madness, of which Maupassant wrote many, challenge our belief in a rational and stable subject. These stories prepare the transition to the new concept of the short story that will emerge in the twentieth century, in which all guidelines will be abolished, and author and reader will no longer be sure of their correctly understanding the world.

Authors at a crossroads

Most of the great authors studied here are also in themselves embodying this transition. Maupassant is one of the major links in the deconstruction of the classic short story: he wrote both lengthy short stories and fantastic tales. His well-known interest in the pathological states of consciousness

---

— it is absolutely normal — and that we, too, would have reacted in the same way. See, for example, Maupassant's *La Peur* (Pléiade, I, pp. 600-06) or *Lui?* (Pléiade, I, pp. 869-75). This type of empathy is never evoked in the realistic classic short story.

and his mastery of the oscillation of meaning were at odds with the neat and effective exotic story. Other major authors who were masters of the classic short story — particularly Akutagawa Ryūnosuke, Anton Chekhov, Luigi Pirandello and Giovanni Verga, as we shall see below — also embodied the transition from one form to the other.

My first goal in studying Akutagawa along with the European authors was to put my structural hypotheses to the test: if stories written in dramatically different circumstances showed the same features, then we could start to generalise about generic conventions. And indeed, in a country with a very different tradition from that of the West, where length has never been considered important as a criterion, we have met with this "classic" form of the short story, of which most of Akutagawa's texts, from *Mikan* (*The Tangerines*) to *Kareno shō* (*Withered Fields*) or *Hana* (*The Nose*), could be taken as canonical examples.[8] But Akutagawa is also acclaimed as a master of what we are accustomed to call the "modern" short story. As a writer of both kinds of texts from 1914 on, Akutagawa proves that the evolution towards short fiction does not result from the creative personality of the author, nor from an automatic, historic evolution.[9]

Tales of madness are again an essential link. Akutagawa writes "formless" texts that are often akin to those of the "stream of consciousness" mode of writing. The one unifying principle tends to be the actual mind it comes from; for example, that of the "dwarf" in *Shuju no kotoba* (*The Words of a Dwarf*), or that of the young man Akutagawa in the autobiographical *Aru hō no isshō* (*The Life of an Idiot*). Even when they follow the chronological order of events, as in *Haguruma* (*The Gears*), the outcome is dramatically different from that of the classic short stories. Paroxysms are rare, and

---

8   As we saw earlier, the Japanese did not have a special word for "short story" prior to the last years of the nineteenth century. Up to that time, the same word, *monogatari*, was used indifferently: for the *Genji monogatari* and its thousands of pages, as well as for Ueda Akinari's *Ugetsu monogatari*, tales of a few pages each. Even at the end of the nineteenth century, when the increasing influence of western culture brought about new trends in Japanese literature, the emerging modern literature was slow to pay attention to the criterion of length. The word chosen to name the new-born novel — *shōsetsu* — was made up of the two sino-Japanese characters for "short" (*shō*) and "story" or "apologue" (*setsu*), although the works in question, such as Futabatei Shimei's programmatic *Ukigumo* (*Floating Cloud*), were often full-length novels. The specific word for "short story", *tanpen shōsetsu*, was created later in response to the multitudinous translations of western short stories, by adding *tanpen* ("brief") to *shōsetsu*. By the second quarter of the twentieth century, this new word was widely used.

9   The narrative short story in its most classic form did not disappear; many stories by Joyce Carol Oates, Isaac B. Singer or Nina Berberova are, to my mind, absolutely "classic".

when they appear occasionally, they are never used to build a strong structure. Nothing is resolved at the end of these texts; in fact, no tension will have been created that could lead to a resolution, let alone a "twist-in-the-tail". We are invited to penetrate the erratic way of thinking rather than contemplating it from afar. One could stress Akutagawa's links with Japanese literary traditions.[10] But this should not overshadow the fact that he is also sharing in the essential preoccupation of writers around the world at that time: the deconstruction of the self, and doubt about reason's grasp of reality.

Moreover, Akutagawa had begun writing with another kind of non-narrative text: the lyrical story, which also had much in common with those of American or European authors of the time.[11] These lyrical stories also rejected the dominance of the anecdote, and they originated at a very early point in Akutagawa's career: *Ōgawa no mizu* (*The River's Water*) and *Shisō* (*The Shadow*) were both written when he was still a student. Again these stories share few of the features that characterise his classic narrative stories. A good example is one of Akutagawa's most beautiful tales, *Bisei no shin* (*The Faith of Wei Cheng*), in which a man, waiting on a river bank for a woman who never comes, is finally drowned by the rising tide.[12] What is striking is that this most unusual situation of a man not trying to escape imminent drowning is not portrayed as strange or uncommon. Even the waiting is not made to seem extraordinary. And neither the water nor the landscape is characterised by any particular tension: there is no paroxystic treatment of the elements here and, as a consequence, no antithesis will emerge. However, unlike most stream of consciousness stories, this text has a strong structure; but it is a structure very similar to that of the musical "rondo", with a refrain: "*Onna wa imada ni konai* (But the lady still does not come)". The effect it produces is closer to that of music or poetry than prose. Nothing in this is reminiscent of the tightly-wound narratives we saw earlier in this book; yet neither is it "formless".

---

10 For example, with the *zuihitsu* — the "following the brush" essay — a form illustrated in the thirteenth century by Kamo no Chōmei's *Hōjōki* (*An Account of My Hut*) or in the fourteenth century by Yoshida Kenkō's *Tsurezuregusa* (*Essays in Idleness*) and practiced by Akutagawa himself.

11 On this topic, see for example Eileen Baldeshwiler, "The Lyric Short Story: The Sketch of a History", in *The New Short Story Theories*, ed. by Charles E. May (Athens, OH: Ohio University Press, 1994), pp. 231-41.

12 Akutagawa, Ryūnosuke, *Akutagawa Ryūnosuke zenshū*, 19 vols (Tōkyō: Iwanami Shoten, 1954-1955), IV, pp. 44-46. There are no published translations that I know of.

Chekhov is perhaps an even more obvious example of the move to "short fiction" or the modern short story — many critics see him primarily as an author of this latter type of writing. However, I would argue that he only wrote a few stories in this mode, generally at the end of his career; most of his stories were perfectly "classic".[13] That is part of the reason why I think that a study of the classic short story is necessary: far from being only a form for minor or inexperienced writers, it was the core practice for most writers at the end of the nineteenth century. Chekhov was interested in the idea of progress and satire, both of which could be illustrated effectively in the classic short story format. Neither *The Mujiks* nor *Enemies*, nor of course *The Death of a Civil Servant* nor *Gooseberries* could be described in the terms generally used for speaking of Chekhov as a writer of nuance and complexity. This, of course, does not mean that the usual criticism on his work does not hold true; only that we need to recognise his other modes of writing. What makes Chekhov so great is the way he was able to use the classic form *and* go beyond it. The same could be said of the other authors studied here. I have been able to use Chekhov's *Lady with Lapdog* to illustrate many points of the classic short story format, although this is a favourite story for the criticism interested in the (hyphened) "short-story" — to use Brander Matthews' term for the modern short story — which for its part insists on epiphany.[14]

One will not be surprised that, for Pirandello, the advent of the dramatic form breeds this motion out of the short story format. *Quando si comprende (War)* begins as a classic short story indeed.[15] In its opening scene, a bereaved mother is literally hauled up into the rail wagon by her husband; she is reified, assimilated to a parcel.[16] Everything in the scene is grotesque. And then, something completely different emerges when the characters begin to communicate with each other in a dramatic dialogue.

---

13 Chekhov's "modern" stories include *The Bishop* (1902) and *The Bride* (1903).

14 Brander Matthews proposed to use the term "short-story" to describe the story that does not only happen to be short, but uses brevity itself as the means of saying more. Brander Matthews, *The Philosophy of the Short-story* (New York: Longmans, Green and Company, 1901).

15 An abridged translation is available in Ruth Spack, *The International Story: An Anthology with Guidelines for Reading and Writing about Fiction* (Cambridge: Cambridge University Press, 1998), pp. 74-77 (hereafter Spack). For the original Italian text, see Luigi Pirandello, *Donna Mimma* (Milan: Mondadori, 1951), pp. 66-70 (hereafter Pirandello).

16 The translation reads: "a bulky woman in deep mourning was hosted in — almost like a shapeless bundle" (Spack, p. 74). In a paragraph not translated: "*il pesante fardello*" is "the heavy bundle" (Pirandello, p. 66).

Suddenly, the characters cease to be ridiculous and pitiful. That the story is called in Italian "When one understands" reminds us this is all a question of renouncing the prejudices we bring to the reading and of re-working the distance usual to the format, to let the characters get a full "voice".

It is the same situation with Verga. Leo Spitzer, in his study of Verga's *I Malavoglia* (*The House by the Medlar Tree*), insisted exactly on this emergence of a full voice for the characters. As we saw in Chapter Nine, the decision of narrating the novel through the eyes and words of one of the characters (the device of *regression*) is a means of hearing their truth, different from ours. But we saw also that the same device in the stories is a means of exoticism.[17] Here again, presence or absence of the anecdote seems to be the dividing line: *The House by the Medlar Tree* "tells" nothing, it only has us enter more and more profoundly in a world distinct from ours, and lose on the way our preconceptions. It is not a question of an author's ripening mastery of his art. *The House by the Medlar Tree* dates from 1881, roughly the same time as his great short story cycles.[18]

******

Such an evolution represents the unravelling of the very form of the classic short story. Boundaries with other genres become blurred. The traits that firmly characterised the short story at the end of the nineteenth century disappear and are not replaced by anything half so clear. Instead of a few structuring traits, the new modern stories showed a variety of features that had little in common with one another. Of course, rhetorical devices were multifarious in the classic short story, but, as we saw, this variety was superficial: the genre relied on a few constant principles. These in-depth features meant that the surface traits did not have to be repetitive. Readers knew a short story when they saw one, and never hesitated to label a text as a "short story" except in a few lengthy examples. The new form is not so

---

17 With the exception of *Libertà* (*Liberty*), a non-narrative tale, which describes the movements of a mob in a popular revolt in 1860. On this story see, for example, Leonardo Sciascia, *La corda pazza* (Turin: Einaudi, 1991), pp. 79-94; and Giuseppe Lo Castro, *Giovanni Verga: una lettura critica*, Saggi brevi di letteratura antica e moderna, 5 (Soveria Mannelli: Rubbettino, 2001), pp. 139-40.

18 The classic short story *Nedda* was published in 1874; the (classic) cycles *Primavera e altri racconti* (*Spring and Other Stories*) in 1877; *Vita dei campi* (*Life in the Fields*) in 1880; and *Novelle rusticane* (*Little Novels of Sicily*) in 1883. Verga's later novel *Mastro Don Gesualdo* (*Master Gesualdo*), published in 1889, has always been considered to be much less innovating than *The House by the Medlar Tree*. See Luigi Russo, *Giovanni Verga* (Bari: Laterza, 1941).

clearly discernible, as is obvious from the very wide use of the term "short fiction" to speak of short stories as well as of other genres. Short texts are considered fiction like any other: lyrical stories sometimes verging on the prose poem, but also short works resembling theatre, as exemplified by Akutagawa on the one hand and Pirandello on the other. By renouncing the classic way of telling stories which had met with such success in the end of the nineteenth century, the genre in its new form joins with other genres to conquer new territories of the mind: polyphony and stream of consciousness rather than anecdote and monologism. What made the authors we have seen so great is that they knew not to stop at the perfect form that they had contributed to shape, but saw beyond it and could in the same years use and renounce its major features and its somewhat awesome efficacy.

Bibliography

Achebe, Chinua, *Hopes and Impediments: Selected Essays* (New York: Doubleday 1989).

Achter, Erik van, "Revising Theory: Poe's Legacy in Short Story Criticism", in *Short Story Theories: A Twenty-First-Century Perspective*, ed. by Viorica Patea (Amsterdam: Rodopi, 2012), pp. 75-88.

Akutagawa, Ryūnosuke, *Akutagawa Ryūnosuke zenshū*, 19 vols (Tōkyō: Iwanami Shoten, 1954-1955).

—, *Exotic Japanese Stories: The Beautiful and the Grotesque*, trans. by Takashi Kojima and John McVittie (New York: Liveright, 1964).

—, *Japanese Short Stories by Ryūnosuke Akutagawa*, ed. by Takashi Kojima (New York: Liveright, 1961).

Alain (Emile-Auguste Chartier), "Avec Balzac", in *Les Arts et les Dieux* (Paris: Gallimard, collection La Pléiade, 1958).

Albert, Pierre and Christine Leteinturier, *La Presse française* (Paris: Secrétariat général du gouvernement, La Documentation française, 1978).

Amaury, Francine, *Histoire du plus grand quotidien de la IIIe République, Le Petit Parisien, 1876-1944* (Paris: Presses Universitaires de France, 1972).

Ambroise-Rendu, Anne-Claude, *Petits récits des désordres ordinaires: les faits divers dans la presse française des débuts de la IIIe République à la Grande Guerre* (Paris: S. Arslan, 2004).

Anesko, Michael, *Friction with the Market: Henry James and the Profession of Authorship* (New York: Oxford University Press, 1986).

Auclair, Georges, *Le Mana quotidien: structures et fonctions de la chronique des faits divers* (Paris: Anthropos, 1982).

Bakhtin, Mikhail, *The Dialogic Imagination: Four Essays*, trans. by Michael Holquist and Caryl Emerson (Austin, TX: University of Texas Press, 1981).

—, *Problems of Dostoevsky's Poetics*, ed. and trans. by Caryl Emerson (Minneapolis, MN: University of Minnesota Press, 1984).

Baldeshwiler, Eileen, "The Lyric Short Story: The Sketch of a History", in *The New Short Story Theories*, ed. by Charles E. May (Athens, OH: Ohio University Press, 1994), pp. 231-41.

Baldi, Guido, *L'artificio della regressione: tecnica narrativa e ideologia nel Verga verista* (Naples: Liguori, 1980).

Barilli, Renato, *La barriera del Naturalismo* (Milan: Mursia, 1964).

Barthes, Roland, *Critical Essays*, trans. by Richard Howard (Evanston, IL: Northwestern University Press, 1972).

—, "Textual Analysis of a Tale By Edgar Poe", *Poe Studies*, 10:1 (1977), 1-12. DOI: 10.1111/j.1754-6095.1977.tb00029.x

Battaglia, Salvatore, "Dall'esempio alla novella", *Filologia Romanza*, 7 (1960), 45-82.

—, *La coscienza letteraria del Medioevo* (Naples: Liguori, 1965).

Beachcroft, T. O., *The Modest Art: A Survey of the Short Story in English* (Oxford: Oxford University Press, 1968).

Bellanger, Claude, *Histoire générale de la presse française. 3, De 1871 à 1940* (Paris: Presses Universitaires de France, 1972).

Bernard, Claude, *An Introduction to the Study of Experimental Medicine*, trans. by Henry Copley Greene (Birmingham, AL: Classics of Medicine Library, 1980).

Bhabha, Homi K., *The Location of Culture* (London: Routledge, 2004).

Bickley, R. Bruce, Jr., *The Method of Melville's Short Fiction* (Durham, NC: Duke University Press, 1975).

Blin, Jean-Pierre, "Enseigner la nouvelle: perspectives et limites d'une didactique", in *La Nouvelle et d'aujourd'hui*, ed. by Johnnie Gratton and Jean-Philippe Imbert (Paris: Éditions L'Harmattan, 1998), pp. 187-9.

Bonheim, Helmut, *The Narrative Modes: Techniques of the Short Story* (Cambridge: D. S. Brewer, 1986).

Booth, Wayne C., *A Rhetoric of Irony* (Chicago, IL: University of Chicago Press, 1974).

Boulez, Pierre, *Orientations* (London: Faber, 1986).

Bourrelier, Paul-Henri, *La Revue blanche: une génération dans l'engagement 1890-1905* (Paris: Fayard, 2007).

Bowen, Elizabeth, *A Day in the Dark and Other Stories* (London: Cape, 1965).

Brahimi, Denise, *Quelques idées reçues sur Maupassant* (Paris: Editions L'Harmattan, 2012).

Brake, Laurel and Marysa Demoor (eds.), *Dictionary of Nineteenth-century Journalism in Great Britain and Ireland* (Gent: Academia Press and London: British Library, 2009).

Brockhaus, F. A. and Efron, I. A. (eds.), *Entsiklopedicheskii slovar'*, 82 vols and 4 supplements (St. Petersburg: Granat, 1890-1907).

Brown, Arthur A., "Death and the Reader: James's 'The Beast in The Jungle'", in *Postmodern Approaches to the Short Story*, ed by Farhat Iftekharrudin, Joseph Boyden, Joseph Longo and Mary Rohrberger (Westport, CN: Praeger, 2003), pp. 39-50.

Brown, Julie (ed.), *Ethnicity and the American Short Story* (New York: Garland, 1997).

Buonvino, Orazio, *Il giornalismo contemporaneo* (Milan: R. Sandron, 1906).

Capuana, Luigi, *Lettere a Luigi Capuana*, ed. by Gino Raya (Florence: Le Monnier, 1975).

—, *Verga e D'Annunzio* (Bologna: Cappelli, 1972).

Castronovo, Valerio and Nicola Tranfaglia, *Storia della stampa italiana* (Rome: Laterza, 1976).

Chavannes-Fujimoto, Edwige de, *Akutagawa Ryūnosuke. L'organisation de la phrase et du récit* (Paris: Inalco, 1979).

Chekhov, Anton Pavlovich, *Anton Chekhov's Short Stories*, ed. by Ralph E. Matlaw, trans. by Constance Garnett (New York: Norton, 1979).

—, *The Kiss and Other Stories*, trans. by Ronald Wilks (Harmondsworth: Penguin, 1982).

—, *Lady with Lapdog and Other Stories*, trans. by David Magarshack (London: Penguin, 1964).

—, *Late-Blooming Flowers and Other Stories*, trans. by I. C. Chertok and Jean Gardner (New York: McGraw-Hill, 1964).

—, *The Oxford Chekhov*, trans. and ed. by Ronald Hingley, 9 vols (London: Oxford University Press, 1971).

—, *Polnoe sobranie sochinenii i pisem*, 30 vols (Moscow: Nauka, 1974-1983).

—, *The Portable Chekhov*, ed. by Avrahm Yarmolinsky (Harmondsworth: Penguin, 1977).

—, *The Schoolmaster and Other Stories*, trans. by Constance Garnett (New York: Macmillan, 1921).

—, *201 Stories by Anton Chekhov*, ed. by James Rusk, trans. by Constance Garnett (Eldritch Press online), available at http://www.eldritchpress.org/ac/jr/147.htm (accessed 21/08/13).

Chevrel, Yves, *Le Naturalisme* (Paris: Presses Universitaires de France, 1993).

Chudakov, Aleksandr P., *Poetika Chekhova* (Moscow: Nauka 1971).

Croce, Benedetto, *Poesia e non poesia* (Bari: Laterza, 1923).

Davison, Ray, "Simone de Beauvoir: 'La Femme rompue'", in *Short French Fiction: Essays on the Short Story in France in the Twentieth Century*, ed. by J. E. Flower (Exeter: University of Exeter Press, 1998), pp. 71-88.

Delaisement, Gérard, *Maupassant, journaliste et chroniqueur; suivi d'une bibliographie générale de l'oeuvre de Guy de Maupassant* (Paris: A. Michel, 1956).

Descombes, Vincent, *Proust: Philosophy of a Novel* (Stanford: Stanford University Press, 1992).

Devoto, Giacomo, *Itinerario stilistico* (Florence: Le Monnier, 1975).

Dietz Faletti, Heidi E., "Interior Monologue and the Unheroic Psyche in Schnitzler's *Leutenant Gustl* and *Fräulein Else*", in *The Image of the Hero in Literature, Media and Society*, ed. by Will Wright and Steve Kaplan (Pueblo, CO: Society for the Interdisciplinary Study of Social Imagery, 2004), pp. 522-57.

Eckermann, Johann Peter, *Conversations with Goethe*, trans. by John Oxenford, ed. by J. K. Moorhead (London: Dent, 1930).

—, *Gespräche mit Goethe in den letzten Jahren seines Lebens* (Frankfurt: Insel, 1981).

Edel, Leon, *Henry James: A Life* (New York: Harper & Row, 1965).

Eikhenbaum, Boris, "How Gogol's 'Overcoat' is Made", in *Gogol's "Overcoat": An*

Anthology of Critical Essays, ed. by Elizabeth Trahan (Ann Arbor, MI: Ardis, 1982), pp. 21-36.

Ellis, John M., *Narration in the German Novelle: Theory and Interpretation* (Cambridge: Cambridge University Press, 1974).

Ellmann, Richard, *James Joyce* (New York: Oxford University Press, 1959).

Elwood, Maren, *Characters Make Your Story* (Boston: Houghton Mifflin, 1942).

Esin, Boris, *Chekhov Jurnalist* (Moscow: Izd-vo Moskovskogo universiteta, 1977).

Etō Jun, "Nichiōbunka no taishōsei to hitaishōsei," in *Bungakkai*, 43-1 (January 1989), 240-52.

Fanon, Frantz, *Black Skin, White Masks* (New York: Grove Press, 1967).

Feddersen, Rick, and Susan Lohafer, Barbara Lounsberry, Mary Rohrberger (eds.), *The Tales We Tell: Perspectives on the Short Story* (Westport, CN: Greenwood Press, Praeger, 1998).

Ferrucci, Franco, "I racconti milanesi del Verga", *Italica*, 2 (1967), 124.

Festa McCormick, Diana, *Les Nouvelles de Balzac* (Paris: Nizet, 1973).

Fowler, Virginia C., *Henry James's American Girl: The Embroidery on the Canvas* (Madison, WI: University of Wisconsin Press, 1984).

Fusco, Richard, *Maupassant and the American Short Story: The Influence of Form at the Turn of the Century* (University Park, PA: Pennsylvania State University Press, 1994).

Gandelman, Claude, *Les Techniques de la provocation chez quelques romanciers et nouvellistes de l'entre-deux-guerres* (doctoral thesis, Paris III Sorbonne-Nouvelle, 1972).

Genette, Gérard, *Figures III* (Paris: Le Seuil, 1972).

— *Narrative Discourse: An Essay in Method*, trans. by Jane E. Lewin (Ithaca, NY: Cornell University Press, 1980).

Genot, Gérard, *Analyse structurelle de 'Pinocchio'* (Pescia: Fondazione Nazionale Carlo Collodi, 1970).

— and Paul Larivaille, *Etude du Novellino* (Paris: Presses de l'Université Nanterre, 1985).

Gerlach, John C., *Toward the End: Closure and Structure in the American Short Story* (Tuscaloosa, AL: University of Alabama Press, 1985).

Goethe, Johann Wolfgang von, *Great Writings of Goethe*, ed. by Stephen Spender, trans. by Christopher Middleton (New York: New American Library, 1958).

Gorki, Maxim, Alexander Kuprin and A. I. Bunin, *Reminiscences of Anton Chekhov*, trans. by S. S. Koteliansky and Leonard Woolf (New York: Huebsch, 1921).

Goyet, Florence, *La Nouvelle au tournant du siècle en France, Italie, Japon, Russie, pays anglo-saxons. Maupassant, Verga, Mori Ōgai, Akutagawa Ryūnosuke, Tchekhov et James* (doctoral thesis, Université Paris 4-Sorbonne, 1990). The second part of the thesis is available at http://w3.u-grenoble3.fr/rare/spip/spip.php?article341 (accessed 7/11/2013).

—, *La Nouvelle, 1870-1925: description d'un genre à son apogée* (Paris: Presses Universitaires de France, 1993).

—, "*Les Plaisirs et les Jours* entre nouvelle classique et nouvelle moderne", *Bulletin d'Informations proustiennes*, 44 (2014).

—, "L'exotisme du quotidien: Maupassant et la presse", in *Maupassant multiple*, Actes du colloque de Toulouse, Presses de l'Université de Toulouse-Le Mirail, 1995, pp. 17-28, available at http://w3.u-grenoble3.fr/rare/spip/IMG/pdf/Maupassant_et_la_presse_-M-_multiple-_Toulouse-.pdf (accessed 04/02/13).

—, *Penser sans concepts. Fonction de l'épopée guerrière* (Paris: Champion, 2006).

Grivel, Charles, *Production de l'intérêt romanesque* (The Hague: Mouton, 1973).

Hanson, Clare, *Short Stories and Short Fictions, 1880-1980* (New York: St. Martin's Press, 1985).

Hashimoto, Kenji, *Amerika tanpen shōsetsu no kōzō* (Ōsaka: Ōsaka Kyōiku Tosho, 2009).

Hellmann, John, *Fables of Fact: The New Journalism as New Fiction* (Urbana, IL: University of Illinois Press, 1981).

Hernández, Rebecca, "Short Narrations in a Letter Frame: Cases of Genre Hybridity in Postcolonial Literature in Portuguese", in *Short Story Theories: A Twenty-First-Century Perspective*, ed. by Viorica Patea (Amsterdam: Rodopi, 2012), pp. 155-72.

Hills, Rust, *Writing in General and the Short Story in Particular* (Boston, MA: Houghton Mifflin, 2000).

Hutchings, Stephen, *A Semiotic Analysis of the Short Stories of Leonid Andreev: 1900-1909* (London: Modern Humanities Research Association, 1990).

Ingram, Forrest L., *Representative Short Story Cycles of the Twentieth Century: Studies in a Literary Genre* (The Hague: Mouton, 1971).

Jablon, Madelyn, "Womanist Storytelling: The Voice of the Vernacular", in *Ethnicity and the American Short Story*, ed. by Julie Brown (New York: Garland, 1997), pp. 47-62.

James, Henry, *The Art of the Novel: Critical Prefaces* (New York: Scribner, 1962).

—, *The Complete Tales of Henry James*, ed. by Leon Edel, 12 vols (London: Rupert Hart Davis, 1960).

—, *Hawthorne* (Ithaca, NY: Cornell University Press, 1967).

—, *Letters: 1883-1895*, ed. by Leon Edel (Cambridge, MA: Harvard University Press, 1980).

—, *The Notebooks of Henry James*, ed. by F. O. Matthiessen and Kenneth B. Murdock (New York: Oxford University Press, 1947).

—, *The Tales of Henry James: Volume 3, 1875-1879*, ed. by Maqbool Aziz (Oxford: Clarendon Press, 1984). *no italics*

Joyce, James, *Dubliners*, ed. by Hans Walter Gabler and Walter Hettche (New York: Garland, 1993).

—, *Dubliners*, ed. by Jeri Johnson (Oxford: Oxford University Press, 2001).

—, *Letters*, ed. by Stuart Gilbert and Richard Ellmann, 3 vols (New York: Viking Press, 1957-1966).

Kalifa, Dominique, and Philippe Régnier, Marie-Ève Thérenty (eds.), *La Civilisation du journal: histoire culturelle et littéraire de la presse française au XIXe siècle* (Paris: Nouveau Monde éditions, 2012).

Kataev, Vladimir, *If Only We Could Know: An Interpretation of Chekhov*, trans. by Harvey Pitcher (Chicago: Ivan R. Dee, 2002).

—, *Literaturnye svyazi Chekhova* (Moscow: Izd-vo Moskovskogo universiteta, 1989).

—, *Proza Chekhova: problemy interpretatsii* (Moscow: Izd-vo Moskovskogo universiteta, 1979).

—, *Sputniki Chekhova* (Moscow: Izd-vo Moskovskogo universiteta, 1982).

Kermode, Frank, *The Sense of an Ending: Studies in the Theory of Fiction* (Oxford: Oxford University Press, 2000).

Kipling, Rudyard, *Plain Tales From the Hills* (London: Penguin, 1995).

—, *Something of Myself: For My Friends Known and Unknown* (Rockville, MD: Wildside Press, 2008).

Krämer, Herbert, *Theorie der Novelle* (Stuttgart: Reclam, 1976).

Levy, Andrew, *The Culture and Commerce of the American Short Story* (Cambridge: Cambridge University Press, 1993). DOI: 10.1017/CBO9780511519345

Llewellyn Smith, Virginia, *Anton Chekhov and the Lady with the Dog* (Oxford: Oxford University Press, 1973).

Lo Castro, Giuseppe, *Giovanni Verga: una lettura critica. Saggi brevi di letteratura antica e moderna*, vol. 5 (Soveria Mannelli: Rubbettino, 2001).

LoCicero, Donald, *Novellentheorie: The Practicality of the Theoretical* (The Hague: Mouton, 1970).

Lohafer, Susan, *Coming to Terms with the Short Story* (Baton Rouge, LA: Louisiana State University Press, 1983).

—, "Preclosure and Story Processing", in *Short Story Theory at a Crossroads*, ed. by Susan Lohafer and Jo Ellyn Clarey (Baton Rouge, LA: Louisiana State University Press, 1990), pp. 249-75.

—, *Reading for Storyness: Preclosure Theory, Empirical Poetics, and Culture in the Short Story* (Baltimore, MD: Johns Hopkins University Press, 2003).

— and Jo Ellyn Clarey (eds.), *Short Story Theory at a Crossroads* (Baton Rouge, LA: Louisiana State University, 1989).

Lugli, Vittorio, *Dante e Balzac con altri italiani e francesi* (Naples: Edizioni Scientifiche Italiane, 1952).

Luperini, Romano, *Verga e le strutture narrative del realismo: saggio su "Rosso Malpelo"* (Padova: Liviana, 1976).

—, *Verga: l'ideologia, le strutture narrative, il "caso" critico* (Lecce: Millela, 1982).

Luscher, Robert M., "The Short Story Sequence: An Open Book", in *Short Story Theory at a Crossroads*, ed. by Susan Lohafer and Jo Ellyn Clarey (Baton Rouge, LA: Louisiana State University Press, 1990), pp. 148-67.

Lynch, Gerald, "The One and the Many: Canadian Short Story Cycles", in *The Tales We Tell: Perspectives on the Short Story*, ed. by Rick Feddersen, Susan Lohafer, Barbara Lounsberry and Mary Rohrberger (Westport, CN: Greenwood Press, Praeger, 1998), pp. 35-46.

Maigne, Vincenette, "Exotisme, évolution en diachronie du mot et de son champ sémantique", in *Exotisme et création. Actes du colloque international* (Lyon: L'Hermes, 1985).

Mann, Susan Garland, *The Short Story Cycle: A Genre Companion and Reference Guide* (New York: Greenwood Press, 1989).

Margarito, Donato, "Verga nella critica marxista: dal 'caso' critico al metodo critico-negativo", in *Verga: l'ideologia, le strutture narrative, il "caso" critico*, ed. by Carlo Augieri and R. Luperini (Lecce: Millela, 1982), pp. 235-89.

Margolis, Anne T., *Henry James and the Problem of Audience: An International Act* (Ann Arbor, MI: University of Michigan Press, 1985).

Matthews, Brander, *The Philosophy of the Short-story* (New York: Longmans, Green and Company, 1901).

Maugham, William Somerset, *Points of View* (London: Heinemann, 1938).

Maupassant, Guy de, *The Complete Short Stories of Guy de Maupassant*, trans. by Artine Artinian (Garden City, NY: Hanover House, 1955).

—, *Contes et nouvelles*, ed. by Louis Forestier, 2 vols (Paris: Gallimard, collection La Pléiade, 1974).

—, *The Entire Original Maupassant Short Stories*, trans. by Albert M. C. McMaster, A. E. Henderson and Mme Quesada (Project Gutenburg, 2004), available at http://ia700204.us.archive.org/9/items/completeoriginal03090gut/3090-h/3090-h.htm#2H_4_0086 (accessed 30/07/13).

—, *Pierre and Jean: And Other Stories* (New York: French Library Syndicate, 1925), p. xvi.

May, Charles E., "The Secret Life in the Modern Short Story", in *Contemporary Debates on the Short Story*, ed. by José R. Ibáñez, José Francisco Fernández and Carmen M. Bretones (Bern: Lang, 2007), pp. 207-25.

—, (ed.), *Short Story Theories* (Athens, OH: Ohio University Press, 1976).

—, (ed.), *The New Short Story Theories* (Athens, OH: Ohio University Press, 1994).

—, "Why Short Stories Are Essential and Why They Are Seldom Read", in *The Art of Brevity: Excursions in Short Fiction Theory and Analysis*, ed. by Per Winther, Jakob Lothe and Hans H. Skei (Columbia, SC: University of South Carolina Press, 2004), pp. 14-25.

May, Charles, "The American Short Story in the Twenty-first Century", in *Short Story Theories: A Twenty-First-Century Perspective*, ed. by Viorica Patea (Amsterdam: Rodopi, 2012), pp. 299-324.

—, "The Unique Effect of the Short Story: A Reconsideration and an Example", *Studies in Short Fiction*, 13 (1976), 289-97.

Melmoux-Montaubin, Marie-Françoise, *L'écrivain-journaliste au XIXe siècle: un mutant des lettres* (Saint-Etienne: Editions des Cahiers intempestifs, 2003).

Miñambres, Garrido, *Die Novelle im Spiegel der Gattungstheorie* (Würzburg: Königshausen & Neumann: 2008).

Montes-Granado, Consuelo, "Code-Switching as a Strategy of Brevity in Sandra Cisneros' *Woman Hollering Creek and Other Stories*", in *Short Story Theories: A Twenty-First-Century Perspective*, ed. by Viorica Patea (Amsterdam: Rodopi, 2012), pp. 125-36.

Moorhead, J. K. (ed.), *Conversations of Goethe with Johann Peter Eckermann* (New York: Da Capo Press, 1998).

Mori, Ōgai, *Mori Ōgai zenshū*, 38 vols (Tōkyō: Iwanami, 1971-1975).

—, *Youth and Other Stories*, ed. and trans. by J. Thomas Rimer (Honolulu: University of Hawaii Press, 1994).

Morson, Gary Saul and Caryl Emerson, *Mikhail Bakhtin: Creation of a Prosaics* (Stanford, CA: Stanford University Press, 1990).

Mullen, Bill, "Marking Race/Marketing Race: African American Short Fiction and the Politics of Genre, 1933-1946", in *Ethnicity and the American Short Story*, ed. by Julie Brown (New York: Garland, 1997), pp. 25-46.

Nagel, James, *The Contemporary American Short-Story Cycle: The Ethnic Resonance of Genre* (Baton Rouge, LA: Louisiana State University Press, 2004).

Nasi, Franco, *100 anni di quotidiani milanesi* (Milan: Comune di Milano, 1958).

Neuschafer, Hans-Jörg, *Boccaccio und der Beginn der Novelle: Strukturen der Kurzerzählung auf der Schwelle zwischen Mittelalter und Neuzeit* (Munich: Fink Verlag, 1983).

O'Connor, Frank, *The Lonely Voice: A Study of the Short Story* (Cleveland, OH: World Publishing Company, 1963).

O'Faolain, Sean, *The Short Story* (Cork: Mercier, 1948).

O'Reilly Herrera, Andrea, "Sandra Benitez and the Nomadic Text", in *Postmodern Approaches to the Short Story*, ed. by Farhat Iftekharrudin, Joseph Boyden, Joseph Longo and Mary Rohrberger (Westport, CN: Greenwood Press, Praeger, 2003), pp. 51-62.

Ōe, Kenzaburō, "Sakka no soba kara", *Bungakkai*, 41:9 (September 1987), 180-83.

Ognev, Aleksandr V., *O Poetike sovremennogo russkogo rasskaza* (Saratov: Izd-vo Saratovskogo Universiteta, 1973). Small u (universitcta)

Orel, Harold, *The Victorian Short Story* (Cambridge: Cambridge University Press, 1986).

Patea, Viorica (ed.), *Short Story Theories: A Twenty-First-Century Perspective* (Amsterdam: Rodopi, 2012).

Pirandello, Luigi, *Donna Mimma* (Milan: Mondadori, 1951).

—, *Il vecchio Dio* (Milan: Mondadori, 1979).

—, *Opere di Luigi Pirandello* (Milan: Mondadori, 1956-60), available at http://lafrusta.homestead.com/riv_pirandello.html (accessed 21/08/13).

Poe, Edgar Allan, "Poe on Short Fiction", in *The New Short Story Theories*, ed. by Charles E. May (Athens, OH: Ohio University Press, 1994), pp. 59-72.

—, *Essays and Reviews*, ed. by Gary R. Thompson (New York: The Library of America, 1984).

Polt-Heinzl, Evelyne, *Arthur Schnitzler: Leutnant Gustl* (Stuttgart: Reclam, 2000).

Pratt, Mary Louise, "The Short Story: The Long and the Short of It", *Poetics*, 10 (1981), 175–194.

Proust, Marcel, *Correspondance*, ed. by Philip Kolb (Paris: Plon, 1970-1993).

—, *Les Plaisirs et les Jours*, ed. by Thierry Laget (Paris: Gallimard, 1993).

—, *Pleasures and Days: And Other Writings* (Garden City, NY: Doubleday, 1957).

Ramsdell, Catherine, "Homi K. Bhabha and the Postcolonial Short Story", in *Postmodern Approaches to the Short Story*, ed. by Farhat Iftekharrudin, Joseph

Boyden, Joseph Longo and Mary Rohrberger (Westport, CN: Praeger, 2003), pp. 97-106.

Reid, Ian, *The Short Story* (London: Methuen, 1977).

Richepin, Jean, *Le Pavé* (Paris: Dreyfous, 1883).

Riffatterre, Michael, *Semiotics of Poetry* (Bloomington, IN: Indiana University Press, 1978).

Rimer, J. Thomas, "Three Stories by Mori Ōgai", in *Approaches to the Modern Japanese Short Story*, ed. by Thomas E. Swann and Tsuruta Kin'ya (Tōkyō: Waseda University Press, 1982), pp. 201-09.

Rohrberger, Mary, *Hawthorne and the Modern Short Story: A Study in Genre* (The Hague: Mouton, 1966).

—, "Origins, Development, Substance, and Design of the Short Story: How I Got Hooked on the Short Story and Where It Led Me", in *The Art of Brevity: Excursions in Short Fiction Theory and Analysis*, ed. by Per Winther, Jakob Lothe, and Hans H. Skei (Columbia, SC: University of South Carolina Press, 2004), pp. 3-13.

Rowe, John Carlos, "The African-American Voice in Faulkner's *Go Down, Moses*", in *Modern American Short Story Sequences: Composite Fictions and Fictive Communities*, ed. by J. Gerald Kennedy (Cambridge: Cambridge University Press, 2011), pp. 76-97.

Russo, Luigi, *Giovanni Verga* (Bari: Laterza, 1941; augmented ed. 1976).

Said, Edward W., *Orientalism* (New York: Vintage Books, 1979).

Saposnik, Irving S., *Robert Louis Stevenson* (New York: Twayne, 1974).

Sarkany, Etienne, *Forme, socialité et processus d'information: l'exemple du récit court à l'aube du XXe siècle* (doctoral thesis, Diffusion Université Lille III, 1982).

Schnitzler, Arthur, *Das erzählerische Werk* (Frankfurt: Fischer Taschenbuch, 1981).

—, *Plays and Stories*, ed. by Egon Schwarz (New York: Continuum, 1982).

Scholes, Robert, "Some Observations on the Text of Dubliners: 'The Dead'", *Studies in Bibliography*, 15 (1962), 191-205.

Scofield, Martin, *The Cambridge Introduction to the American Short Story* (Cambridge: Cambridge University Press, 2006). DOI: 10.1017/CBO9780511607257

Sempoux, André, *La Nouvelle*, in *Typologie des sources du moyen âge occidental*, 9 (Turnhout: Brepols, 2009).

Shaw, Valerie, *The Short Story: A Critical Introduction* (London: Longman, 1983).

Sheridan, David, "The End of the World: Closure in the Fantasies of Borges, Calvino and Millhauser", in *Postmodern Approaches to the Short Story*, ed. by Farhat Iftekharrudin, Joseph Boyden, Joseph Longo and Mary Rohrberger (Westport, CT: Praeger, 2003), pp. 9-24.

Schorske, Carl E., *Fin-de-siècle Vienna: Politics and Culture* (New York: Knopf, 1980).

Sciascia, Leonardo, *La corda pazza* (Turin: Einaudi, 1991).

Shklovsky, Viktor, *Theory of Prose*, trans. by Benjamin Sher (Elmwood Park, IL: Dalkey Archive Press, 1990).

Shubin, Eduard Anatol'evich, *Sovremennyi russkii rasskaz: voprosy poetiki zhanra* (Moscow: Nauka, 1974).

Spack, Ruth, *The International Story: An Anthology with Guidelines for Reading and Writing about Fiction* (Cambridge: Cambridge University Press, 1998).

Spitzer, Leo, "L'Originalità della narrazione nei *Malavoglia*", *Belfagor*, 11 (1956), 37-53.

Springer, Mary Doyle, *Rhetoric of Literary Character: Some Women of Henry James* (Chicago: University of Chicago Press, 1976).

Steele, Karen, *Women, Press and Politics During the Irish Revival* (Syracuse, NY: Syracuse University Press, 2007).

Tarde, Gabriel, *L'Opinion et la foule* (Paris: Presses Universitaires de France, 1989).

Thiesse, Anne-Marie, *Le Roman du quotidien* (Paris: Le Seuil, 2000).

Tieck, Ludwig, *Ludwig Tieck's Schriften* (Berlin: G. Reimer, 1828-55).

Todorov, Tzvetan, *The Fantastic: A Structural Approach to a Literary Genre*, trans. by Richard Howard (Cleveland, OH: Case Western Reserve University Press, 1973).

—, *Grammaire du* Décaméron (The Hague: Mouton, 1969).

Tolstoy, Lev Nicolaevich, *Sochineniya*, 90 vols (Moscow: Khudozhestvennaya literatura, 1935-1964).

Topia, André, "Joyce et Flaubert: les affinités sélectives", in *James Joyce: Scribble 2: Joyce et Flaubert* (Paris, Minard, 1990), pp. 33-63.

Tsutsui, Yasutaka, *Tanpen shōsetsu kōgi* (Tōkyō: Iwanami Shoten, 1990).

Verga, Giovanni, *The She-Wolf and Other Stories*, trans. by Giovanni Cecchetti (Berkeley: University of California Press, 19730.

—, *The House by the Medlar Tree* (Berkeley, CA: University of California Press, 1983).

—, *Lettere a Luigi Capuana*, ed. by Gino Raya (Florence: Le Monnier, 1975).

—, *Tutte le Novelle*, ed. by Carla Ricciardi, 2 vols (Milan: Mondadori, 1983).

—, *Under the Shadow of Etna: Sicilian Stories from the Italian of Giovanni Verga*, trans. by Nathan Haskell Dole (Boston: Joseph Knight, 1896).

Vial, André, *Guy de Maupassant et l'art du roman* (Paris: Nizet, 1954).

Voloshinov, V. N., *Marxism and the Philosophy of Language*, trans. by Ladislav Matejka and I. R. Titunik (Cambridge, MA: Harvard University Press, 1973).

Watelet, Jean, *La presse illustrée en France 1814-1914* (Villeneuve d'Ascq: Presses Universitaires du Septentrion, 2000).

Wendt, Albert (ed.), *Nuanua: Pacific Writing in English Since 1980* (Honolulu: University of Hawaii Press, 1995).

Winther, Per, "Closure and Preclosure as Narrative Grid in Short Story Analysis" in *The Art of Brevity: Excursions in Short Fiction Theory and Analysis*, ed. by Per Winther, Jakob Lothe, and Hans H. Skei (Columbia, SC: University of South Carolina Press, 2004), pp. 57-69.

Zola, Émile, *The Experimental Novel, and Other Essays*, trans. by Belle M. Sherman (New York: Cassell, 1893).

Index

more space between entries

This book does not end here...

At Open Book Publishers, we are changing the nature of the traditional academic book. The title you have just read will not be left on a library shelf, but will be accessed online by hundreds of readers each month across the globe. We make all our books free to read online so that students, researchers and members of the public who can't afford a printed edition can still have access to the same ideas as you.

Our digital publishing model also allows us to produce online supplementary material, including extra chapters, reviews, links and other digital resources. Find *The Classic Short Story* on our website to access its online extras. Please check this page regularly for ongoing updates, and join the conversation by leaving your own comments:

http://www.openbookpublishers.com/isbn/9781909254756

If you enjoyed this book, and feel that research like this should be available to all readers, regardless of their income, please think about donating to us. Our company is run entirely by academics, and our publishing decisions are based on intellectual merit and public value rather than on commercial viability. We do not operate for profit and all donations, as with all other revenue we generate, will be used to finance new Open Access publications.

For further information about what we do, how to donate to OBP, additional digital material related to our titles or to order our books, please visit our website.

OpenBook
Publishers
Knowledge is for sharing